Who Owns Football?

The commercialisation of football in Europe since the 1990s has had a number of consequences for the game, not all of them beneficial to its wellbeing. The market forces that have defined these developments have impacted upon the financial future of clubs as key social and cultural institutions and some continue to see their existence threatened. The inevitable result is enforced sale of club assets for commercial development; their relocation to towns and cities many miles from their original locale, or the acquisition of clubs by individuals of whose motives many fans are rightly suspicious. In recent years one of the most high profile responses to these developments has been for groups of supporters to join together and purchase ownership of part of the club, or in some cases the entire club, to run it on a non-commercial basis. It mimics the successful membership model deployed by FC Barcelona and upon which entire organisations, like the Gaelic Athletic Association (GAA) has successfully existed for 125 years.

This book will explore the background to this movement and its practical outworking by providing individual case studies from several European countries.

This book was previously published as a special issue of *Soccer and Society*.

David Hassan is a Senior Lecturer at the University of Ulster. He is Academic Editor of *Sport in Society* and joint Editor of *Foundations in Sport Management*, a new Routledge series. Dr. Hassan has published extensively in the politics and governance of sport in a range of international academic journals.

Sean Hamil is a Lecturer in the Department of Management at Birkbeck College, University of London. A co-founder of Birkbeck College's Sport Business and Consultancy Network he has edited a number of books on football governance including Hamil, S., Michie, J., Oughton, C., and Warby, S. (eds) (2001) *The Changing Face of the Football Business: Supporters Direct*, London: Frank Cass and Hamil, S., Michie, J., Oughton, C. and Warby, S. (eds) *Football in the Digital Age: Whose Game is it Anyway?* Edinburgh: Mainstream.

Who Owns Football?

The Governance and Management of the Club Game Worldwide

Edited by
David Hassan and Sean Hamil

Routledge
Taylor & Francis Group

LONDON AND NEW YORK

First published 2011
by Routledge
2 Park Square, Milton Park, Abingdon, Oxon, OX14 4RN

Simultaneously published in the USA and Canada
by Routledge
711 Third Avenue, New York, NY 10017

Routledge is an imprint of the Taylor & Francis Group, an informa business

First issued in paperback 2012

This book is a reproduction of *Soccer and Society*, vol. 11.4. The Publisher requests to those authors who may be citing this book to state, also, the bibliographical details of the special issue on which the book was based.

Typeset in Times New Roman by Taylor & Francis Books

British Library Cataloguing in Publication Data
A catalogue record for this book is available from the British Library

ISBN13: 978-0-415-44570-2 (hbk)

ISBN13: 978-0-415-66124-9 (pbk)

Disclaimer
The publisher would like to make readers aware that the chapters in this book are referred to as articles as they had been in the special issue. The publisher accepts responsibility for any inconsistencies that may have arisen in the course of preparing this volume for print.

Contents

SPORT IN THE GLOBAL SOCIETY – CONTEMPORARY PERSPECTIVES

Series Editor: Boria Majumdar

WHO OWNS FOOTBALL?
The Governance and Management of the Club Game Worldwide

Sport in the Global Society – Contemporary Perspectives
Series Editor: Boria Majumdar

The social, cultural (including media) and political study of sport is an expanding area of scholarship and related research. While this area has been well served by the Sport in the Global Society Series, the surge in quality scholarship over the last few years has necessitated the creation of *Sport in the Global Society: Contemporary Perspectives*. The series will publish the work of leading scholars in fields as diverse as sociology, cultural studies, media studies, gender studies, cultural geography and history, political science and political economy. If the social and cultural study of sport is to receive the scholarly attention and readership it warrants, a cross-disciplinary series dedicated to taking sport beyond the narrow confines of physical education and sport science academic domains is necessary. Sport in the Global Society: Contemporary Perspectives will answer this need.

Titles in the Series

INTRODUCTION

Models of football governance and management in international sport

David Hassan[a] and Sean Hamil[b]

[a]School of Sports Studies, University of Ulster at Jordanstown, Newtownabbey, UK;
[b]Department of Management, Birkbeck, University of London, London, UK

Introduction

Historically, the governance of professional sport has been understood in relatively straightforward, indeed taken for granted, terms. Essentially, this has meant that association football clubs, for example – but the same is true of other professional sports clubs – have remained under the ownership of private companies or mutual associations and that these entities appropriately reward athletes of varying abilities for their role in delivering a sporting 'product'. In doing so, they have mostly operated within systems of governance that have presented sport as something of a deviation from normal business practices, but this has meant that, as in this case, football began to constitute anything but a conventional industry. Clubs did not seek to profit maximize and did not regard themselves as part of the 'entertainment business', even if they did effectively provide this through their participation in various sporting competitions. Instead, 'utility maximization', or simply the achievement of success on the field of play, remained the key objective for most if not all clubs regardless of what levels of the professional game they competed at. For the most part, this was a relatively benign business approach because, despite many clubs 'living beyond their means', the financial stakes were sufficiently low that overall equilibrium was retained and the game followed a largely predictable course. However, significant and wide-reaching changes have taken place in a range of national sports settings, especially over the last two decades, which have begun to distort this picture – in certain cases dramatically so – and that, in turn, give rise to some worrying trends. This is a situation that has become especially apparent since the turn of the new millennium and has begun to raise questions about the very purpose of elite professional football clubs across Europe; in some cases this has included a debate over their continued existence.

These and similar issues were placed under the spotlight in January 2008 following the remarks of UEFA (the governing body of European football) President Michel Platini, who, according to UEFA's own website[1] – uefa.com, issued:

> … an impassioned plea for the safeguarding of the essential values and specificity of football and sport in an address to the Council of Europe's winter parliamentary Assembly in Strasbourg.

It is worth reprising Michel Platini's comments in detail, as they go to the heart of the current debate surrounding to which realm – social, economic/commercial or political – sport truly belongs. Under a sub-heading entitled 'Negative influences' UEFA.com stated that:

> … Mr Platini expressed his concern that football's fundamental social and cultural values were coming under pressure from various negative influences. He called for preservation of the European sports model based on elements such as financial solidarity and openness of competitions with promotion and relegation, and urged the assembly's support for a draft resolution on sport's specific nature and the European sports model.

> 'European sport has always been a powerful catalyst for social and cultural integration', said Mr Platini. 'Two key aspects make the European model of sport both unique and completely fair: the financial solidarity between the different levels of European sport and the openness of competitions thanks to the system of promotion and relegation. Any attempt to undermine these two elements would sound the death knell of the fundamental relationship that exists between sport and society in our continent.'

In essence, these comments represented a fundamental critique of the American sports 'entertainment' model, as exemplified by American Football's NFL, a closed league with few solidarity arrangements and one that may be understood as having more in common with the US entertainment industry than with any comparable sports league operating within Europe.

Later in his comments, Mr Platini made explicit reference to the importance of nurturing football's grassroots and the volunteer tradition, which together with European sports organizations, he argued, helped maintain the balance which enabled sports' values to be passed on perpetually. Critically he spoke of:

> … an explosion of sectoral and corporate interests at both league and club levels in all team sports that are played professionally. These initiatives, which often attract enormous media coverage, are designed to benefit one element, particularly if it is powerful and rich, rather than the masses. Attempts are made to reduce a discipline into a show, to demean a sport in order to convert it into a product. It is becoming more important to make a profit than to win trophies.

This was interpreted in some quarters as a very thinly veiled attack on the elite football clubs of Europe. Of course it should be recognized that UEFA has itself become quite adept at harnessing the power of commercial sponsors and broadcasters to market and develop its own competitions. However, it argues that because its core objective is to redistribute this income back to the base of the football pyramid, this distinguishes its commercial activities from those of some elite clubs who seek only to make a financial profit for themselves and have no interest in nurturing football's grassroots or addressing any wider social or cultural agenda.

UEFA.com concluded the report under the heading 'Social Problems':

> … many social problems were reflected in sport, particularly football, since it is by far the most popular sport and attracts the most media attention. In addition to violence, he (Platini) said: 'Society has also passed other scourges on to the world of sport: money-laundering, match-fixing, illegal betting, racism and xenophobia, doping, child trafficking. The list is long but enables us to identify all the areas in which close cooperation between sports bodies and public authorities is both necessary and unavoidable'. Mr Platini reflected that if professional sport were treated as a kind of commercial activity

like any other business, all sporting activity would ultimately be viewed through the 'terribly distorting prism of competition law'.

In his comments, Michel Platini was throwing into sharp relief an age-old argument in the history of organized sporting activity, the encroachment of commercial forces into sport. He was also concerned with how to manage these forces without losing something potentially very valuable – sport's wider contribution to the social and cultural 'balance sheet' of society. More explicitly, Platini was also reasserting the primacy of sports' traditional governing bodies to have overall responsibility for the governance and regulation of their sport, in all its social, cultural, political, economic and commercial facets; and that this responsibility should not and, if he received broad support for his views, would not be acceded to primarily commercial organizations. For it is this perception – that in essence a takeover of the control of sports is underway (and in some cases in full flow) underpinned by purely commercial forces – that lies at the heart of Mr Platini's concerns. Interestingly, shortly after the speech to the European parliament by the UEFA president, it was announced that the independent organization of European elite clubs, G14, was to be disbanded and that a new independent European Club Association (ECA) was being formed. Significantly, the latter was to operate within the terms of UEFA's existing framework of consultation with stakeholders in European football.[2]

In his comments, Mr Platini illustrates another central reality of sport as a sector; that it truly does have multiple objectives spanning the social, cultural and economic spheres, as reflected in its diverse and numerous stakeholders. This makes the terrain of sports governance and regulation impossible to analyse effectively other than by adopting a rounded interdisciplinary approach. For even in the context of economic analysis, as Walter Neale's[3] seminal paper outlines, the economics of sport has 'peculiar' characteristics that make it particularly challenging to analyse when compared with conventional economic marketplaces. These include an understanding that:

(1) Clubs and leagues constitute a form of joint production. There is a need for strong competitors to have a healthy league competition, or to achieve competitive balance; whereas under conventional market arrangements businesses seek to eliminate other strong competitors to increase their market share. Ultimately, therefore, sports competitions require the presence of effective governance mechanisms to ensure an adequate level of competitive balance is maintained.

(2) Redistribution is critical: in order to create a reasonable level of competitive balance there is a need for some degree of revenue redistribution to ensure that unequal financial power in the sport labour market does not distort overall competitive balance. Once again, therefore, sports competitions need effective governance mechanisms to ensure adequate competitive balance is maintained.

(3) Supporters of all sports clubs exhibit an extraordinary degree of loyalty to their clubs – what some have described as 'fan equity',[4] to the extent that they will not substitute their support for other clubs even if their own team proves to be unsuccessful. This area of consumer–producer relationships in sport is unique in business terms and therefore needs to be nurtured and protected by governing bodies the world over.

(4) Business objectives in sport are often different to those in other industries. Private businesses that own sports teams are unique in the business world in

that they frequently prioritise winning (utility) over financial profit. Yet this creates a built-in incentive for clubs to be financially irresponsible in the pursuit of sporting success. It follows that any successful sports competition or league needs to design and enact a proper regulatory system to counter this growing tendency.

(5) Players in sports, particularly in professional sports, as a consequence of their unique talents, possess monopoly power, which again creates a built in incentive for wage inflation in sports' labour markets. It hardly needs to be said that any successful sports competition needs to design regulation to address this trend as unchecked it contains the seeds of its own destruction.

(6) For all this, the health of any professional sports league is ultimately dependent on the strength of a particular sport's grassroots programme, as it is from the grassroots that future players, and indeed spectators, emerge. Sports' organizations need to regulate to ensure that there is a degree of redistribution from the commercial revenue generation sectors of their respective industries to the grassroots to enable the sport at this level to prosper.

(7) It is broadly accepted that sport has a deep social significance beyond the purely economic sphere. For example, a high level of sports participation helps governments to achieve objectives regarding the health and well-being of the population. There is, therefore, a shared governance agenda on the part of state administrations and sports governing bodies to regulate for increased participation.

(8) Similarly, sport has a deep *cultural* significance beyond its perceived commercial imperative. It can help to create a sense of identity and group loyalty that can contribute to improved levels of social cohesion, for example, the role of anti-racism campaigns in English football as a vehicle for addressing wider problems of racism behaviour in English society. Once again, government and sports governing bodies have a vested interest in promoting the positive cultural values of sport.

(9) Critically, as has become a central theme here, effective regulation is required by football and sports authorities, and government, to ensure efficient outcomes against all the above criteria.

In summary, the central reality of sport as a sector is that sports organizations have multiple objectives ranging across the social, cultural and economic spheres, as reflected in their multiple stakeholders. An understanding of how these objectives can best be achieved is ideally suited to a multi- or interdisciplinary framework of analysis. As such, this is the principle which underpins the approach adopted within this collection of articles; that the analysis and governance of sports' organizations requires an interdisciplinary approach, which attempts to address the influences of all its stakeholders, albeit within a particular sporting environment or national setting. It follows that this collection is deliberately eclectic and seeks to examine the challenges of sport governance from a number of different angles. It does not claim to be comprehensive and readily accepts that different case studies may give rise to confounding views and experiences to those relayed through the pages of this series of articles. For all this, this collection of articles is designed to make a serious contribution to the ongoing debate surrounding the future governance of sport by presenting a wide-ranging series of perspectives and, in turn, demonstrate the heterogeneous (if occasionally the homogeneous) nature of the challenges faced in achieving a more sustainable sporting future for all those who wish to see this become a reality.

The collection

Since the foundation of the Premier League in 1992, English football has embarked on an extraordinary financial expansion. Between the 1992/1993 season and the 2006/2007 season the combined financial turnover of the clubs in the Premier League increased by 900% from £170m to £1530m.[5] This is a significant achievement by any standards. However, it is an astonishing fact that there has not been a single year since its foundation in which the combined Premier League clubs have made a collective pre-tax profit. This is also the case for the Championship and Divisions One and Two of the Football League. The clubs have only been able to survive through the receipt of new investment from owners or investors, or through shedding debt through the financial administration process. Worryingly, in the case of this latter point, nearly 50 clubs went bankrupt between 1992 and 2009. This raises a fundamental question. Is it possible for any industry to sustain losses on the consistent annual basis that has characterized the English football industry and not eventually be faced with a catastrophic industry-transforming crisis?

In their article the 'Financial performance in English professional football: "an inconvenient truth"' Sean Hamil and Geoff Walters outline the key data on the financial performance, or nonperformance, of English football in general. They then present a series of case studies of individual clubs and their respective challenges and conclude by questioning why it is that, in the face of seemingly obvious and extremely challenging economic conditions, the leading English clubs appear so resistant to any regulatory reform that might attempt to address the twin and related problems of chronic indebtedness and unprofitability. To explain this phenomenon, the article utilizes an analogy from the policy arena around the climate-change phenomenon and its threat to the world ecosystem. In his best-selling book, *An Inconvenient Truth: The Planetary Emergency of Global Warming and What We Can Do About It*, former US vice president Al Gore[6] argues that the climate crisis is an 'inconvenient' one because it will be expensive to address over the long-term and there is a natural tendency to put off until tomorrow what requires financial commitment today. Nevertheless, even though its effects are happening slowly, if left unchecked the consequences of climate change will be catastrophic; and so it will require an expensive transformation in the way we live our lives, and in the way the global economy is organized, to avoid these consequences. But in order to begin the process of addressing the crisis there must first be recognition among global leaders that there is indeed a global climate change crisis. Gore then poses the question – why is it that some leaders seem not to hear the clarion warnings?

Although the crisis in English football finance will only be a footnote in history compared with the issue of climate change, in terms of their response to the issue of rising debt and chronic unprofitability, the Premier League and its member clubs share many of the same characteristics of those who seek to play down the significance of climate change, and represent another 'inconvenient truth'? And if this view is accepted and no proactive action is taken, is it then inevitable that the problem of chronic unprofitability and unsustainable debt will quickly lead to a major financial crisis in English football? What is clear is that English football is entering uncharted waters with its future far from clear.

Because this collection aims to locate the theoretical alongside the applied, we continue with an account of football governance in Italy – 'The governance and regulation of Italian football' – by a group of both Italian and UK scholars, Sean Hamil, Stephen Morrow, Catharine Idle, Giambattista Rossi and Stefano Faccendini. Based on the performance criteria of success on the field of play, Italian football would appear to be in rude health; the Italian national team won the FIFA World Cup in 2006, and the national club champions AC Milan won the UEFA Champions League in 2007. Constituting, as it does, one of the five largest and most lucrative sports broadcasting TV markets in Europe, the Italian football industry should also be in good financial health given the very high financial revenues it generates. However, in reality, it is now widely recognized that Italian football is in a state of severe financial, sporting and public order crisis. The Calciopoli match-fixing and refereeing scandal of the 2005/2006 season saw Serie A champions Juventus FC stripped of the title and demoted to Serie B, with a number of other clubs suffering penalty points deductions. On top of this, in recent years Italian football has faced a severe public order problem at its grounds. Most Italian clubs are financially unstable and unprofitable, and attendances have been in decline since the 1990s. Of course, as recently as 1999, there was also a major player-doping scandal at Juventus FC, and viewed in their entirety, these incidents present a picture of an industry in almost permanent crisis.

Drawing on a range of published secondary sources (in Italian as well as English), the authors analyse the reasons why this crisis has come about, in particular focusing on the various regulatory shortcomings of Italian football. The article focuses on the power relationship between the Italian Football Federation and the leading football clubs and their owners; and the impact of individual (as opposed to collective) selling of TV broadcasting rights on financial instability with its anti-redistributive effect. The article discusses the apparent reluctance of those in positions of authority in Italian football to resolve issues of governance and corruption; instead through initiatives such as the 2002 Salva Calcio law, the Italian government allowed clubs to bend accounting rules to flatter their accounts. Finally, the article addresses whether the failure of Italy to win the bid to host the 2012 UEFA European football championships, which would have provided much-needed capital to modernize stadia, and which it seems likely was unsuccessful in part due to factors such as the frequent tax irregularities reported in Italian football, will prove a catalyst for a thoroughgoing programme of reform of the Italian football industry.

At one level, the situation in Ireland could hardly be more different from the picture presented of the domestic football scene in Italy. Here, as the article by Hassan entitled 'Governance and the Gaelic Athletic Association: time to move beyond the amateur ideal?' outlines, the success of the Gaelic Athletic Association (GAA), Ireland's largest sporting organization, has been nothing short of remarkable and stands testimony to what can be achieved when a community-based model of sport governance is afforded serious consideration. The GAA has a membership of almost 1 million people and a presence in every part of the island. It has advanced an amateur ideal for the 125 years of its existence, although in recent years there has been a considerable growth in the professional administration of gaelic games activity in the country. This article deals with the question of corporate governance within the GAA, an issue that to date has not received any form of academic coverage. Despite the overall positive nature of the GAA, David Hassan argues that the current approach to governance in the association is outdated, unwieldy and inefficient. An argument for the adoption of a stewardship model, with the appointment of a professional board of directors, is outlined throughout the article. This is seemingly all the more pressing when one considers the growing number of stakeholders who would wish to have a say in how the GAA manages its affairs. Indeed, it is notable that many of the Association's fiercest critics on this matter have emerged from within its own ranks. Because these are the same individuals on whom the GAA has relied to secure its current position of strength, their growing levels of dissent should be of concern to those in positions of authority within the organization.

Returning to an issue outlined earlier – the apparent conflation of fundamentally different models of sport governance in the USA and in Europe – John Nauright and John Ramfjord's provocatively entitled article 'Who owns England's game? American professional sporting influences and foreign ownership in the Premier League' is a critical examination of English club football by two American-based scholars. Changes to the organization of the Barclay's Premier League in England and its apparent unrelenting commercialization has made some of its member clubs attractive to international investors. Recently, in particular, there has been a rapid increase in American ownership of Premier League teams with Aston Villa, Liverpool, Manchester United and Sunderland owned by Americans, while a large minority shareholder at Arsenal FC is also American. Beyond directorship/ownership issues, North American organizational and marketing structures of professional sport have increased their influence within the Premier League. These include a focus on diverse revenue streams including media rights, luxury seating, commodification and branding of clubs and their heritage, and diversified services such as club-branded credit cards. While these have merged with English traditions within professional football, there is no doubt that North American influences have begun to change the nature of marketing within the game and have also made leading English clubs attractive to North American and other international investors. Of course, the result of increasing 'Americanization' of English professional football marketing and management strategies has placed it on a collision course with English traditions of organization as well as supporters' consumption of the game itself.

In contrast to the global reach and popularity of the association football game, rugby union enjoys the position of being the national sport of New Zealand. This position is sustained by an exceptional model of governance with central control by the national administration. It was established before the turn of the twentieth century and has remained New Zealand's governance model in the new professional era. In '"Club versus country" in rugby union: tensions in an exceptional New Zealand system', Camilla Obel offers a comparative discussion of the different organizational structures in the northern and southern hemispheres and explains how the sport is vulnerable to the contrasting governance systems characterized as 'club versus country'. Drawing on Leifer's account of the transformation of the major leagues in North America, this article investigates how the tension between hierarchical control by a central authority and the drive for local autonomy by clubs is resolved. It details the early establishment of local and national amateur rugby union competitions in New Zealand and argues that these 'professional-like' competitions constituted a strategic compromise by the New Zealand Rugby Union (NZRU). In the global professional era, the NZRU has retained central control over the sport and players through the establishment of NZRU contracts to players and coaches in the five New Zealand Super 14 teams. While the wealthy English clubs exercise a considerable degree of control relative to the English RFU on the issue of player releases for national representation, the current tension in the New Zealand system resides in the saturation of the local player/coach labour market and the ability of players and coaches to exit for better-paying contracts in the northern hemisphere.

In their article entitled, 'The impact of televised football on stadium attendances in English and Spanish league Football', which is the combined contribution of Babatunde Buraimo, Juan Luis Paramio and Carlos Campos, the authors remind their readership of a salient truth, which is that since at least the early 1990s, sports broadcasting has emerged to become an important part of the sports' industry. This is particularly important in the case of European football because revenues generated from the sport broadcast market tend to dominate and overshadow those generated from gate attendance, which has traditionally been the main source of income to football clubs and leagues. In this article, the authors critically review the broadcast regimes of the English Premier League and the Spanish Primera Liga (Liga de Primera Division) and examine the impacts that televising games from these leagues has had on their respective match-day attendances. They conclude that, although stadium attendances in both leagues respond to a series of factors in a similar manner, the effects of broadcasting on match-day attendance vary across the two leagues. Towards the close of their fascinating article the authors examine the economic issues and policy implications of these findings for a wider market.

For the final article in this collection, the focus remains on Spain, albeit by focusing specifically on the governance arrangements of the Catalan giants FC Barcelona. In this case, Sean Hamil, Geoff Walters and Lee Watson present their argument in an article entitled 'The model of governance at FC Barcelona: balancing member democracy, commercial strategy, corporate social responsibility and sporting performance', which acts as a timely reminder that all is seemingly not lost amid the suggestion that football clubs across Europe now constitute the worst excesses of sport's unrelenting drive to commercialize itself. In this vein, a popular justification for takeovers of English football clubs by millionaire private owners is that in order to be successful a club needs to be able to attract major private investment to compete in the international football player labour market. The debate that unfolded in the UK through spring 2008 as to whether Liverpool FC would be better served being owned by Dubai International Capital (DIC), as opposed to its current owners the American investors Tom Hicks and George Gillett, on the grounds that DIC would likely be more aggressive in its forays into the football transfer market, exemplifies this particular terms of reference concerning an ideal model of ownership for a football club. By extension, this explicitly implies that a successful football club is best structured as a private or public limited company with shareholders as opposed to members or indeed any form of mutual or collective ownership.

However, by contrast, FC Barcelona, one of Europe's most successful clubs, is a not-for-profit sporting club owned by over 150,000 members, or socios. This article critically considers the reasons why the atypical ownership and governance structure of FC Barcelona does not appear to hamper its ability to compete on financial and sporting terms, examines the reasons why this is the case, and discusses the extent to which the Barcelona governance and strategic 'model' might be generalized across the elite European football sector. Utilizing a case study analysis, the first part of the article considers how the membership model at FC Barcelona initially came under threat during the presidency of Josep Nunez (1978–2000). It then charts the activity of L'Elefant Blau, an organization that campaigned for member democracy from 1999 to 2003 until its leader, Joan Laporta, was elected FC Barcelona president, and which specifically presented a vision of the club's future where it remained in mutual ownership and did not become a privately owned corporation. The article then critically considers the record of Joan Laporta and his board of directors against four key stated strategic objectives: (1) a re-assertion of member democracy and transparency of club governance, (2) a commitment to significantly increase commercial revenues through more effective business management, (3) an explicit commitment to develop a corporate social responsibility strategy (CSR) policy, and (4) a commitment to dramatically improve the club's sporting performance. It concludes by discussing the extent to which the distinctive Barcelona governance and strategic 'model' might be generalized across the elite European football sector.

Conclusion

The analysis contained within the various articles addresses developments in a number of countries, including England, Ireland, Italy, New Zealand and Spain. But perhaps more critically, a number of key themes emerge across the various contributions, of which the following represent the most important. First, the income-generating power of traditional fan cultures as the well-spring of virtually all successful economic models of sport be they professional, for example English and Italian football, the remarkable model of the supporter-owned FC Barcelona in Spain's La Liga or amateur (or more appropriately perhaps those 'with amateur roots', for example, Ireland's GAA and rugby union in New Zealand). Second, the economically de-stabilizing effect of very strong labour power, the key engine of rising costs in English Premier League football, which is also now beginning to manifest itself in, for example, the amateur sporting arena represented by the GAA through the establishment of a players' union, the Gaelic Players Association (GPA). Third, as sports become more economically productive a tendency has emerged for their leading representatives to wield greater (possibly disproportionate) degrees of power. This has been a defining development in English football where the major clubs, through the Premier League, have emerged as possibly the most dominant stakeholder in the industry. The recent experience of New Zealand rugby illustrates similar tendencies in this regard. Fourth, at the same time that commercial influences are challenging the European model of sport, universally all sporting bodies, be they traditional or commercial, seek to extract revenue from the public purse. For example, in Italy, bankrupt Italian clubs pinned their hopes on the right to stage the 2012 European Championships as a means to leverage the refurbishment of publicly owned football stadia. Finally, but by no means of any lesser concern, has been the extraordinary influence of TV broadcasting on the economics of sports, and on the stability of sporting competitions generally.

Indeed it is worth examining how this issue – the impact of television broadcasting of sport – manifests itself in each of the geographical contexts addressed in this collection, as a means of demonstrating the appropriateness of an interdisciplinary approach such as the one adopted here. It is a truism that in all sports the development of the pay-TV market and its influence cannot be underestimated. It has increased income, but it has also increased instability. And in all sports it has led to either increased pressure to restructure or the actual restructuring of leagues and other competitive contexts. This is because income from TV broadcasting flows disproportionately to elite professional sport, potentially undermining the role of traditional governing bodies where they do not retain control of TV income distribution. As Nauright and Ramjford argue, sport originally professionalized because spectators were prepared to pay at the gate to enter an enclosed arena to watch football. More latterly, television has simply adopted the same principle by presenting the opportunity of 'pay to view' to a wider audience. As a result of this, the means of distribution for viewing became extended, occasionally to include a global reach.

Thus the commercial pressures that sport currently faces from television are only a more aggressive re-run of those instigated following the introduction of stadia designed to accommodate paying customers. As Hassan notes in his analysis of the situation in Ireland, TV has both popularized elite intercounty gaelic football and increased incomes that can be redistributed to the grassroots. Yet simultaneously, this same TV-contract-inspired income has contributed to the development of the GPA, a players' union that is seeking to take a share of these incomes and in the process is threatening to destabilize the GAA as an organization. Ironically, the GAA is rare among sports organizations in that it is currently profitable, probably because it does not pay its players. In examining the situation within rugby union, Obel observes that in both hemispheres, the introduction of televised sport and the broadcasting of the alternative rugby league code almost certainly boosted the position of the major gate-taking clubs in England and the larger provincial unions in New Zealand, who were both in favour of national competitions. In a similar vein, and picking up on an earlier point, Hassan also indicates that the GAA changed the structure of its competitions in part as a response to TV interest. In this case, the knockout system used in elite level gaelic sports, and the risk that leading teams could be eliminated after only one match, became unacceptable to players, television executives and the GAA itself, the latter ever more mindful of its commercial responsibilities. Indeed, within the sport of football, UEFA amended the Champions League for the same reason. But of course it had faced the additional pressure from privately owned 'super-clubs' that became increasingly ambitious around their commercial direction. In terms of these specific issues, Hamil *et al.* illustrate the extraordinarily destabilizing effect that the individual selling of TV rights by clubs, as opposed to collective selling by the league, has had on the competitive balance of Italian football. Earlier, Hamil, in his co-authored piece with Geoff Walters examining the English game, details the emergence of the pay-TV industry in England, which in turn was a key driver behind the creation of the English Premier League. Thus it is appropriate that it is to this article that we now turn, a piece that complements the overarching aim of this entire compendium, which is to initiate a debate surrounding the corporate governance of sport, to begin to raise questions about the direction being taken by those managing sport across a range of national settings and in so doing demonstrate the importance of a synthesised, interdisciplinary approach to this task when assessing the challenges that lie ahead for all.

Notes

1. UEFA.com. 'Platini Plea for Values', 24 January 2008.
2. UEFA.com. 'European Football the Winner', 7 March 2008.
3. Neale, 'The Peculiar Economics of Professional Sports'.
4. Hamil, 'A Whole New Ball Game', 29–32.
5. Deloitte, *Annual Review of Football Finance*.
6. Gore, *An Inconvenient Truth*.

References

Deloitte. *Annual Review of Football Finance*. Manchester: Deloitte, 2008.
Gore, A. *An Inconvenient Truth: The Planetary Emergency of Global Warming and What We Can Do About it*. London: Bloomsbury Publishing, 2006.

Hamil, S. 'A Whole New Ball Game: Why Football Needs A Regulator'. In *A Game of Two Halves: The Business of Football,* ed. S. Hamil, J. Michie, and C. Oughton, 23–39. Edinburgh: Mainstream, 1999.

Neale, W. 'The Peculiar Economics of Professional Sports; a Contribution to the Theory of the Firm in Sporting Competition and in Market Competition'. *Quarterly Journal of Economics* 78, no. 1 (1964): 1–14.

UEFA.com. 'Platini Plea for Values', 24 January 2008. http://www.uefa.com/uefa/keytopics/kind=64/newsid=649269.html. Accessed 7 March 2009.

UEFA.com. 'European Football the Winner', 7 March 2008. http://www.uefa.com/magazine/news/kind=128/newsid=669554.html. Accessed 7 March 2009.

Financial performance in English professional football: 'an inconvenient truth'[1]

Sean Hamil and Geoff Walters

Department of Management, Birkbeck, University of London, London, UK

This article presents an analysis of the financial performance of English football since the creation of the Premier League in 1992. It demonstrates that despite large increases in revenue, in particular from broadcasting, football clubs in the Premier League and Football League have year-on-year collectively failed to post a pre-tax profit; there have been many examples of clubs in the Football League having to enter into administration; and debt levels have risen. The article argues that, in their denial that the financial crisis in the wider economy will seriously impact the economic health of English Football, many of the industry's leading figures share many of the same hugely optimistic assumptions of those who seek to play down the significance of climate change. In doing so they overlook the 'inconvenient truth' coined by former US Vice-President Al Gore in the context of the climate change debate, that English football is not immune from the impact of wider financial instability. The article questions whether, given the current economic climate, a failure to implement pro-active regulatory action to address the problem of chronic unprofitability and unsustainable debt will lead to a major financial crisis in English football.

Introduction

Since the foundation of the Premier League (Premiership) in 1992, English football has embarked on an extraordinary financial expansion. Between the 1992/1993 season and the 2006/2007 season the combined financial turnover of the clubs in the Premier League increased by 900% from £170m to £1530m.[2] This is a significant achievement by any standards. This financial success is not confined only to the Premier League. All levels of the English professional game have increased financial turnover, if not as spectacularly as the Premiership. By way of example, between the 1997/1998 and 2006/2007 seasons, the combined financial turnover of clubs in the second tier of English professional football, the Championship, increased 179% from £186m to £329m.[3]

However, it is an astonishing fact that there has not been a single year since its foundation when the combined Premier League clubs have made a collective pre-tax profit. This is also the case for the Championship and Divisions 1 and 2 of the Football League. The clubs have been able to survive only through the receipt of new investment from owners or investors, or through shedding debt via the financial administration process, as nearly 50 clubs went bankrupt between 1992 and 2009.

This raises a fundamental question. Is it possible for any industry to sustain losses on the consistent annual basis that has characterized the English football industry and not eventually be faced with a catastrophic industry transforming crisis?

The stock answer to the lack of profitability by English football insiders is that owners of English clubs have always recognized that few clubs make money; they are in fact motivated primarily by nonfinancial considerations, for example, by the desire to pursue sporting success on the field of play at the expense of profit because they themselves are fans, for the public relations benefits to their wider business interests, or for the celebrity and vanity assuaging benefits that club ownership brings. By this logic, there will always be a sufficient pool of willing investors prepared to sacrifice some investment in order to, to echo the well-worn phrase, 'live the dream', if only for a short period. Certainly, the fact that the Premier League has managed to sustain 17 years of uninterrupted pre-tax losses since its foundation while simultaneously being lauded as the most successful soccer league business in the world would seem to support this folklore. However, that was before the 'credit crunch'.

In September 2008, the world entered a economic slowdown of a severity not experienced since the great depression of the 1930s. A number of major British banks had to be rescued either by the British state taking a significant shareholding via a cash injection, as in the case of Royal Bank of Scotland, or by straight nationalization, as in the case of Northern Rock. Fundamental to their difficulties was the issue of over-indebtedness. It does not seem an extraordinary leap in logic to suggest that, with some of the country's major financial institutions brought to their knees by the 'credit crunch', it was at best rather optimistic to suggest that English football would be immune from its effects. That was certainly the view of Lord David Triesman, chairman of English football's main governing body the Football Association (FA). In a controversial speech[4] to the Leaders in Football conference in October 2008 at Chelsea's Stamford Bridge Premiership stadium he observed regarding indebtedness of English clubs:

> The best estimate I could get in the City yesterday was that debts in English football as a whole have probably edged to the £3bn mark.

Critically, Lord Triesman observed that such 'toxic debt' could cause massive damage to the game and called for a review of the Fit and Proper Persons test in order to make football club ownership more transparent. The test, first introduced by the Football League in 2003, with the Premier League following shortly after, effectively bars from ownership of a football club anyone with a criminal record. However, Lord Triesman expressed concern about the current format of the test:

> Transparency lies in an unmarked grave. Nobody has real confidence in what they cannot see. The Fit and Proper Persons Test does not do the job sufficiently robustly. A review is now inevitable because football clubs are not mere commodities. They are the abiding passion of their supporters. We forget that at our peril.

Essentially, Triesman was arguing that the test should be extended to ensure that only those who could demonstrate a clear ability to finance a football club as an ongoing concern should be able to take ownership of an English football club. And that English football needed a much stronger financial regulatory framework if it was to avoid major problems in the near future.

Premier League chief executive Richard Scudamore responded robustly, arguing that the Premier League clubs' debts were not out of line with their revenues (although he made no mention of profitability),[5] and that the established framework of light touch self-regulation had served the industry well and did not require significant amendment. However, a week later, the government minister with responsibility for sport, Andy Burnham,[6] Secretary of State for Culture, Media & Sport, entered the debate. Speaking at the annual conference of the supporters' organization Supporters Direct, he opined that English football risked losing touch with its core supporters but that it also needed to 're-assess its relationship with money'. He then asked the FA, as well as the Premier and Football Leagues to consider whether:[7]

- the rules governing finances could be made consistent between the leagues;
- there could be greater transparency and scrutiny of clubs' ownership, including the amount of debt used to finance a takeover and an assessment be made as to whether that debt is 'sustainable and in the wider interests of the game';
- the rules which penalize clubs falling into insolvency needed to be reviewed;
- the rule which requires insolvent clubs to pay football debts in full (the Football Creditors' Rule), unlike other debts, should be reviewed;
- the Fit and Proper Person test for club directors and 30% shareholders needed to be strengthened;
- 'competitive balance' [unpredictability of league outcome] should be promoted, 'preventing the game becoming too predictable';
- everything possible was being done to bolster the national side, and whether there is 'a case for introducing a specified number of homegrown players' into club sides.

As with Lord Triesman's comments, at the heart of Minister Burnham's comments was a concern that football clubs' perceived reckless approach to financial management was creating a risk of spiralling financial instability, leading to the possible demise of some clubs and the collapse of the traditional relationship between English football and its supporters.

Although the Premier League's response was more restrained than it had been for Lord Triesman's comments – a spokesman simply noted the comments and said they would await formal communication – clearly there was not much appetite in this quarter for the implied significant overhaul of the regulatory regime in football. So, while in the rest of the economy major companies collapsed with startling regularity, the view from the commanding heights of the major professional football league in the Europe was that, in all likelihood, English football would ride out the economic trauma of global recession relatively unscathed, and certainly without the need for the kind of dramatic regulatory intervention seen elsewhere in the economy. To repeat a comment made earlier, this seems an extraordinarily optimistic assumption in light of the wider economic circumstances that pertained toward the end of the 2008/09 season.

An effective analogy that might be drawn with the 'optimist' position on English football finance in 2009 can be found in the policy arena around the climate-change phenomenon and its threat to the world ecosystem. In his best-selling book, *An Inconvenient Truth: The Planetary Emergency of Global Warming and What We Can Do About It*, former US vice president Al Gore[8] argues that the climate crisis is an 'inconvenient' one because it will be expensive to address over the long-term and there is a natural tendency to put off until tomorrow what requires financial commitment today. Nevertheless, even though its effects are happening slowly, if left unchecked, the consequences of climate change will be catastrophic; so it will require an expensive transformation in the way we live our lives, and in the way the global economy is organized, to avoid these consequences. But in order to begin the process of addressing the crisis, there must first be recognition among global leaders that there is indeed a global climate change crisis. Gore then poses the question – why is it that some leaders seem not to hear the clarion warnings?

In its first season in 1992/1993, the Premiership commenced with four key supporting trends:

(1) English clubs had just been re-admitted to European football competitions in 1990, with the consequent boost to revenue, after a five-year ban following the Heysel disaster (Brussels 1985), when 39 Juventus fans died at the European Cup Final between Juventus and Liverpool following crowd disorder.
(2) The rebuilding of all English football stadia had commenced, following the recommendations of the Taylor Report into the Hillsborough disaster which saw 96 Liverpool fans die at an FA Cup semi-final with Nottingham Forest due to flawed stadium management and policing strategies. This meant conversion to all-seater status and a consequent improvement in stadia conditions and services which attracted a much wider and more affluent spectator to English football grounds. This rebuilding received a significant subsidy from the state via a levy on pools betting duty.[9]
(3) Premiership clubs were benefiting from the first season of revenues from a brand new and highly lucrative source – pay-per-view television via the first BSkyB contract.
(4) Coming out of recession, the world and UK economies were beginning 15 years of uninterrupted growth which lasted into 2007; as economies grow a disproportionate amount is spent on leisure and so the Premiership benefited disproportionately from this trend.

In 2009, the economic landscape for English football changed radically:

(1) European competition revenues were an established requirement not an additional boost.
(2) Investment in new stadia had to be financed independently and involves some trade-off with player expenditure.
(3) Domestic TV income was comparatively stable and the years of exceptional growth were over. The latest domestic Premier League broadcasting deal (2010–2013) is worth £1.782bn, compared with £1.7bn over the period 2007–2010, a marginal increase.
(4) Both the world and the UK economies were contracting and commercial and sponsorship incomes, and the incomes of many of those who support Premiership football clubs, were contracting with them.

In summary, for the first time since its foundation, the Premiership was facing an environment in which the economic stars were not universally aligned favourably.

Although the crisis in English football finance will only be a footnote in history compared with the issue of climate change, in terms of their response to the issue of rising debt and chronic unprofitability does the response of the Premier League and its member clubs, and indeed those of the Football League, also share many of the same characteristics of those who seek to play down the significance of climate change, another 'inconvenient truth'? And if this view is accepted and no proactive action is taken, then is it inevitable that the problem of chronic unprofitability and unsustainable debt will quickly lead to a major financial crisis in English football? Whatever the answer, it is clear that English football is entering uncharted waters.

Some history

English professional football is widely held up as the definitive success story of European football over the last decade; and by extension the role model for other European leagues to follow. Drawing on data from the authoritative Deloitte *Annual Review of Football Finance* there is certainly a lot of evidence to support this contention:[10]

- The top tier Premier League is the richest league in Europe by some margin in terms of financial turnover.
- Over the 10-year period 1996/97 to 2006/2007 the combined turnover of the 20 clubs in the Premier League, when expressed in euros to allow cross-comparison with other European peer leagues, increased by 330% from €689m to €2273m.
- The next most lucrative league, the German Bundesliga, increased from €444m to €1379m.
- The second tier English league, the Championship, is itself the fifth richest league in Europe in terms of financial turnover.
- The Premier League has the most lucrative television broadcasting deal and derives the most income from sponsorship.

In the 2007/2008 season, the average Premiership team stadium operated at around 93% capacity – a capacity utilization figure most airlines would be delighted with:

- Total crowds for the season were 13.7m, the highest since the foundation of the Premier League in 1992/1993.
- The Championship was the fourth best-attended league in Europe after the Premiership, the Bundesliga and La Liga; again illustrating the strength in depth of the performance of English football across a number of key performance indicators.

Average match-day revenue per game attendee at a Premiership match in 2006/2007, at €61, was by far the highest in Europe (the comparative figure for La Liga was €35). This again underlines the extraordinary commercial power of the Premier League:

- Not surprisingly, the Premier League paid the highest wages in Europe. The total Premiership wage bill in 2006/07 was €1440m; the total for the next highest, Spain's La Liga, was €822m.
- Equally unsurprisingly, Premier League clubs had a dominant position in the global market for football players. It was therefore widely perceived as being the highest quality league in Europe in terms of the quality of football, and the most glamorous in terms of the number of celebrity players it could attract.
- This, in turn, made it more attractive to TV broadcasters, which is why the Premier League has the most lucrative TV broadcasting deal of any league in the world.

Across a range of key indicators therefore it is clear that English football does deserve the accolade of being described as Europe's most successful league. However, on the most critical financial indicator of all, English football's performance is deeply problematic. For the top flight of English football – that is the Premier League, and also the three divisions of the Football League below it, the Championship, League One and League Two – is chronically unprofitable as the data in Table 1 illustrates for just the seasons 2005/2006 and 2006/2007.

English football is unprofitable

So, at the pre-tax level (profit after taking account of player transfer trading) total losses in the 2006/2007 season at Premiership clubs reached a new high of £285m (Table 1). The pre-tax losses of the 72 clubs in the Football League were also significant totalling £86m; while aggregate debt levels for the 18, of 24, Championship clubs for which Deloitte had information at the time of publication, totalled £289m. Total debt in the Premier League reached £2.47billion (making the combined Premier League clubs debt-to-turnover gearing a very high 161%) with some clubs, notably Manchester United (owned by the Glazer family; debt of £605m), Chelsea (owned by Russian oligarch Roman Abramovich; debt of £620m), Arsenal (a company quoted on the London's MyPlus stock market but controlled by a group of private investors none with a dominant share together with several thousand small shareholders who were mainly supporters; debt of £268m), West Ham United (controlled by Icelandic investor Bjorgolfur Gudmundsson; debt of £142m) and Fulham (owned by Mohammed Al Fayed, who also owned London's iconic Harrods department store; debt of £167m) maintaining especially high levels of debt. With the exception of the consistently well-managed Arsenal, all of these clubs made substantial pre-tax losses in the 2006/2007 season. For example, Fulham made a loss of £15.9m and West Ham United lost £22m.[12] Unless these clubs are able to trade their way out of debt, which for the vast majority, given the long history of unprofitability in the Premier League is unlikely, the only way they will ultimately be able to address their debt issues is either by debt write-off through new investment from existing or new investors, or by entering administration via a bankruptcy. Essentially English football is almost entirely dependent for its continued stability on the willingness of individual owners, increasingly non-UK citizens, to sustain losses and underwrite debt and pay the related interest payments. This situation would be regarded as intolerable and unsustainable in any other industry.

Table 1. English football – pre-tax profitability (£ sterling).

	2006/07		2005/06	
	Pre-tax profit	Turnover	Pre-tax profit	Turnover
Premier League	−£285m	£1530m	−£200m	£1379m
Championship	−£62m	£329m	−£36m	£318m
League One	−£20m	£102m	−£17m	£102m
League Two	−£4m	£63m	−£4m	£61m

Source: Deloitte, *Annual Review of Football Finance.*[11]

Nevertheless, although Premier League clubs are loss making, as of the beginning of the 2008/2009 season, almost all owners appeared willing to sustain these losses – perhaps for reasons of prestige they regard their ownership of a club as a 'trophy asset' the benefits of which are largely non-pecuniary. As such, the finances of Premiership clubs are more stable than clubs in the Football League. For example, they are at least profitable at the operating level (before transfers) making a cumulative operating profit of £1312m in the 15 seasons to 2006/2007. By contrast, in 2006/2007 the cumulative operating losses of the 72 clubs in the three divisions of the Football League in the 15 seasons up to 2006/2007 were £932m. In other words, Football League clubs do not even break even before transfer spending. This can be explained by the fact that they spend a much higher proportion of their income on wages. In 2006/07 the wages-to-turnover ratio for the Premier League was a record 63%; whereas the comparative figures for the Championship, League One and League Two were 79, 74 and 67%, respectively. The wages-to-turnover ratio in the Championship in the 10 seasons from 1997/1998 to 2006/2007 has never been below 71%, and was as high as 101% in 2000/2001. Deloitte recommend a wages-to-turnover ratio no higher than 60% as part of a prudent financial strategy.

In effect, the reality is that the vast proportion of increased revenue that has been generated by the English football industry since its restructuring with the establishment of the Premier League in 1992/93 has been transferred to the elite players in increased wages.

Bankruptcy – a common occurrence in English football

While there has been a history of financial instability at clubs below the Premiership in the Football League, prior to the 1990s, financial crisis was often averted due to the intervention of local businessmen, with few cases of administration or insolvency (bankruptcy leading to dissolution of the club). Administration is the process whereby failed companies which are unable to meet their financial obligations are given protection from their creditors while being 'administered' by an insolvency practitioner until such time as they are restructured. Yet from 1992 to 2008, the period when English football entered an unprecedented period of financial revenue expansion through increased attendances, the most lucrative television broadcasting deals in Europe and very beneficial sponsorship deals, financial problems at Football League clubs resulted in 48 cases of administration[13] (well over half of the 72 clubs in the Football League) or bankruptcy. This was because they overspent on player wages to achieve sporting success, although some clubs in the Championship were committed to unaffordable player contracts upon relegation from the Premier League; in effect, clubs which got into difficulties while taking on debt in a failed bid to stay in the Premiership only crystallized the financial consequences of this reckless behaviour on exiting the Premier League, thus flattering the overall financial performance of the Premier League in the process. The experience of Leeds United exemplifies this effect. Having reached the UEFA Champions League semi-final in the 2000/2001 season, the club narrowly missed qualification the following season and began an inexorable spiral of decline as players were sold at less than their purchase price to service debt, sporting performance then declined, until finally the club was relegated from the Premiership at the end of the 2003/2004 season, entering administration in 2007. A further relegation followed and they were playing in League One in the 2008/2009 season, a shadow of the great big city club they once were.

Sustained operating losses in the Football League have also served to increase debt levels, which proved too difficult to service. In England, if a club emerging from administration wishes to retain its place in the league then it must first pay all its football-related debt (player wages and transfer payments to other clubs) under a condition known as the Football Creditors' Rule. This is a football industry-specific rule which is designed to protect football clubs from the reckless financial behaviour of those peer clubs which fall into bankruptcy and financial administration. As a result, a particularly dubious scenario results whereby other creditors receive proportionately less from the reconstruction of the business. Often significant losers are the UK tax authorities. So, in effect, a large part of the cost of failing English football clubs is being carried by the public purse, in effect, a public sector subsidy to a failing private business sector.[14] Again this is a situation that would not be tolerated in any other industry, with the exception of the strategically critical UK financial services sector which was bailed out by the British government over the 2008/2009 period. In effect, football trades on its status as one of the most powerful cultural and social assets in the country. In reality, no state body, such as the tax authorities, wants to be the organization that ultimately liquidates a football club, such is their iconic status in English popular culture.

Why is English football unprofitable?

Prominent businessman (and star of the UK TV hit show *The Apprentice*) and former owner of Tottenham Hotspur Sir Alan Sugar has referred rather coarsely to 'the prune juice effect' (prune juice being a laxative – increased revenues enter the mouth of a football club and exit swiftly out the rear in player salaries). When Sugar sold his controlling interest in Tottenham in 2001, he publicly stated that owning an English football club was not a viable business proposition, but a very expensive 'hobby' or leisure pursuit.[15]

> With the exception of one football club – Manchester United – it is questionable whether they are good investments or not. I've got my [13% of Tottenham – down from 40%] and I'm quite happy. We're all entitled to a little hobby.

He subsequently sold the balance of his investment in Tottenham.

There has always been some debate as to why Alan Sugar originally involved himself in football by purchasing Tottenham in 1991. Clearly, he had another interest in the football industry as his Amstrad company was the main supplier of satellite dishes for the Sky pay-per-view television company (soon to be BSkyB as it took over its only rival BSB), who established the market for pay-per-view television in 1992 largely on the back of broadcasting the first season of Premiership football. However, having bought Tottenham, he did try to run it as a conventional profit-making business. As Szymanski & Kuypers[16] have outlined, the consequences are instructive. Refusing to compete with the inflationary wage awards of competitors, the club was profitable (although only marginally) but sporting performance suffered. It moved from being a team challenging for qualification to European competition to one flirting with relegation (in the 1997/98 season) and crowds also declined affecting revenues. To avoid relegation, Alan Sugar had to sanction the signing of former Tottenham, and German international player, Jurgen Klinsmann and a very significant uplift in player transfer spending. Relegation was avoided, but the expenditure involved in achieving this objective negated the attempt to run a profitable business in the process. As noted above, Sugar exited Tottenham soon after highly disillusioned with football's economics.

The experience of Alan Sugar's tenure at Tottenham illustrates a central reality in sports economics. The source of competitive advantage on the field of play is obvious for all to see – the best players. Every year the Deloitte *Annual Review of Football Finance* charts the close relationship between expenditure on players and sporting success.[17] In a situation such as pertains in the English Premiership and Championship leagues where there is a free, unrestrained market for player contracts and player salaries, then all clubs are free to engage in what is essentially a labour market version of the Cold War 'arms race' to hire and retain the best playing talent, in the process driving a highly inflationary spiral in players' wages and transfer fees. In a league which is not closed and where there is promotion and relegation there are clear incentives for all clubs, not just those seeking to win the league title, but those seeking to compete to qualify for European competition or to avoid relegation, to spend beyond their means to achieve their immediate sporting objectives. In this situation, only one team can really plan on being consistently profitable; the one with the highest turnover who can therefore afford to outbid all other teams in the league for the best labour but still have a margin left over for profit. Until the arrival of Roman Abramovich at Chelsea, this was the position occupied by Manchester United, who as Alan Sugar rightly observed, have been the only consistently profitable (at a significant level) club in England since the establishment of the Premiership. Of course, there are occasions where spending power alone cannot buy absolute success. It is a tribute to the extraordinary managerial ability of Sir Alex Ferguson that he has been able to sustain Manchester United's sporting dominance with significantly inferior spending power than Chelsea (while also, as we will see below, having to tolerate a situation where significant revenues go to service the debt the Glazer family used to buy the club in the first place). But this is a rare achievement and is untypical of the industry.

In reality, the reason why the American NFL football competition operates as a closed league with a highly equalized redistribution of centrally controlled broadcasting and commercial income together with a highly regulated player recruitment market with a salary cap is because: (1) they want to achieve a high level of competitive balance (uncertainty of outcome) in order to enhance the attractiveness of their 'product' to spectators and TV viewers; but also (2) critically, because they wish to create an environment where all owners of NFL club franchises can make profits and the league is financially stable.[18]

Or put another way, why do the owners of NFL franchises accept aggressive redistribution of TV and merchandising revenues by a central body – the office of the NFL Commissioner – a salary cap, a draft system – the worst performing team gets to pick the best players from the College (university) competition system which sits below the NFL in the sport's organizational hierarchy – and strict ownership eligibility criteria? The reason is because this acceptance of restraints on individual business autonomy creates competitive balance and hence sporting uncertainty which drives spectator/TV interest, because it guarantees financial stability, and most critically of all because the franchises are then profitable for virtually all owners. In contrast to the UK, the NFL owners understand the implications of one of the key descriptive principles of sports economics – in order to be profitable individual clubs need to sacrifice some control over their own business because sports leagues are joint products and you need strong competitors for the league to be successful, and if you are to be profitable you need to eliminate the built-in incentive to engage in labour cost competition.

These conditions do not exist in English football which is why it is chronically unprofitable. Essentially, English football is a not-for-profit industry for its owners, from which other stakeholders, notably the players, TV companies and merchandising companies make money. This central reality was disguised over the 1992–2007 period because every year saw further increases in revenues and so it was possible to generate profit through selling on clubs to the next ambitious (and dare we say, optimistic) owner. However, with overall revenues likely to be at best static in 2008/2009 and increasing only incrementally thereafter logic dictates that the challenge of lack of profitability will be harder to disguise. It is useful to examine some individual case studies to illustrate the potential problems which may lie ahead.

The case of Manchester United

The 'credit crunch' makes it much more difficult for owners to refinance debt in the event that they struggle to meet interest payments if financial performance declines and could conceivably lead to the financial collapse of some clubs. This should be a particular concern for Manchester United.

In 2005, the American Glazer family bought Manchester United, historically the only English club to consistently make a pre-tax profit,[19] through a mechanism known as a leveraged buyout, i.e. they borrowed the money to purchase Manchester United and intend to pay it back out of the club's profits. However, in order to achieve this they are totally dependent on team manager Sir Alex Ferguson continuing to produce a highly competitive team on the field of play, the wellspring from which financial revenues are derived. To give some idea of the challenge, for the 2006/2007 financial year, the ultimate holding company for Manchester United had a financial turnover of £212.2m, made interest payments of £81m, made a pre-tax loss of £62.6m, but still actually saw total debt rise to £605m. Were Manchester United to fail to qualify for the Champions League by finishing below the top four in the Premier League placings, then the Glazer business plan would come under severe pressure. It would not be over-dramatic to say that such a failure would threaten the very financial stability of the club. The Glazers are in fact almost completely dependent on Sir Alex Ferguson to continue to work his particular brand of coaching magic by not only always qualifying for the Champions League, but also reaching the latter stages of the competition. Should he retire, the challenge of organizing a successor will be challenging – as the history of Chelsea since the departure of Jose Mourinho at the end of the 2006/2007 season demonstrates, with the club, at the end of the 2008/2009 season, onto to its third manager since Mourinho's departure and struggling to meet the competitive standards achieved during his time at the club.

The case of Liverpool

In March 2007, Liverpool football club was acquired by American businessmen George Gillett and Tom Hicks[20] using a similar debt-financed model to the Glazer takeover of Manchester United. In January 2008, the vehicle they used to take over Liverpool, Kop Football Limited, secured a £350m financing package, a proportion of which was intended to fund commencement of the club's proposed new stadium in

Stanley Park, Liverpool. In October 2008, Liverpool announced that it was delaying commencing the new stadium development due to financing problems related to the 'credit crunch'.[21]

Going forward, this delay puts Liverpool at a major competitive disadvantage because it can only have 45,000 paying customers in its Anfield ground to drive revenue for players (and to meet interest payments on Kop Football Limited's debt) against Manchester United's capacity of 76,000. Critically, Liverpool lacks scale to compete with Manchester United. How it can overcome this disadvantage while staying profitable enough to meet interest payments on its debt and also building a new stadium is a very challenging question.

It has been estimated that the immediate benefit to Liverpool of qualifying for the group stages of 2008/2009 Champions League via a last minute goal by Dutch striker Dirk Kuyt against Standard Liege in the third-round qualifier was £10m.[22] Were Liverpool to fail to qualify for the Champions League the business model of Gillett and Hicks, already under stress, would come under very severe pressure.

The case of Chelsea

When Chelsea released their financial results for 2007/2008 in February 2009 the accounts revealed that Russian oligarch Roman Abramovich had spent a total of £679.6m on the club since he took over in 2003. In effect, the club have been totally dependent on subsidy by Mr Abramovich, although the club's chief executive, former Manchester United chief executive Peter Kenyon, continued to emphasize that it was the short-term aspiration of the organization to start to operate on at least a break-even basis.

In 2007/2008, Roman Abramovich converted half of the £679.6m historic subsidy, which was constituted as a loan, into shares in Chelsea. As *Guardian* journalist David Conn[23] observed:

> Putting the money in as shares is a genuine financial investment in Chelsea, not repayable, as loans are, unless he sells the club. It is by far the largest equity contribution ever made to a football club.

However, regardless what the form that Roman Abramovich's investment in Chelsea takes, it does not obscure the fact that should he decide to exit the business in the future, in order to avoid Mr Abramovich making a loss a new owner would have to pay at least £700m. This is a challenging price in today's marketplace. The example of Chelsea would appear to underline the hypothesis that prospective owners of Premier League clubs need to have motives, other that a simple desire to run a profitable business, if they are to justify their investment.

The case of Manchester City

In July 2007, the former president of Thailand, Thaksin Shinawatra, became the owner of Manchester City football club. Under criminal investigation for fraud/corruption in Thailand – where his wife had been convicted of fraud – the Thai government had frozen his financial assets in his homeland. Questions abounded over the extent to which he had actually invested his own money in Manchester City or had in fact borrowed against future season ticket sales and broadcasting income to buy out the previous owners and sign new players. His motive for buying Manchester City was widely reputed to be to further his political campaign to rehabilitate himself in

Thailand and keep himself in the public eye in a country where Premiership football is a major attraction. In the summer of 2008 rumours began to circulate that Manchester City were in severe financial difficulties. A further complication was that it appeared increasingly likely that Shinawatra would be convicted in the criminal courts in Thailand (in fact this did happen subsequent to his sale of the club and in November 2008 the UK government renounced his visa rights to enter the UK). The consequences of Manchester City collapsing into administration and not being able to pay their star players their contractual obligations, raising the spectre that the club might not be able to complete its fixtures, can only be imagined but they would clearly have been severe for the credibility of the Premier League competition, particularly in overseas markets. Fortunately, in early September 2008, Abu Dhabi-based Abu Dhabi United Group Investment and Development Limited took over the club.

Similarly, if Shinawatra had been convicted of criminal charges while owner of Manchester City he would then have posed a very significant problem for the Premier League. As Premier League Chief Executive Richard Scudamore observed in an interview in the *Daily Telegraph* in early August 2008 regarding Shinawatra's legal status:[24]

> We have to establish the status of his [Shinawatra's] return to England [Shinawatra was out of the country at the time] and where that leaves him as regards to the legal process in Thailand. Our rules are clear. Somebody has to be convicted of something before they fall under the remit of the 'Fit and Proper Person' act. Until such a time as he is convicted, he falls within the rules. But we have always said that the test is meaningful and has to be applied. We need to make sure that if he is guilty of anything we will deal with it.

The Abu Dhabi takeover saved the Premier League from having to make some very difficult choices. But for how long? Will the Premier League have to face similar challenges over future owners with questionable sources of finance?

Potential problems at Arsenal

Arsenal has long been regarded as a model for English football clubs. It has consistently broken even financially, with a board largely made up of long-term shareholders widely regarded as effective and reliable custodians of the club as a sporting institution as well as a business. The Arsenal board executed a bold move to a state-of-the-art new ground at the Emirates Stadium for the beginning of the 2006/2007 season, quite close to their old ground at Highbury. The old ground was the subject of a real estate development meant to pay for the new stadium. However, with the property market in the doldrums due to the 'credit crunch' the club was left vulnerable to a predatory takeover.

In February 2009, Arsenal and the Premier League faced a major challenge in the face of new investor Alisher Usamov, an oligarch from Uzbekistan, who had taken control of 25% of the shares in the club. When Usamov first emerged as an investor in 2007 *Guardian* journalist David Conn summarized the problem as follows:[25]

> Controversy over Usmanov's record has surfaced since he paid Arsenal's former vice-chairman [David Dein] £75m for a 14.5% stake… In 1980 he was convicted of offences reported to include fraud, corruption and theft of state property and served six years in prison, but after the collapse of the Soviet Union he insisted the charges had been

politically motivated and that he has since been formally pardoned by the Russian government. This version of events has been contested by Craig Murray, the British ambassador to Uzbekistan from 2002 to 2004.

Alisher Usamov is a controversial figure in the Shinawatra mould.

Regardless of who owns Arsenal, going forward, the club's business plan is fundamentally dependent on qualifying for the group stages of the Champions League, which necessitates a top four finish in the Premiership. In 2008/2009 they were, for the first time in a number of seasons, facing stiff competition for this position from a fifth club – Aston Villa. Failure to qualify for the group stages for the Champions League, in this or any other season, would throw the financial stability of the club into jeopardy and uncertainty.

Some lessons from Scotland – Gretna FC

Although English football is facing some severe economic challenges the situation in Scottish football is significantly worse. Because of the cultural and economic similarities between the football industries in the two countries, it is useful to look at some recent examples of financial difficulty in Scottish football as a guide to some of the problems that might occur in England if proactive regulatory initiatives are not embarked on.

In February 2008, one of the twelve members of the Scottish Premier League (SPL), Gretna FC, collapsed with a reported £4m worth of debt. Gretna was an unusual club. From a town with fewer than 10,000 inhabitants its rise from non-league English football to the top division of the Scottish football, a Scottish Cup final appearance followed by one round of the UEFA Cup, was financed entirely by idiosyncratic millionaire Brooks Mileson who spent £4m of his own money 'living his dream'. However, in February 2008, when Mileson fell seriously ill (a condition from which he ultimately did not recover, dying in November 2008), funding was withdrawn and the club collapsed into financial administration. In fact it was only able to fulfil the rest of its fixtures through advance payments on prize money from the SPL.[26] At the end of the season, the club was liquidated and left the league. Gretna supporters subsequently formed a new club in non-league football using the fans' owned supporters' trust model.[27]

The collapse of Gretna mid-season raises a critical question. What if a bigger club than Gretna had collapsed mid-season with running costs too large to be sustained to the end of the season by the SPL and with no obvious bail-out buyer? Would the integrity of the league have been compromised if the club's fixtures had been declared void? This was a problem which Gordon Smith, Chief Executive of the Scottish Football Association, alluded to in an interview in June 2008 on the subject:[28]

> The SFA, the SFL, the SPL will need to look very closely at these aspects of how the game is structured and financed… It's very sad… Unfortunately, the problem with Gretna was their success was down to the money of one person and there was no stability behind it because of that. That's something that maybe lessons have to be learned about, the stability in the game. If someone is putting a lot of money into a team and it's getting a bit of success for a while, is there any future for that team if that one person pulls out? I think all of us in Scottish football need to look at that, all the bodies, everybody involved in the game.

Table 2.   Hearts Football Club – key financial indicators (2005 to 2007).

	2005/06	2006/07
Turnover	£10.3m	£10.3m
Pre-tax loss	£5.8m	£12.9m
Debt (held by Lithuanian owner Vladmir Romanov's bank)	£21.5m	£37.6m
Wages/turnover ratio (%)	102	121

Source: PriceWaterhouseCoopers, *Season 2006/2007 19th Annual Review of Scottish Football.*

And this is a problem that they might have to address quite soon. For, as in England, the level of indebtedness of many Scottish clubs is alarmingly high. Table 2 illustrates the case of Scotland's third biggest club, Hearts, which is owned by Lithuanian financier Vladmir Romanov.

With debt at nearly three times the level of turnover the club is entirely dependent on its owner for survival. Business consultants PriceWaterhouseCoopers observed:[29]

> Hearts' wage costs have nearly tripled in three seasons ... the wage to turnover ratio now sits at an unsustainable 121%.

Twice in the 2008/2009 season it was reported in the Scottish press that Hearts had played their players late.

In December 2006, prominent Scottish tabloid newspaper pundit Jim Traynor had this to say on the issue of club ownership in Scottish football prompted by a dispute at Hearts between Vladmir Romanov and senior players,[30] the culmination of what many observers felt was a highly aggressive and eccentric style of management by the owner:

> ...we don't have any kind of proper screening programme in this country. We have three governing bodies yet not one of them can be bothered running rigorous checks on anyone who wants to own a club. That's why the world's most wanted man, Osama Bin Laden, could fund a buy-out of any club in Scotland and no one would know. Worse still, our administrators wouldn't know where to start with background checks even if they did wish to find out a little about buyers. This also is why not a single one of them has any right now to criticise or complain about what is happening at Hearts, who have become a joke under the Romanov regime.

However, no action has been taken by the SFA or the SPL to address the issue of owner suitability.

Financial instability threatens ground ownership

On the back of this financial instability, an increasingly common development in English football has seen some owners of failing clubs separating ownership of the club from ownership of their club's ground. Then, when the club enters administration they can at least salvage something from the wreckage by selling the ground for building development. So, for example, in July 2008, League Two club Rotherham United were seeking to relocate from Rotherham to Sheffield's Don Valley Athletics Stadium as a temporary measure after over 100 years' tenure at their Millmoor stadium due to a financial crisis which had seen their previous owners retain ownership of the ground.[31] However, securing and financing a new ground without the benefit of finance from the sale of the old ground is a major challenge. So when a club loses its ground it often sets in train a prolonged period of instability and decline, as was the case after former Premiership club and FA Cup winners (1988) Wimbledon FC's Plough Lane ground was sold to a supermarket company without any suitable alternative stadium being made available.

After a long period of ground-sharing with south London neighbours Crystal Palace, the club's, by then Norwegian, owners ultimately generated a *cause celebre* by relocating the club to the English city of Milton Keynes, 55 miles north of London, (England's first, and so far only, case of football club franchising) where it was reformed as the MK Dons in the 2003/2004 season. Predictably, the club then went into administration due to financial difficulties (from which it has since emerged having shed its considerable debts), and the vast majority of its traditional fanbase chose to support the establishment of a new supporters owned club, using the supporters' trust model, called AFC Wimbledon, currently thriving in the non-league football pyramid below the level of the Football League.

In February 2009, Barry Hearn, owner of Leyton Orient, separated ownership of the football club from ownership of Orient's Brisbane Road ground. This caused much anxiety among Orient's supporters.[32]

At the beginning of the 2008/2009 season, the financial challenges facing the Football League clubs could best be illustrated by a direct quotation from the management consultants Deloitte:[33]

> In general, a Championship club can only hope to significantly reduce its net debt in the short/medium term via either promotion to the Premier League or an injection of equity funding from its owner... [in Leagues One and Two] ... managing the risks taken by some boards of directors will, without correction, lead to a continuing flow of insolvency cases in the seasons to come.

That club owners would seek to cash in on land values is hardly surprising given that grounds are more valuable for non-football purposes, as illustrated in stark terms by a 2006 study by Cass Business School.[34,35] However, this trend poses a significant threat to the stability of the English football industry because in order to participate in a league a club must have a ground. And ground purchase and development is an expensive undertaking for any new investor thinking of purchasing from an administrator a club which does not have its own ground. In fact, it raises the question that some clubs which find themselves in this situation may, in fact, end up following the example of Gretna and being liquidated as they lose their grounds and their place in their respective leagues, destroying decades of history, tradition and fan investment in the process.

Conclusion

There is no doubt that there is much to admire in the recovery of English football from its status in the 1980s as a chronically poorly managed industry with declining attendances whose clubs were banned from playing in Europe from 1986 to 1992 due to the blight of hooliganism following Brussels' Heysel stadium disaster of 1985 when 39 Italian supporters died at the European Cup final between Liverpool and Juventus. English stadia have been completely rebuilt to a very high standard, crowds have flocked back and the Premiership in particular is regarded as the most attractive elite league in Europe with the most lucrative TV broadcasting deal. Both BSkyB and the Premier League have done an excellent job in marketing their product.

However, it is an 'inconvenient truth' that English football remains, as it always has been, chronically unprofitable; and the scale of the losses, as reflected in the enormous debts carried by the 92 clubs collectively, would not be sustainable in any other industry, and so, we would argue, are unlikely to be sustainable in the football industry over the medium term. Although at the time of writing no major club had yet to collapse completely, anecdotal evidence was emerging that very many clubs were suffering severe financial pressures, as we have illustrated through the selection of case study evidence above. By way of further example, in an interview[36] with *Guardian* journalist David Conn, in December 2008, Adam Pearson, chairman of newly relegated from the Premiership Derby County – who lost £12.5m in the year to June 2007 – warned starkly that clubs need to bring wages under control:

> The game is close to meltdown at all levels… Boards are under pressure to gain success and that leads to them paying ridiculous wages. It cannot carry on or it will end in disaster. There is a growing feeling now that some sort of wage cap has to come in.

Up to now, the chronic loss-making exemplified by Derby County has only been sustained by shedding debt through the administration process (following wholesale bankruptcies); this is in fact a form of *de facto* state subsidy because the majority of the tax debt is rarely repaid, and through equity investment by new owners and investors seeking trophy assets. However, by the beginning of 2009 evidence suggested that the supply of rich overseas investors was drying up. As no less a figure than Keith Harris, executive chairman of investment bank Seymour Pierce, the leading broker in almost all the major sales of Premiership football clubs since the turn of the millennium, told David Conn[37] in January 2009:

> The clubs have been spending too much and the club owners were looking for richer people to buy the clubs and take on the losses… But we are in a different climate now, where the football clubs have to realise it is back to the fundamental basics of managing their costs. The supply of richer people has proved to be finite [authors' underlining].'

A similar argument was being made at Premiership club Middlesbrough. Deloitte's reported that Middlesbrough made a loss of £13.3m in the 2006/07 season[38] and had total debt of £85m.[39] Most of the debt was believed to be owed to club owner Steve Gibson who was neither paid a salary or received a dividend from his shareholding.[40] In a December 2008 newspaper interview, Middlesbrough manager Gareth Southgate[41] amplified Keith Harris' theme:

> At the moment quite a few [clubs] are dependent on billionaire owners. But if those people walk away you're reliant on finding someone else with those sorts of funds… We're all marvelling at how strong our league is but I'm not sure quite where we go after billionaire owners, especially as a lot of them are losing a lot of their money at the moment… I don't see why the chairman should keep footing the bill here… It's my belief that we should run it as a sound business.

In other words, English football clubs are going to have to start operating on a break-even financial basis. But their ability to do so is greatly complicated by the extraordinary high level of debt they were collectively carrying as they entered 2009.

It is the view of these authors that unless the issue of chronic unprofitability is addressed through some form of pre-emptive regulatory action then a major financial crisis in English football that will threaten the very existence of a number of clubs is inevitable. In this respect, both Lord Triesman, Chairman of the FA, and Andy Burnham, Minister of State for Culture, Media & Sport, were absolutely right to raise their concerns about the level of indebtedness of English football clubs and their related financial instability.

What pre-emptive regulatory action that might be embarked upon is open to debate, and the authors have made some suggestions of possible ways forward in a submission to the All-Party Football Football Group *Inquiry into English Football and its Governance*.[42] What seems absolutely clear is that some form of renewed regulatory intervention is necessary, and indeed inevitable.

We would conclude by quoting the remarks of former UEFA General Secretary Lars-Christer Olsson[43] in 2004 in the context of a debate about chronic indebtedness and unprofitability of clubs competing in the European Champions League which was perceived to be distorting the quality and balance of the sporting competition:

> In recent years, too many clubs have been indulging in, if you like, financial doping [authors' underlining] – sometimes not paying transfer fees and even having to delay salaries in some cases. The big problem is not so much on the income side, but on the cost side. They have to think more about their investment. Financial planning is often conducted on a far too short-term basis… In future, clubs … [should] have to prove they have sound finances to play in our competitions [authors' underlining].

What Lars-Christer Olsson's remarks demonstrate is that the understanding of the impact of reckless financing on the integrity of sporting competition is already well-established. All that is missing in English football is the will to tackle this 'inconvenient truth'.

Postscript

In February 2010 Portsmouth FC became the first Premier League club to enter financial administration.

Notes

1. Gore, *An Inconvenient Truth*.
2. Deloitte, *Annual Review of Football Finance*, 34.
3. Ibid., 35.
4. Bryant, 'English Football is £3bn in Debt, Warns FA Chairman'.
5. BBC Sport, 'FA Chief Fears £3bn "Club Debts"'.
6. BBC Sport, 'Burnham Demands Football Reforms'.
7. Conn, D. 'Burnham Poses Seven Questions for Football's Authorities'.
8. Gore, *An Inconvenient Truth*.
9. Hamil, 'A Whole New Ball Game', 26.
10. Deloitte, *Annual Review of Football Finance*.
11. Ibid., 24.
12. Ibid., 59, appendices, 5.
13. Ibid., appendices, 15.
14. BBC News, 'Football Clubs Owe Tax Millions'.
15. Daniel, 'Only Sweet Nothings From Sugar'.
16. Szymanski, and Kuypers, *Winners & Losers*, 291–4. This text provides an excellent, highly accessible introduction to sports economics for non-economists.
17. Deloitte, *Annual Review of Football Finance*, appendices, 37.
18. For a useful summary of how the NFL is organized see Staudohar, P. 'Governance in the National Football League'. In *Governance and Competition in Professional Sports Leagues*, ed. P. Rodriguez, S. Kesanne, and J. Garcia. Oviedo, Spain: University of Oviedo, 2007.

19. For a more detailed analysis of Manchester United's business strategy and the challenges it faces see Hamil, 'Manchester United'. See Deloitte, *Annual Review of Football Finance*, 59–60, appendices 4–5, for data on Manchester United's financial performance in 2006/2007.
20. Deloitte, *Annual Review of Football Finance*, 60.
21. BBC Sport, 'Liverpool Stadium Plans on Hold'.
22. Rich, 'Liverpool Leave It Late to Secure a Place in the Next Round of the Champions League'.
23. Conn, 'Abramovich Digs Deep Again to Cover Chelsea Losses'.
24. Winter, 'Soap Opera Involving Thaksin Shinawatra and Manchester City Damaging Our Game'.
25. Conn, 'Hill-Wood'.
26. BBC Sport, 'Gretna Relinquish League Status'.
27. For details of the new supporter-owned Gretna, see www.gretnasupporterssociety.co.uk
28. BBC Sport, 'SFA Chief Wants No More Gretnas'.
29. PriceWaterhouseCoopers, *Season 2006/2007 19th Annual Review of Scottish Football*, 13.
30. Traynor, 'Osama Bin Laden Could Buy Out a Scottish Club and Our Ruling Bodies Wouldn't Bat an Eyelid'.
31. Rotherham United Football Club, *Move to Don Valley Stadium*.
32. Website of Leyton Orient Supporters Trust http://www.leytonorientfanstrust.com/index.asp. Accessed March 3, 2009.
33. Deloitte, *Annual Review of Football Finance*, 57.
34. Pickard, 'Football Clubs Urged to Sell Off Stadiums'.
35. Cass Business School, *Rival Football Clubs Should Share Grounds to Ease Financial Problems*.
36. Conn, 'Fear of Bust has Clubs Looking for a Salary Ceiling'.
37. Conn, 'Financial Nightmare has Disrupted Dream of Club Ownership'.
38. Deloitte *Annual Review of Football Finance*, appendices, 4–5.
39. Deloitte, *Annual Review of Football Finance*, 59.
40. Taylor, 'League's Boom Could Turn to Bust Says Southgate'.
41. Ibid.
42. Walters and Hamil, *All Party Parliamentary Football Group*.
43. The Football Association, 'Keeping Football Together', March 12, 2004. http://www.thefa.com/TheFA/NewsFromTheFA/Postings/2004/03/Olsson_UEFA.htm. Accessed March 3, 2009.

References

BBC News. 'Football Clubs Owe Tax Millions', *BBC News*, November 23, 2008. http://news.bbc.co.uk/1/hi/uk/7741859.stm. Accessed March 3, 2009.

BBC Sport. 'Gretna Relinquish League Status', *BBC Sport*, June 3, 2008. http://news.bbc.co.uk/sport1/hi/football/teams/g/gretna/7433470.stm. Accessed March 3, 2009.

BBC Sport. 'SFA Chief Wants No More Gretnas', *BBC Sport*, June 3, 2008. http://news.bbc.co.uk/sport1/hi/football/scot_div_1/7434685.stm. Accessed March 3, 2009.

BBC Sport. 'Liverpool Stadium Plans on Hold', *BBC Sport*, October 5, 2008. http://news.bbc.co.uk/sport1/hi/football/teams/l/liverpool/7653369.stm. Accessed March 3, 2009.

BBC Sport. 'FA Chief Fears £3bn "Club Debts"', *BBC Sport*, October 7, 2008. http://news.bbc.co.uk/sport1/hi/football/7656862.stm. Accessed March 3, 2009.

BBC Sport. 'Burnham Demands Football Reforms', *BBC Sport*, October 16, 2008. http://news.bbc.co.uk/sport1/hi/football/7674838.stm. Accessed March 3, 2009.

Bryant, T. 'English Football is £3bn in Debt, Warns FA Chairman', *The Guardian*, October 7, 2009. http://www.guardian.co.uk/football/2008/oct/07/footballpolitics.premierleague. Accessed March 3, 2009.

Cass Business School. *Rival Football Clubs Should Share Grounds to Ease Financial Problems*. Press release, Cass Business School, April 6, 2006.

Conn, D. 'Hill-Wood: We Do Not Want Usmanov Here: Arsenal Chairman Opposed to Involvement of Uzbek', *The Guardian*, September 26, 2007. http://www.guardian.co.uk/news/2007/sep/26/topstories3.mainsection. Accessed March 3, 2009.

Conn, D. 'Burnham Poses Seven Questions for Football's Authorities', *The Guardian*, October 17, 2008. http://www.guardian.co.uk/football/2008/oct/17/premierleague-andyburnham. Accessed 3 March 2009.

Conn, D. 'Fear of Bust has Clubs Looking for a Salary Ceiling', *TheSportBlog: Guardian.co.uk*, December 3, 2008. http://www.guardian.co.uk/sport/blog/2008/dec/03/championship-credit-crunch-recession. Accessed March 3, 2009.

Conn, D. 'Financial Nightmare has Disrupted Dream of Club Ownership', *TheSportBlog:Guardian.co.uk*, January 7, 2009. http://www.guardian.co.uk/sport/blog/2009/jan/07/west-ham-newcastle-football-finances. Accessed March 9, 2009.

Conn, D. 'Abramovich Digs Deep Again to Cover Chelsea Losses', *The Guardian*, February 13, 2009. http://www.guardian.co.uk/football/2009/feb/13/roman-abramovich-chelsea. Accessed March 3, 2009.

Daniel, C. 'Only Sweet Nothings from Sugar for the Tech Sector's Losers', *Financial Times*, September, 27 2001.

Deloitte. *Annual Review of Football Finance.* Manchester: Deloitte, 2008.

Gore, A. *An Inconvenient Truth: The Planetary Emergency of Global Warming and What We Can Do About it.* London: Bloomsbury Publishing, 2006.

Hamil, S. 'Manchester United: The Commercial Development of a Global Football Brand'. In *International Cases in the Business of Sport*, ed. S. Chadwick, and D. Arthur, Chapter 9. Oxford: Butterworth-Heinemann/Elsevier, 2008.

Hamil, S., J. Michie, and C. Oughton ed. *A Game of Two Halves: The Business of Football.* Edinburgh: Mainstream, 1999.

Pickard, J. 'Football Clubs Urged to Sell Off Stadiums', *Financial Times*, April 7, 2006.

PriceWaterhouseCoopers. *Season 2006/2007 19th Annual Review of Scottish Football.* PriceWaterhouseCoopers, 2008.

Rich, T. 'Liverpool Leave It Late to Secure a Place in the Next Round of the Champions League', *The Telegraph*, August 28, 2008. http://www.telegraph.co.uk/sport/2634883/Liverpool-leave-it-late-to-secure-a-place-in-the-next-round-of-the-Champions-League---Football.html. Accessed March 9, 2009.

Rodriguez, P., S. Kesanne, and J. Garcia. *Governance and Competition in Professional Sports Leagues.* Oviedo, Spain: University of Oviedo, 2007.

Rotherham United Football Club. 'Move to Don Valley Stadium', June 2, 2008. http://www.themillers.co.uk./page/NewsDetail/0,,10360~1321047,00.html. Accessed May 13, 2010.

Szymanski, S., and T. Kuypers. *Winners and Losers: The Business Strategy of Football.* London: Penguin Books, 1999.

Taylor, L. 'League's Boom Could Turn to Bust Says Southgate', *The Guardian*, December 18, 2008. http://www.guardian.co.uk/football/2008/dec/17/gareth-southgate-middlebrough-credit-crunch. Accessed March 9, 2009.

Traynor, J. 'Osama Bin Laden Could Buy Out a Scottish Club and Our Ruling Bodies Wouldn't Bat an Eyelid', *The Daily Record,* December 4, 2006. http://www.dailyrecord.co.uk/comment/columnists/sport-columnists/jim-traynor/2006/12/04/osama-bin-laden-could-buy-out-a-scottish-club-and-our-ruling-bodies-wouldn-t-bat-an-eyelid-86908-18204016/. Accessed March 3, 2009.

Walters, G., and S. Hamil. *All Party Parliamentary Football Group – Inquiry into English Football and its Governance. Memorandum of Evidence.* London: Birkbeck Sports Business Centre, July 2008. http://www.sportbusinesscentre.com/images/APPFG%20Written%20EvidenceFinal20October2008_2_.pdf. Accessed March 9, 2009.

Winter, H. 'Soap Opera Involving Thaksin Shinawatra and Manchester City Damaging Our Game: Normally People in England Go On the Run to Thailand', *The Daily Telegraph*, August 12, 2008. http://www.telegraph.co.uk/sport/football/leagues/premierleague/mancity/2542658/Soap-opera-involving-Thaksin-Shinawatra-and-Manchester-City-damaging-our-game---Football.html. Accessed March 3, 2009.

The governance and regulation of Italian football

Sean Hamil[a], Stephen Morrow[b], Catharine Idle[b], Giambattista Rossi[a] and Stefano Faccendini[c]

[a]Department of Management, Birkbeck, University of London, London, UK; [b]Department of Sports Studies, University of Stirling, Stirling, UK; [c]Freelance Writer

Italian football represents a paradox. It produces teams which, at the elite level, are the most successful in European club competitions, and second only to Brazil in national competitions. The quality of its players, in terms of sporting excellence, make it one of the most admired football cultures in the world. The romance and tradition of Italian football captures the imagination of a global sporting public. On the other hand, the industry is chronically unprofitable and unstable, and characterized by a long history of financial scandal. The 2007/2008 season saw it continue to endure an ongoing crisis of confidence in the wake of financial and sporting scandals, an upsurge of spectator violence in dilapidated stadia and crowds well below their peak in the 1990s. This article presents a comprehensive case study of the recent history of Italian football focusing on its administration, governance and regulation. The objective of the case study is to provide a detailed context, in one of the big five European football markets (the others being England, France, Germany and Spain), against which to analyse and inform fresh thinking on how more effective systems of corporate governance in European football might be developed. Much of what is written about the governance of football tends to focus on the English industry. A premise of this article is that it is necessary to move beyond an anglo-centric orientation and analyse the systems and experience in other European football markets and cultures. This is because football in individual countries forms part of a pyramid structure ultimately governed by the European football governing body, UEFA. What happens in individual country markets has the potential to affect what happens in other markets either by way of example, through influencing UEFA policy, or through precedent-setting rulings in the courts, such as the Bosman ruling of 1995 which allowed players free movement at the end of their contracts without a transfer fee having to be paid as had hitherto been the case. The case study is interdisciplinary in its focus – economic, social and political dimensions are all important in trying to understand what constitutes the Italian model of football, a European model of football or indeed the European model of football. Critically the article asks the following questions: (1) Is it possible for Italian football to prosper in an environment in which there appears to have been significant shortcomings in governance? (2) If not, what should be the key planks of an agenda for reform? (3) Is there potential for 'contagion' of negative Italian experience in the rest of the European football market?

Introduction

On 14 July 2006, the champions of Italy, FC Juventus, were stripped of the 2005/2006 Serie A title and demoted to Serie B. This followed an investigation into the

Calciopoli match-fixing and refereeing scandal which began in May 2006. Several other clubs, including AC Milan, were forced to begin the following season in Serie A with a points deduction. The initial penalty imposed by the Italian football association, or Federazione Italiana Giuoco Calcio (FIGC), included a retrospective deduction of 44 points from the total with which AC Milan had earned second place in Serie A in the 2005/2006 season, which resulted in AC Milan dropping out of the Champions' League qualification positions at the end of season 2005/2006. However, after appeal, the points reduction was reduced to 8 allowing AC Milan to claim third place in Serie A and a place in the Champions' League. European football's governing body, UEFA, was unable to take action as, under its rules, the national associations have sovereignty over which clubs are put forward for UEFA club competitions and there was nothing in UEFA's statutes and regulations which permitted its intervention. In the midst of the *Calciopoli* investigation, on 9 July 2006, the Italian national team won the FIFA World Cup[TM]. Nearly a year later, on 23 May 2007 AC Milan won the 2006/2007 Champions' League beating Liverpool in the final.

Such a juxtaposition of events begins to provide some insight into the extraordinary and complex world that is Italian football. It is difficult to overstate the importance of the game in Italy. How many other countries can claim that a prime minister, Silvio Berlusconi, was also the owner of one of the country's top football clubs, AC Milan, not to mention one of the country's main media companies, Mediaset? How many countries have had political parties whose name, Forza Italia, was taken from a football chant? How many other parliaments can claim to have introduced a decree – *Salva Calcio* (literally 'save football') – designed to alleviate the related financial reporting, regulatory and licensing problems faced by its clubs?[1]

On the field of play, its record of four victories in the World Cup, the most recent of which came in 2006, is second only to Brazil. Its clubs have also dominated UEFA competitions winning more than any other nation. More than 44 million Italians are interested in the game; hours of television are dedicated each week to football-related output; while around 20 million people read about football in newspapers each day.[2] As an industry, football is among the top 20 in Italy, and its total turnover is estimated at around €4200m.[3] As impressive as these figures are, its importance or 'specialness' does not arise simply from competitions won: it is also about how the game is played. Although criticized at times outside Italy for being dull and defensive, Italian football is subject to elaborate commentary at home. Arguably, Italian football supporters have a passion for the intricacies of the game that is unmatched elsewhere. And ultimately Italian football captures the imagination of the global sporting public in a way not matched by many other footballing nations; as acknowledged by the plethora of literary and journalistic accounts of its history, most recently by Agnew (2007),[4] Foot (2006)[5] and Jones (2007).[6]

However, it is also widely acknowledged that in Italy the display of cunning and craft in the team tactics is also widely admired,[7–9] perhaps best exemplified by the famous *catenaccio* defensive formation perfected by leading Italian teams in the 1960s and 1970s; a view underpinned by a desire to win at all costs. While purists might view such playing tactics as unsporting, their tolerance in Italy also goes some way to offer a reflection of the broader issues at play in the political culture of modern Italian society – with all its scandal, financial crises and disorganization. As Kuper[10] observes, 'many of Italian football's problems are the problems of Italy'. For while Italy does not stand alone as a nation with a murky past of footballing scandals and political corruption, it does appear unique in western Europe in the apparent frequency with which such events occur, and the depth of their intensity. More seriously, at the time of writing (March 2009), it seems legitimate to ask whether these shortcomings might actually fatally undermine the capacity of Italian football to maintain its place as a leading football market place.

The historical and political context

Despite scant literary evidence, popular belief holds that football in Italy was introduced by the English in the 1860s. Emigrants arriving in the port towns of Livorno, Genoa, Palermo and Naples began playing and the first football clubs were formed in Turin in 1881 – International Football Club – and in Genoa in 1893 – Genoa Cricket and Athletic Club.[11] Links to the origin of the game continue today with the anglicized club names of CFC Genoa and AC Milan, while it is claimed that the black and white colours of FC Juventus represent a link to Notts County. The early governance of the game was also influenced from outside Italy, with club presidents, referees, players and much of the terminology used being imported from England, France, Germany and Switzerland.[12]

The Italian football association, la Federazione Italiana Giuoco Calcio (FIGC), was founded in 1898 and the first league championship took place at Torino (Turin) in 1898. It took all of one day to complete and was won by CFC Genoa.[13] Although initial support for football was limited, public interest quickly began to grow and other cities developed football clubs. The following year, the second championships lasted three days, the third in 1900 lasted twenty days and were also won by CFC Genoa, who won the first six league championships ever staged in Italy.

For several years thereafter, the participating clubs remained concentrated in the north of the country and it was not until 1929 that the first national league was formed. Despite this, the geographical distribution of football clubs in Italy has remained skewed towards the north and centre of the country. Of the 20 teams in Serie A in 2006/2007, only four were based in the south, while in more than 100 years' history, the Italian league has been won by a team from south of Rome on only three occasions,[14] by Napoli (2) and Cagliari (1).

For many supporters from the south, this pattern of league success reflects wider economic and social realities. An enduring characteristic of Italy is the existence of wide regional disparities in terms of economic measures of performance such as GDP,[15] with a 2007 labour force survey report[16] suggesting that the so-called north–south divide is continuing to widen in every social and economic sector. Unsurprisingly, resentments arise between southerners who feel they are overlooked by political decision-makers in the north and the northerners who begrudge what they see as subsidies made to the struggling economy and high unemployment of the south. Taken further, this resentment and political difference is given a sporting outlet through heightened – and occasionally violent – rivalries between football clubs on match days. A classic example of north/south division of national loyalties was seen during the Italian-staged 1990 World Cup when Napoli's Argentinean hero, Diego Maradona, sought to encourage local fans to support Argentina rather than Italy in the semi-final being played in Naples, by reminding them of how they were not considered as proper Italians by northerners for the rest of the year.[17]

The politicization of football in Italy has a long history. Benito Mussolini's fascist regime was the first to exploit football for propaganda purposes with leading fascists taking over the running and organization of the game.[18] Today some supporters of clubs like SS Lazio continue to be associated with far-right extremism, while clubs like FC Bologna and AS Livorno have strong links with the left wing arising out of those urban centres' left-wing traditions. More recent is the 'footballization' of politics, where football is used as a metaphor in politics.[19] Prior to entering the 1994 general election candidate race with his Forza Italia party, Silvio Berlusconi was more renowned for his wealth and business achievements rather than any political acumen. However, it was the association made by many that the success of Serie A football club AC Milan, which he bought in 1986, was directly related to Berlusconi's influence as president of the club that assisted in bringing together the detached worlds of politics and football for his advantage. In further support to this proposition, it became commonplace for daily newspapers to use football vocabulary in their reporting of politics.[20] Almost imperceptibly, traditional football terms became associated with political expressions, bolstering the discussion of politics into the mainstream and strengthening the influence of one on the other.[21] The division between political and football governance became more opaque.

Silvio Berlusconi, the owner of AC Milan since 1986, and prime minister three times – 1994 to 1995; 2001 to 2006; 2008 to date – is a man who utilized the huge success of the club in football – for example, winners of the European Champions' League competition in 1988/1989, 1989/1990, 1993/1994, 2002/2003 and 2006/2007 – to support the launch of, and afterwards to sustain, his political career, lifting even the name of his new political party Forza Italia from a terrace chant[22] (Forza Italia has since been renamed Il Popolo Della Liberta). Agnew[23] notes the fact that even though AC Milan under Berlusconi's ownership has always been loss-making, he still saw its value as a trophy asset:

> By June 2003 ... AC Milan [was estimated] to be €142.8m in debt, while the club returned a €51.5m loss for the financial year 2003/2004. Berlusconi, however, understood that, in terms of image, AC Milan was well worth the investment, and each year he came up with the cash to meet the club's debts. For someone with huge commercial and ultimately political ambitions in a country where football is encoded into the national DNA, four [then five with another in 2006/2007] European Cup/Champions' League trophies and seven Serie A league titles over the next 19 seasons [since 1986] were worth more than money could buy.

However, as Agnew[24] and Jones[25] recount, he is a man with a controversial history. Jones notes that Berlusconi has been convicted of bribing former disgraced Prime Minister Bettino Craxi and sentenced to 30 months in prison, only to be acquitted on appeal due to the statute of limitations. While Berlusconi blames the political left for many of his problems which end up in the courts, there is clearly concern about his behaviour from more mainstream sources. In 2002, *The Economist* magazine ran a front page with Berlusconi's portrait under the headline: 'Why Berlusconi is unfit to govern Italy'.[26] In September 2008, Berlusconi lost a libel case he had brought against *The Economist* in a Milan court and was ordered to pay the magazine's costs.[27]

Critically, in a country where politics and football are closely intertwined, and where politics is itself so characterized by scandal, it would be surprising if the football industry was unaffected by a general malaise in the body politic.

The institutional structure of football in Italy

Italian football is organized in a hierarchical, and, on the face of it, straightforward manner. The FIGC is the governing body of football in Italy and is a founding member of both UEFA and FIFA. Its activities include the organization of the main Italian football competitions, including its league and cup competitions. It also oversees the country's national side, the U-21 and Olympic teams, as well as the Italian national side fixtures. The president of the FIGC is its legal representative. Assisted by a federal board and a presidency committee, the president gives all directives for the association's activity, supported by the general manager and the general secretary of the federation. The general manager is in charge of all aspects related to managing the FIGC's operations, including issues like sponsorship, media deals and human resources. The general secretary's position focuses on issues relating to the laws and regulations of the FIGC.[28]

The federal board includes representatives from Italian football's three leagues: (1) the professional league of Serie A and B; (2) the professional league of Serie C (now called Lega Pro); and (3) the amateur league. In addition, it also includes representatives from the AIAC (the Italian Coaches' Association) and AIC (the Italian Players' Association). The clubs are affiliated to the FIGC and to the league body which organizes the relevant championship (e.g. the Lega Nazionale Professionisti, more commonly known as Lega Calcio, for Serie A and B clubs). The leagues are independent clubs' associations but are governed by the statutes and directives of the FIGC. The president and board of directors of each league are appointed by the member clubs. Up until 2009, one difference between Italy and countries like, for example, England, was that the top professional leagues in Italy, Serie A and Serie B, had not formed break-away league structures, instead remaining under the control of the Lega Calcio, and by extension the FIGC (but in April 2009 it was announced that Serie A was to split from Serie B – see postscript).

League football in Italy is organized in a pyramid system of interconnected leagues. While the FIGC provides the guidelines for the operation of the Italian League Championships, the Serie A and B leagues are organized by Lega Calcio. Serie C1 and C2 (now called Prima Divisione and Seconda Divisione respectively) are organized by the Lega Italiana Calcio Professionistico or Lega Pro. Serie D is nonprofessional and organized by the Comitato Interregionale (Interregional Committee) of the Lega Nazionale Dilettanti (National Amateur League). The FIGC receives significant public funding from the Italian Ministry of Sport. In 2008, the sum received from the State, via the Italian Olympic Committee (CONI), was €81m.[29]

In addition to acting as the licensor for the UEFA Club Licensing system, the FIGC acts as the licensing body for professional football in Italy through a financial commission called Co.Vi.Soc.[30] The FIGC's internal rules delegate its inspection powers in respect of the financial performance of football clubs to Co.Vi.Soc which is supposed to act autonomously and ensure that clubs operate to minimum financial standards so that there is financial stability in order to ensure the regular running of championships. Its responsibilities do not extend to issues like the verification of clubs' payments to the tax authorities; issues which fall within the remit of clubs' auditors.[31] In theory, failure to meet the requirements set by to Co.Vi.Soc will result in a club not being licensed and hence excluded from participation in the Championship.

Ostensibly then there is a clear and transparent system of regulatory oversight for the Italian football industry. Transgressions of the rules can be punished. In particular, the licensing system suggests that a high standard of club governance should exist. However, there is a very serious gap between theory and practice, a gap which has had significant consequences for the health of the Italian football industry.

A history of scandal

Italian football has been embroiled in a number of major scandals in recent decades. Indeed the history of Italian football is strewn with examples of deviance from best practice in corporate governance and administration as illustrated in some detail in the popular and journalistic accounts of Agnew (2007),[32] Foot (2006)[33] and Jones (2007).[34] The biggest of them all has been the *Calciopoli*[35] match-fixing scandal which came to light shortly before the 2006 World Cup in Germany. It is worth examining the progress of these scandals in order to illustrate the deep-seated nature of the culture of malpractice. Moreover, a striking aspect is the way in which, so frequently, even where perpetrators are identified, penalties are few and fundamental reform does not follow. Jones[36] observes this phenomenon in the wider political sphere of Italian political life:

> Investigations go on for years... When someone is finally brought to court it seems almost *de rigueur* that if they've been condemned in *Primo Grado* (first grade), they will be absolved in *Secondo Grado*... No one is ever entirely guilty, no-one is ever simply innocent... Sooner or later the accusation will be dropped anyway, because the deadline for a judicial decision has been superseded.

The long history of scandal in Italian football has prompted questions about the authority and political will of the Italian football authorities to address the regulatory implications of such scandals. In turn, it raises a question as to whether such inaction may ultimately undermine the Italian sporting public's faith in the integrity of the sporting contest of Italian football, and see the game begin to lose its grip on the Italian public's popular imagination, with significant business as well as sporting consequences.

Beginning in 1980, Italian football was confronted with the totonero scandal, surrounding illegal betting on the outcome of league matches.[37] Similar to the English weekly Football Pools' coupon, Totocalcio was a state-run football betting system where wagers were placed on the outcome of matches selected from Serie A and B. The system was very limited in scope, with no opportunity for participants to predict the scores of individual matches or goal scorers. To meet this illicit market demand, totonero was launched. Although illegal, totonero betting points were frequently located within the legal counterpart Totocalcio betting shops. With this new opening in the betting market came the opportunity to influence the outcome of matches, through bribery of match officials, clubs and players. The scandal of 1980 revolved around attempts to 'fix' the results of individual matches, then place bets on their final scores. Far less clandestine in their operations than those implicated in the subsequent *Calciopoli* scandal, those involved in totonero were quickly arrested. SS Lazio, AC Milan and FC Bologna received points deductions, with the former two clubs being relegated to Serie B; and players received bans, although all were later acquitted due to a failure in the legal system of the time to provide for 'sporting fraud' (subsequently amended in 1986 and 1989). Among the people implicated in the scandal was national team star Paolo Rossi who received a two-year ban. Nevertheless, he was able to rejoin the national squad in time to assist Italy to win the 1982 World Cup. Another gambling scandal erupted in 1986.[38]

AC Milan became embroiled in scandal in 1992. Jones[39] recounts how in the summer of 1992, Milan (by then owned by three-time Italian prime minister Silvio Berlusconi) paid Torino 18.5bn lira for the young player Gianluigi Lentini. The deal ended up in the courts amid accusations of improper financial dealings. The president of Torino alleged that 6.5bn lira of the transfer fee was paid to a Swiss bank account without receipts or a contract, an obvious way to avoid taxes. Further, Jones[40] recounts that the Torino President alleged that Lentini:

> ...had his proposed salary slashed (with the obvious suspicion ... that he was 'topped up' in cash from Berlusconi's slush funds in Switzerland); most damning of all, it was claimed that when the Milan directors had paid a seven billion deposit on the player, they didn't ask for the usual 'receipt' of payment, but instead wanted shares in Torino ... it meant that Milan had played much of the end of the 1992 season owning shares in another club. All the allegations were denied by Berlusconi.

Further match-fixing allegations emerged in the 1990s.[41] In 1999 it was revealed that the President of Roma had sent Rolex watches to leading referees. Other referees had enjoyed holidays paid for by Juventus. Others, as Jones[42] recounts: '...enjoyed the company of what is called in Italian a *sexyhostess* courtesy of various clubs'.

Luciano Moggi, the pivotal figure in the *Calciopoli* scandal of 2006 while a senior employee of FC Juventus, featured prominently in a match-fixing scandal in 1995. Then an official of Juventus' Turin rival, Torino FC, he was investigated over allegations that attempts had been made to bribe referees for UEFA Cup matches with the use of prostitutes. Foot[43] quotes the court conclusion that:

> ...there was clearly an attempt to sweeten the severity of the referees, in favour of Torino ... and render them less free in their judgements.

But the court was unable to come to a concrete judgement against Moggi. As Foot[44] observed:

> Cheating appeared to have taken place, but nobody could prove who had ordered the cheating.

A further match-fixing and betting scandal emerged in the 2000/2001 season[45] involving clubs in the lower divisions.

Moggi emerges as a pivotal player in the history of corruption of Italian football. Wherever he worked in Italian football scandal was never far behind.[46] As far back as the 1980s he was an executive at SSC Napoli during the period when Diego Maradona brought success to the club; Napoli won Serie A in 1987 and 1990 and the UEFA Cup in 1989. It was also in this period that Maradona's addiction to cocaine accelerated, culminating in a positive drug test in 1991 and a subsequent playing ban (as well as embroilment in a police investigation into organized crime). With regard to his descent into drug addiction, some commentators allege, at the very least the SSC Napoli club management turned a blind eye to it.[47] Agnew[48] also draws attention to the poor quality of the FIGC and CONI's (the Italian Olympic Committee, and ultimate sporting authority in Italy) drug-testing regime, subsequently revealed in a separate investigation in 1998. Given that Maradona's drug problems were the stuff of popular rumour, Agnew questions why it was only when he was in decline as a player and becoming something of an embarrassment in Italian football that he tested positive?

Doping

In 1998 a different type of 'fixing' scandal emerged. AS Roma manager Zdeněk Zeman accused FC Juventus physicians of doping their players from 1993 until

1998;[49–51] a period of great success for the team – three Serie A titles in 1994/1995, 1996/1997 and 1997/1998; European Champions' League winner in 1995/1996 and beaten finalist in 1996/1997. During this time they were coached by Marcello Lippi, who later went on to coach Italy to victory in the 2006 World Cup. Zeman implied that two leading Juventus players and national favourites, Gianluca Vialli[52] and Alessandro Del Piero, might be involved given their physical development, charges both denied vehemently. In an aside Zeman also referred[53] to Maradona's situation, stating that:

> ...if blind eyes had not been turned he could have been saved from his decline and fall. But at this stage, business considerations dominate everything. Football is controlled by the world of high finance, as well as by pharmaceutical products.

Turin judge, Raffaele Guarinello, launched an investigation into doping at Juventus. Agnew observes, following a raid on their training ground, 281 different medicines were found to be kept by Juventus representing 'the normal stock of a small-sized hospital'. Later evidence would show an almost five-fold increase in expenditure on medicines by Juventus between 1991 and 1995, the latter just as their winning streak was beginning.[54]

In the 2000/2001 season, some stars of the game, such as Dutch midfielder Edgar Davids, a Juventus player, tested positive (while playing for Holland) for the use of the banned substance, Nandrolone, which boosts muscle growth and so physical strength, prompting further outcry from the public and bringing more unwelcome attention to the Italian game. Davids was ultimately banned from the game for four months, though as he served most of the ban over the summer period and returned to play in mid-September, the real impact of the ban was much shorter.[55]

When the trial for 'sporting fraud'[56] announced its verdict in 2004 the Juventus doctor was found guilty of supplying and administering illegal substances, though the club escaped punishment. The pharmacist who allegedly supplied the drugs, Dr Giovanni Rossano, accepted a plea bargain and got a five-month suspended sentence.[57] As Foot[58] notes:

> The court had found that doping had taken place, involving Juventus, but they couldn't prove the club had *ordered* the drug use.

Ultimately, even the Juventus doctor was cleared on appeal in December 2005, despite the wealth of circumstantial evidence presented throughout the investigations indicating widespread drug abuse. But only after immense damage had been done to the reputation of Juventus; the judge in the case was particularly damning in his assessment of players' evidence which was described as 'inadequate and unreliable'.[59]

The reputations of the drug-testing capabilities of both the FIGC and CONI, which had ultimate responsibility for organizing drug testing in Italian sport, were also severely damaged. Agnew[60] reported that conditions at the CONI laboratory were chaotic and incompetent and its head was sacked. The CONI president, Mario Pescante, also resigned.

Agnew's[61] closing observation on the arc of the investigation makes particularly depressing reading for those seeking to reform the regulation of Italian football:

> Sadly, I found the whole Juventus trial process predictable. It fits in with an Italian judicial syndrome whereby we move from initial, media-driven clamour through a complex,

often difficult trial, which ultimately ends in acquittal… Legally, Juventus were in the clear, but morally and ethically?

A question arises as to why players would agree to take illegal drugs in the first place. The answer is simple. In such incredibly competitive environments as Serie A, the Champions' League and national competitions in which players might be performing for their respective countries, the tests on their physical endurance over a typical season were enormous. However, as Agnew[62] outlined, a subsidiary element of the Guarinello investigation unearthed evidence that the misuse of illegally acquired drugs might be causing severe long-term damage to the health of many players. Again, Agnew[63] makes an important point; do the assorted sponsors, governing bodies and team owners, all of whom benefit significantly from the top players playing as many games a season as possible, not have an ethical responsibility to assess what the health impact might be on these players?

In a bizarre footnote, Jones[64] observed that many Italian commentators seemed to be more offended by the idea that muscle-promoting drugs might promote an 'ugly' form of football and so 'threatened the *bellezza* of Italian football'. Zeman himself is judged by many to have damaged his career by making the allegations and has never subsequently managed a Serie A team other than Lecce which is not one of the top teams.[65]

False passports

In 2001, it was discovered that several top Serie A players had used false passports to gain entry to the national Italian leagues. For example, Argentinean-born midfielder, Juan Sebastian Veron enjoyed a very successful career in Serie A but was found to have come to Italy under a false passport. Although ultimately he was completely absolved of any personal wrong-doing, over the course of the investigation it emerged that in order to evade the limit placed on foreign players in the Italian leagues many clubs had been falsifying passports by manufacturing fictitious Italian grandparents, mainly of South American players. As Jones[66] notes, this had the added advantage that once a player became 'Italianized', their transfer value tended to rise by up to 30%. Jones further recounts that so many teams had been involved in illegally importing overseas players, that to prosecute all of them would have left too few 'clean' clubs in the league.[67] So, in a paradox reflective of broader Italian politics, the law regarding foreign players was changed to suit the circumstances and, suddenly, all restrictions on buying foreign players were removed mid-season. Again, the reputation of Italian football was damaged in the process.

Bribery and match-fixing

In 2004, another bribery scandal erupted, with evidence presented of influence by Neapolitan organized crime group the Comorra, which saw the Lega Calcio punish five clubs (Como, Pescara, Modena, Sampdoria and Siena), six players from different clubs and two Siena officials.[68] In 2005, a separate investigation by the Lega Calcio concluded that an end-of-season Serie B game between CFC Genoa and SSC Venezia had been fixed (through the payment of a bribe) in order to allow CFC Genoa to be promoted to Serie A. CFC Genoa was demoted to Serie C and a number of club officials received five-year bans from football; a number of SSC Venezia players were also banned.[69,70]

In a general sense, there is some evidence of organized crime involvement in lower league football. Although in any sporting context where match-fixing to facilitate betting coups exists, the influence of organized crime is usually not far behind. This has certainly seemed to be a problem in Italy in recent times.[71] But despite obvious possibilities for money-laundering, Agnew[72] quotes an investigator in Calabria as follows: '…the Ndrangheta seems to be especially interested in lower league football. [But] For them, it's more about winning consensus in the local community than making money.'

Calciopoli

There has, therefore, been a long history of scandal in Italian football. However, in 2006 the worst scandal of all was to emerge, which became known as *Calciopoli*.[73,74] In May 2006, it was revealed that investigations by police in a number of Italian cities into separate matters had, with the use of telephone wiretaps, uncovered a network of close relationships between team managers, referees, agents and club executives which was being used to fix the results of matches. At the heart of the network was FC Juventus General Director Luciano Moggi. (One of the police enquiries was into the activities of the GEA World football agency where Moggi's son was one of the principals and which had close links to Juventus – the activities of GEA are discussed in detail below and are themselves the subject of legal action.) Transcripts of recorded telephone conversations published in Italian newspapers suggested that Moggi regularly spoke with a number of officials of Italian football with the aim of influencing referee appointments and decisions.[75] In particular, 'favourable' referees had been chosen to officiate at a number of league matches to ensure the chances of positive results for some clubs, notably Juventus. This was the same Mr Moggi who, while at Torino, had survived accusations that he had procured prostitutes for referees in order to influence their decisions in UEFA Cup matches.

As Jones[76] noted, the sheer scale of Moggi's venality was extraordinary:

> Moggi was revealed as a phone-slinger, a man with six handsets and 300 sim cards, a man who made an average of 416 calls a day … What emerges from those conversations is that Moggi was a tireless dispenser of favours and threats. He could get a 23% discount on Fiat cars [Fiat is owned by Juventus owners, the Agnelli family] which he could then supply to anyone – a referee, linesman, policeman – who had helped his cause. He would arrange for children of financial investigators to get tickets for glamorous Juventus fixtures abroad … Pierlugi Pairetto was the man responsible for picking the referees [at the FIGC] and he was in constant contact with Moggi. On one occasion Pairetto even pleaded with one of his referees to 'be good so that you can see what's not there sometimes'.

In the phone taps, Moggi[77] also boasted of being of being able to secure international caps for players, as this would help to boost their value in the transfer market.

Following the publication of the transcripts, on 11 May 2006 FC Juventus' entire board of directors resigned together with Moggi. On 14 May FC Juventus won the 2006 Serie A championship. As well as FC Juventus, AC Milan, ACF Fiorentina, SS Lazio and Reggina Calcio were also implicated in the scandal. As were the afore-mentioned Pierluigi Pairetto, vice chairman of UEFA's referees' commission and head of the FIGC's refereeing selection, and Paolo Bergamo co-head of the FIGC's refereeing selection. Senior Italian referee Massimo de Santis was also implicated.

Having been selected by FIFA to referee at the World Cup he was barred by the FIGC from officiating after coming under investigation.[78]

The FIGC president, Franco Carraro, and the vice president, Innocenzo Mazzini, resigned on 8 and 10 May 2006 respectively. Carraro had received information on Moggi's activities before the scandal broke in the press but had taken no action. Some of the tapes also recorded him seeking to influence Pairetto, head of the FIGC's referee section, to take action to favour SS Lazio in a forthcoming game.[79] The subsequent campaign by Carraro to have the punishment awarded him for his role in *Calciopoli* overturned is instructive in explaining why it has proven so difficult to implement reform in Italian football. Initially banned from exercising any kind of sporting responsibility for four and a half years, the FIGC tribunal of enquiry found him guilty of 'acting with a view to altering the results of a match'. Carraro immediately appealed the ban to the FIGC's appeals arbitration body which altered the decision to a warning and a fine of €80,000 for failing to conduct himself 'in accordance with the principles of honesty, fair play and moral integrity in all relations in any way connected with sports.' Carraro appealed again, this time to the conciliation and arbitration body of the Italian Olympic Committee (CONI) which decided that the previous decision to issue a warning had no legal basis and annulled it leaving Carraro with a fine. Carraro has gone on to appeal the fine as well.[80] Paradoxically, ousted from the FIGC due to his connections to *Calciopoli*, rules allowed Franco Cararro to continue in his roles as head of FIFA's Internal Audit Committee, UEFA Executive Board member, CONI member, and as an active member of the International Olympic Committee (IOC).

Following Carraro's resignation as President of the FIGC, Professor Guido Rossi, a 75-year-old expert on company law and a well-respected 'super manager' was appointed temporary FIGC President.[81] He, in turn, appointed 76-year-old retired judge Franceso Saverio Borelli, a veteran of the 'Clean Hands' anti-political corruption investigations of the early 1990s, to put together a team to carry out an internal football industry investigation. On 14 July 2006 the initial verdicts condemned Juventus to relegation to Serie C, together with a 30 point deduction, coupled with the stripping of their two Serie A titles in 2004/2005 and 2005/2006. SS Lazio was relegated to Serie B as were Fiorentina. AC Milan was deducted 44 points which meant they would not qualify for the 2006/2007 Champions League.

The judgements were appealed, and following the established pattern were ultimately reduced. On 26 October 2006, the final sentence confirmed the relegation of FC Juventus to Serie B. Juventus were also stripped of their 2004/2005 and 2005/2006 Serie A titles. AC Milan, ACF Fiorentina, SS Lazio and Reggina Calcio were respectively sentenced to 8, 15, 3 and 11 points deductions, but without relegation to Serie B. ACF Fiorentina and SS Lazio were banned from the 2006/2007 UEFA Champions' League and UEFA Cup respectively. The fact that AC Milan was able to avoid a ban from the 2006/2007 Champions League was significant as they subsequently went on to win the tournament.

Referee Massimo de Santis was banned from football for four and a half years. Referee boss Pieluigi Pairetto was banned for three and a half years. Luciano Moggi and former Juventus managing director Antonio Giraudo were banned from the game for five years, having been found guilty of influencing the appointment of referees on behalf of FC Juventus. SS Lazio president Claudio Lotito received a two-and-a-half-year ban. AC Milan vice president Adriano Galliani[82] was banned from Italian football for five months (after an appeal reduced the sentence from nine months).

As an aside, Adriano Galliani, the AC Milan CEO, and former FIGC president, is a man with an interesting past. In 1991, as AC Milan were losing 1–0 to Marseille in a European Cup quarter-final, Galliani entered the pitch to encourage Milan captain Franco Baresi to argue with the referee that it was too dark to play after a minor flood-light failure. The match was abandoned, but subsequently awarded to Marseille. UEFA subsequently banned Milan for one year from UEFA competitions and Galliani received a two-year ban.[83]

The extent of the *Calciopoli* scandal did arouse massive public intrigue and prompted much heated discussion. Newspaper sales rose markedly as a result,[84] particularly as the complex web of relationships between those involved began to be unravelled. Remarkably, as the *Calciopoli* scandal was breaking in May and June 2006, the Italian national side were about to go on to win the FIFA World Cup™ for the fourth time.

However, Italy was less successful on another key front. Its bid to stage the 2012 UEFA European Championship was rejected in favour of a joint bid by Poland and Ukraine. Commentators speculated that in part this reflected a view at UEFA that it would be improper to be seen to 'reward' Italy in the context of the *Calciopoli* scandal (although the 2009 UEFA Champions' League final was awarded to Rome by UEFA). This presented Italian football with a major problem. Almost all major football stadia in Italy are owned by public authorities. Most had not been refurbished since the 1990 World Cup which was staged in Italy. It had been hoped that by winning the right to stage the 2012 European Championships Italian football would have been able to leverage public funding to refurbish and rebuild these stadia. This option was now closed off, leaving the industry with a crumbling, ageing stadia infrastructure which was both dangerous and also inadequate in terms of its capacity to offer the kind of high value-added, high-end customer services such as corporate box and banqueting facilities that are such a significant contributor to revenues at major English clubs. The 2006/2007 season added to this mix with a significant escalation of serious football-related violence.

Foot's[85] observation on *Calciopoli* again makes depressing reading for reformers:

> …all attempts at reforming Italian football from the inside had failed. Only one body of people was powerful enough to take on Moggi and his cronies: the judiciary.

He also quotes Rossi, in his resignation letter as temporary FIGC president in September 2006 (he left to become president of the Italian Telecom company), having overseen the investigation into the scandal:

> It has become clear to me that everyone (or nearly everyone) is against real renewal of the world of football.

Foot was jaundiced about the long-term appetite for reform, arguing that with Italy's victory in the 2006 World Cup, and substantial penalties having been meted out, there was a widespread desire among Italy's football establishment to move on without undertaking root and branch reform.

In January 2009, Luciano Moggi was found guilty in one of the trials emerging from the *Calciopoli* scandal relating to the activities of the GEA World agency company and sentenced to 18 months in prison. His son, Allesandro, was given a 14-month sentence. Both appealed the conviction.[86] There was widespread scepticism as to whether either would spend any time in jail.

Football-related violence

From the beginning of the twenty-first century Italian football has been experiencing an upsurge in football-related violence which bears serious comparison with England in the 1980s.[87–89] Although not necessarily the most serious that has occurred, a number of incidents at UEFA Champions' League matches have served to highlight the problem to an international audience and led to heavy penalties being applied to the teams involved. In 2004, at a match between AS Roma and FC Dynamo Kiev, the referee was hit with a coin requiring stitches for his injuries; AS Roma forfeited three points and played their next two home games behind closed doors.[90] In 2005, during a Champions' League quarter-final between Inter Milan and AC Milan, AC goalkeeper Dida was hit by a flare and the match was later abandoned. Inter Milan was heavily fined by UEFA and played the first four home games of its 2005/2006 Champions' League campaign behind closed doors.[91]

Similarly, the scourge of racism had made its presence felt at Italian football matches.[92] In spring 2001, SS Lazio defender Sinisa Mihajlovic was forced to denounce his own racism publicly over the club's public address system after having racially abused Arsenal's Patrick Viera in an earlier UEFA Champions' League match. Then in November 2005, Messina's Ivory Coast defender Mark Zoro tried to have an away match at Inter Milan abandoned by threatening to walk off the field after being racially abused by a section of the Inter support.[93] To the credit of the FIGC, all the following week's games started five minutes late, with players entering arenas carrying 'No to Racism' banners.

The response of the Italian authorities to the upsurge in violence has imitated that of the British authorities in the 1980s, with a major escalation in the policing and regulation of the behaviour of Italian football supporters. In 2005, the then Interior Minister Giuseppe Pisanu sponsored controversial and draconian legislation designed to control attendance at football matches, particularly by away fans, which included a requirement that all tickets must have the ticket-holder's name printed on them. Away fans were not allowed to buy tickets on the day of a game. And there was a general increase in the utilization of paramilitary style policing to control visiting supporters.[94] However, despite these measures the football-related violence continued to escalate.

On 2 February 2007 a riot broke out at the Serie A Sicilian derby between Calcio Catania and US Città di Palermo in which a police officer was killed. This led the FIGC to immediately cancel for a week all football-related events in the country. The Italian government demanded that teams would have to play 'behind closed doors' where stadia did not meet new minimum safety and security standards.[95] This raised the obvious question as to why these new minimum standards had not been imposed in the past.

The demand to meet new safety and security requirements sparked frantic moves to improve short-term security measures at stadia across the country. Only 6 of the 18 stadiums in Serie A then met the standards set by the new regulations. To give an idea of the scale of the challenge the BBC[96] reported that:

> Under the new rules all the top stadiums will have to be fitted with closed circuit television cameras, numbered seating and electronic turnstiles.

In other words, the safety and security standards in Italian stadia fell well below what would be expected in England or Germany for example.

The government also introduced a raft of new draconian anti-hooligan measures.[97] A key objective of the measures appeared to be to break the power of the *ultra* fans' groups so prominent at all Italy's major clubs. For example, supporters from the away teams were banned from attending games in Serie A in the 2007/2008 and 2008/2009 seasons at the discretion of the Osservatorio,[98] a committee of the Interior Ministry. Despite these measures, football-related violence continued to keep the shortcomings of Italian football in the international spotlight. In November 2007, the shooting by a policeman of a SS Lazio supporter at a motorway service station in highly controversial and disputed circumstances led to large-scale violent demonstrations at matches across Italy.[99,100] Meanwhile on the field of play, Italy travelled to Glasgow and defeated Scotland to secure its place in the Euro 2008 finals, demonstrating yet again the ability of Italian football to deliver sporting success against a background of scandal.

However, while the national team appeared able to rise above the problems besetting domestic Italian football, against the backdrop of football-related violence and escalating security counter-measures, crowds at Italian league football continued to stagnate as Italian football's contraction of the 'English disease' of hooliganism became obvious. Between 1997/1998 and 2007/2008 crowds in Serie A declined by 26%, whereas those in England, France, Germany and Spain all increased[101] (this trend is analysed in more detail below). This suggested that the Italian footballing public, long fed a diet of corruption and maladministration, were finally beginning to become jaded with what Italian football had to offer. Clear parallels can be drawn with the state of English football in the direct aftermath of the Hillsborough stadium disaster in 1989 in which 96 Liverpool supporters died at a FA Cup semi-final game. The UK government enquiry into the disaster, The Taylor Report,[102] had criticized both the stadium and police management on the day of the disaster, and the leadership and governance of the English game were also subjected to severe criticism. English football had, of course, staged an extraordinary recovery over the subsequent 20 years, certainly in terms of financial turnover (if not in profitability – English football has been chronically unprofitable for decades[103]), quality and safety of stadia, increases in attendances both at grounds and via subscription television, and sporting success. However, it is worth noting that this recovery had very little to do with draconian policing initiatives; at its heart were comprehensive improvements in the quality, safety and security of UK football stadia all of which were either replaced or extensively modernized in the early 1990s. There was clearly a lesson here that an Italian recovery strategy focused primarily on policing-orientated measures might have limited prospects for success.

This raised the obvious question as to whether the Italian football authorities were capable of engineering a similar recovery in their own industry. And in particular, of avoiding one of the alleged shortcomings of the English 'modernization', the over-sanitization of the stadium experience. Guschwan,[104] in his study of modern Italian fan culture, succinctly summarized the challenge:

> The difficult task facing Italian government, soccer league and fans is to balance the requirements of safety and civility with the passion and expression that makes Italian soccer matches so compelling.

In an interview in 2005, FIGC president Franco Carraro, acknowledged the following problems with Italian football: (1) its stadia were not good enough; (2) ticket sales were poorly organized; (3) clubs' relationships with their fans were poor, some clubs didn't talk to their fans, others were subject to too much influence by *ultra* elements within the fans' groupings; and (4) hooliganism was not adequately or consistently punished.[105] The problems had therefore been diagnosed to some extent, but the move from diagnosis to action was stalled. No stranger to controversy, in 2002 Carraro had previously remarked in relation to issues of accounting practice that '...the irregularity of accounts is a matter of opinion...'.[106] In May 2006, Carraro, as outlined earlier, had to resign as president of the FIGC as a consequence of the *Calciopoli* scandal (he would later be found guilty of exercising improper influence). Notably, having received incriminating tapes relating to the scandal from judicial investigators three months earlier in February 2006 he failed to take any action.[107] This again raised the question as to whether Italian football had the calibre of leadership necessary to drive though an agenda for real reform.

Governance and power: the role of Italian clubs

It might be argued that perhaps one reason for the weak response by the Italian football authorities to the challenges faced by the industry was the very high level of power of Italy's major clubs. Jones[108] observes what many in Italy believe, that there is a culture in Italian football where it is deemed legitimate to seek to create a climate of influence for your team. It could be argued that the particular structure of ownership in Italian football clubs makes the exercise of such influence more likely.

The ownership and governance structures prevalent among Italian football clubs largely reflect those that exist in the wider corporate environment. Within the Italian corporate governance system, a prominent ownership role is played by family groupings, and particularly in listed companies through holdings by other nonfinancial or holding companies in pyramidal group structures, a structure designed at least theoretically, in part to separate ownership and control.[109] Several Italian clubs are controlled either directly by individuals or families or indirectly via corporate groupings. However, in contrast to companies in the wider economy, often there is little evidence of separation between ownership and control.

The importance of this familial style of corporate structure is heightened by the wider Italian passion for football, with in many cases wealthy individuals or families owning the club that they support. A prominent example of direct family control is Inter Milan through the Moratti family (who are prominent industrialists in the oil sector), while the foremost examples of the corporate/familial ownership structure are FC Juventus, which is controlled by the Agnelli family, through its holding company, Istituto Finanziario Industriale (IFI), which includes the Fiat motor company among its subsidiaries; and AC Milan, whose majority shareholder, Fininvest, is a company owned and controlled by Silvio Berlusconi, Italy's second richest man, media billionaire and three times prime minister. Around the turn of the twentieth century a few Italian clubs began to make use of the Stock Exchange to raise funds. However, even in these cases, it was not common for the controlling family or grouping to relinquish control of the club, or more accurately company, with the original families remaining in control after the public flotations at FC Juventus, SS Lazio and AS Roma and certainly in the case of the two Rome clubs, continuing to operate them as if they were family businesses.[110]

A distinctive aspect of Italian corporate culture which strengthens the ownership and control structures discussed previously is the relationships, both direct and indirect through families and other companies, between politicians and major corporations.

While these relationships can be opaque, they are an accepted part of the governance of Italian corporate society. What emerges in football are networks consisting of powerful individuals connected with clubs, governing bodies, political parties and the media, which are in prominent positions to influence decision making within football and the business of football. The eruption of several scandals has also drawn attention to many potential conflicts of interest within Italian football. As Jones[111] observes:

> The most obvious conclusion from watching Italian football is that the country is based upon a few, very powerful, oligarchies. It's not dissimilar to the Renaissance....

But the very concept of conflict-of-interest, so highly debated in Anglo-American business and political culture, remains underdeveloped in Italian society. The scandal surrounding the player agency company GEA, the scandal so intimately entwined with the *Calciopoli* scandal itself (in part the wider *Calciopoli* scandal was revealed through investigator wiretaps in a separate investigation into GEA), clearly illustrates this aspect of Italian corporate culture. Imagine a scenario where a club director in charge of player purchases has to negotiate with his own son to determine the cost of players signed up with his son's contract management company; dealings that would naturally entail transfer commissions. Such behaviour could leave the transfer market open to manipulation, running the risk of inflating values as the two parties saw fit, leaving open the opportunity for 'under-the-counter' tax-free payments. This was indeed the case regarding the football management company, GEA World, managed by the sons and daughters of four prominent Italian men.

Founded in September 2001 following the merger of the activities of three parties, General Athletic, Football Management, and Riccardo Calleri, the latter a son of a former president of SS Lazio and Torino FC, GEA World described itself as a flexibly structured organization whose aim was to define, improve and consolidate the image of companies. It also offered to optimize the career prospects for athletes, who they suggested may be too busy spending their money to manage it properly. The structure of the company, its key actors, and its complex web of connected parties are illustrated in Figure 1.

The significant shareholders in one leg of the organization, General Athletic, included the following children of very influential figures in Italian football. Francesca Tanzi was the daughter of Calisto Tanzi. Calisto Tanzi was the former head of the Parmalat dairy conglomerate and former president of AC Parma. (In December 2003 Parmalat collapsed after a £13bn hole was found in the group's accounts.[112] The trial of those involved in the collapse, including Calisto Tanzi the group's founder, began in Rome in March 2008.) Andrea Cragnotti was the son of Sergio Cragnotti. Sergio Cragnotti was the former head of the Cirio food business conglomerate and former president of SS Lazio. (Cirio collapsed in 2002 amid allegations of false accounting, nearly bankrupting SS Lazio in the process with Sergio Cragnotti spending February–August 2004 in prison. SS Lazio were then bought by Claudio Lotito, the industrial cleaning magnate, who went on to feature in the *Calciopoli* scandal.) Chiara Geronzi was the daughter of Cesare Geronzi. Cesare Geronzi was one of the most influential bankers in Italy, who was investigated in connection with the Parmalat dairy conglomerate collapse. His bank, Capitalia, had been a major investor in SS Lazio.

Another significant shareholder in General Athletic was Romafides, a company owned by Capitalia bank, which subsequently merged with Unicredit bank. Capitalia was the major investment bank in football, financing clubs like SS Lazio, AC Parma, AC Perugia and AS Roma. All these clubs faced several financial difficulties and this investment bank had influence, directly or indirectly, with the respective club boards. Capitalia's role in the collapse of both Cirio and Parmalat was prominent as it was a leading advisor to both companies. Capitalia owned shares in MMC, an investment bank.

The Football Management company was controlled by the most prominent Italian football agents; Alessandro Moggi, the son of former FC Juventus general director, Luciano Moggi (the key figure in the *Calciopoli* scandal), and Franco Zavaglia. Other leading figures connected to the company through collaborative business links were Giuseppe De Mita, son of Ciriaco De Mita, former Italian prime minister; and Davide Lippi, son of Marcello Lippi, former Juventus and Italy 2006 World Cup Champions' team manager.[113]

Data from an investigation by the Italian Anti-Trust Commission[114] outlines the scale and significance of the influence of the GEA World organization. It managed around 200 contracts for managers, club directors and players. The majority of these were players (154), 99 of whom played in Serie A and Serie B. Considering the volume of players' contracts dealt with from 2002 to 2006, it was estimated that GEA's share of the player transfer market was approximately 10.2%, while the share of its prominent agents, Alessandro Moggi and Francesco Zavaglia, was estimated at 4.3% and 3.74% respectively, the highest of any football agents operating in Italy. Moreover, GEA World controlled 18.9% of all football agencies' total turnover in Italy, double the share of rival PDP, listed as the second largest Italian football agency. Over the shorter period from 2004 to 2006, GEA World's share was approximately 17.9%, while the share of its prominent agents was 12.3% and 4.8%. These figures revealed the dominant market position obtained by GEA World.

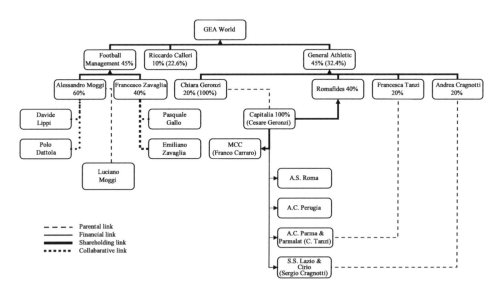

Figure 1. GEA World Structure and Network.
Source: Marcoliguori Blog[115], *Corriere Della Sera* (2003)[116] & AGCM (2006)[117].

On 1 August 2006, GEA World was dissolved; in theory the cartel had been destroyed.[118] Following the *Calciopoli* scandal and several allegations and investigations, most of its leading executives were sent for trial with the accusation of manipulating the transfer market by using threats or violence. At the time of writing the trials continue.

Jones[119] summarizes the problem of GEA as follows:

> In the last two seasons [2004–2006] the agency's share of the entire football transfer market was 17.9%. Allesandro Moggi alone enjoyed 12.3% of the market. The overlap of interests whereby Moggi senior could buy a player represented by his son, or Lippi could sell a player represented by his son, meant that, as always, nothing was ever 'disinterested'. There was always a hidden agenda to most deals which had absolutely nothing to do with football tactics and talent. Because of the practise of the *cartellino* … a human being could be divided into percentages, and, for example, Juventus could own 50% of a player's *cartellino* and another club 50%. When those two teams actually met the players were obviously subject to pressure from competing masters. Juventus deliberately had an enormous squad so that frequently they could loan players to other teams; again when those two teams met, key players for the opposition would be injured or suddenly find themselves short of form.

As Foot concluded regarding GEA World's activities:

> This grotesque monument to nepotism and patronage was a cancer within the game, with its huge costs and corrupt dealings. GEA dealings often led to ridiculous exchanges of players, or absurd prices being paid, or frequent movements for no apparent reason.

The GEA World system was of course wide open to abuse, and so it was.

The economics of Italian football

Given the instances of financial malpractice in Italian football over the last 30 years, the question arises as to why they have been allowed to continue for so long. A short answer to this question might be that up until the turn of the twentieth century Italian football was perceived as being just too successful to be deflected by such malpractice. This is not a world outlook exclusive to Italy. When, in the 1990s, the Football Association in England invited Sir John Smith, to carry out a review of corporate governance and values following the banning of Arsenal manager George Graham in 1995 for taking £425,000 in illegal financial sweeteners from Norwegian agent Rune Hauge[120] to facilitate transfers, he[121] made the following prescient observation:

> Since it is so successful, why should football bother about its occasional scandals? Why meddle with a success story? Does it matter if the world of football is tarnished by rumours of financial misbehaviour? There is a tendency for people within the game to dismiss this subject with a cursory statement: 'that's football' as if it were the natural order of things for financial misconduct to be part of the game.

Given that the report was published only nine years after the Hillsborough disaster and the deaths of 96 supporters, the subsequent report into which by Lord Chief Justice Taylor[122] damned the English football industry for its incompetence and political in-fighting, Sir John Smith's findings revealed a remarkable complacency in the English game. However, an examination of the economic structure of the Italian football industry reveals a similar high level of complacency and a failure to anticipate the long-term consequences of weaknesses in governance and financial malpractice, which when allied to an overall trend whereby the industry is chronically loss-making and resources and influence are beginning to move toward the bigger clubs, leads to competitive imbalance on the field of play.

Table 1 illustrates that, like all major leagues across Europe the combined income of Serie A clubs has increased dramatically over the last decade, largely on the back of increased television revenues and associated commercial and sponsorship deals. However, bearing in mind that international accountancy firm Deloitte recommend a wages-to-turnover ratio of not more that 60%, Table 1 also illustrates that Italian clubs expenditure on players' wages has been excessive, particularly in the early seasons of this century.[123]

The data in Table 1 demonstrate that throughout this period Serie A clubs incurred substantial operating losses. Given that operating profits are calculated before any player transfer trading is taken into account and that Serie A clubs traditionally are net transfer spenders, it is quickly apparent that pre-tax losses are greater still.

That said, the clubs of most top European football leagues tend to report losses after transfer activity is taken into account. However, the top leagues in England (€1562m), France (€337m) and Germany (€1038m) all made combined operating profits over the 1996/1997 to 2006/2007 period.[126] On the other hand, Italy, made an operating loss of €1355m over the same period. In other words, by the standards of its peers, at the operational level Italian football is chronically loss-making before even taking into account any further deficit on transfer spending.

How then was it possible for Italian Serie A football to sustain such losses? One explanation is the aspect, discussed previously, that most major Italian clubs are owned and controlled by prominent business individuals and families who tend to be extremely wealthy; or, as was the case with formers owners Sergio Cragnotti at SS Lazio and Calisto Tanzi at AC Parma, who controlled the finances of private companies which they could at least partially direct toward the football clubs they also controlled (as outlined above both Cragnotti and Tanzi were of course subsequently jailed for fraud at their main private businesses). This type of ownership structure results in the functions of ownership, control and residual claimant (entitlement to any outstanding assets in the event that the business is wound up) being internalized.[127] One consequence of the lack of separation between ownership and control is a reduction in the pressure for external monitoring, as owners are essentially monitoring themselves and risking their own investment. Taken together with football's significance and role within Italian society, business decisions can be taken with the objective of seeking to maximize an owner or dominant family's utility. At its simplest an owner could define his utility as seeking to win *lo scudetto* (the league title) or to qualify for the Champions' League, as opposed to seeking a financial profit. Such an objective, coupled with the ownership structure, may also act to reduce external pressure for monitoring (e.g. from supporters concerned about the future existence of their club due to financial instability), as ostensibly, the utility function of many supporters may be assumed to be similar to the owner's.[128] They both prioritize success on the sporting field of play (utility) over profitability.

This type of decision-making can have implications for financial performance, in that emphasis on a dominant owner or family's utility may act to distort the operation of the industry, particularly through inflationary pressure on player wages. In simple terms, owners of different clubs all seeking to prioritize football success compete for the scarce resource of high-quality players, encouraging an upward spiral in wage costs.

Table 1. The finances of Italian Serie A clubs (€m).

| | Season | | | | | | | | |
	1998/1999	1999/2000	2000/2001	2001/2002	2002/2003	2003/2004	2004/2005	2005/2006	2006/2007
Turnover (€m)	714	1,059	1,151	1,127	1,162	1,153	1,336	1,339	1,163
Operating loss (€m)	-114	-46	-216	-404	-265	-234	(+1)	-1	-40
Salary cost (€m)	512	660	868	1014	884	845	830	806	722
Salaries/turnover (%)	72	62	75	90	76	73	62	58	62

Source Deloitte, 2008.[124]

Note: Operating loss figures for seasons 2002/2003 to 2004/2005 have been restated to exclude player contract amortisation relating to the *Salva Calcio* legislation[125] – see text for explanation.

As the evidence from Serie A indicates, this results in clubs trying to live beyond their means: business models become unsustainable and rational financial management is de-emphasized. In this context it should come as no surprise that a significant number of Serie A club have collapsed into bankruptcy in the last decade, notably ACF Fiorentina, SSC Napoli and AC Parma. ACF Fiorentina were sent down to Serie C2 as a result, losing their name and symbol which had to be repurchased at public auction.[129]

Problematic accounting practices

However, rather than address the core structural problem, the response of the Italian government and the football authorities was to focus on financial reporting presentation issues, attempting to legitimize the most favourable possible presentation of clubs' financial position and performance in their financial statements. So, in response to a critical financial crisis of financial mismanagement in 2002 the Italian government, with Silvio Berlusconi as its prime minister, introduced the *Salva Calcio* decree;[130] literally 'save football'. This was introduced as a direct response to a financial crisis in Italian football when it appeared that many clubs would not be able to secure clearance from the FIGC's financial regulator, Co.Vi.Soc., to start the 2002/2003 league season because of the extent of their debts. In its initial form this allowed clubs to amortize the asset of players' registration rights over an arbitrary period of 10 years rather than over the length of the players' contracts, thus improving the reported financial position and performance of its clubs. One practical consequence of adopting the decree was that it became simpler for clubs to receive an operating licence from the FIGC, thus authorizing them to take part in professional football. Importantly, the licensing criteria were based, in part, on balance sheet, debt-to-income ratios. Given football's perceived importance in Italy, allowing clubs to continue to participate in professional football was an outcome deemed to be in both the public and political (government) interest. Unsurprisingly, the decree was challenged by the EU Minister for Internal Markets. A compromise of allowing the asset to be written off over five years was accepted in 2005.

A major beneficiary of the spirit that informed *Salva Calcio* was SS Lazio. In 2005, the club was facing imminent financial collapse in particular because it had built up substantial liabilities in unpaid taxes. However, a deal was brokered with the tax authorities, with the direct approval of Prime Minister Silvio Berlusconi, which allowed the club to stagger payments on a €140m tax bill over a 23-year period.[131] The negotiations took place against the backdrop of threats of violent disorder by SS Lazio supporters, a hard core of whom demonstrated outside the court during one of the hearings relating to the case waving banners saying:[132] 'If S.S. Lazio goes bust we'll burn down Rome'. Silvio Berlusconi[133] commented on the deal:

> S.S. Lazio's case is a particular one… We are talking about a team with a huge number of supporters and there could have been public disorder and grave consequences [if the deal had not gone through].

The mayor of Rome was also pleased with the deal if for different reasons. Walter Veltroni commented:[134]

> [S.S. Lazio was a] … national heritage for the sport and deserved to be bailed out simply on that account … the tax authorities were wise to help S.S. Lazio because if the club had gone under it would have been a major blow to Italian sport.

What both Berlusconi and Veltroni appeared to overlook was that the deal conferred a major, state-subsidized, advantage to SS Lazio in relation to those clubs who attempted to manage their affairs in an efficient fashion and paid their taxes.

As a postscript to the affair, in March 2009, the president (and controlling shareholder) of SS Lazio, Claudio Lotito was sentenced to two years in jail[135] and fined €65,000 for breaking stock-market rules and withholding information about the true extent of his shareholding in SS Lazio club shares. He had earlier been found guilty of malpractice in the *Calciopoli* scandal. The prosecutors in Milan explained that an intermediary purchased 14.6% of SS Lazio FC shares on behalf of Lotito but this was not disclosed. This enabled Lotito, when he purchased the club in 2004, to avoid having to put up a bid for the rest of the shares by not disclosing his connection to the additional share purchase.

Salva Calcio was not the only mechanism utilized by Italian clubs to flatter their balance sheets. Concerns have also been raised about the practice of Italian clubs manipulating their balance sheets by artificially inflating the costs of players bought and sold and engaging in reciprocal transactions, a practice known as *plus-valenza*.[136] Agnew[137] is particularly scathing on this practice:

> Take the case of the two Milan clubs, which for years now have regularly been selling players to one another ... goalkeeper Paolo Ginestra, striker Matteo Bogani, midfielder Davide Cordone, midfielder Marco Bonura, and defenders Andrea Pollizzano and Fabio Di Sauro? Between 1999 and 2002, these players were all involved in cross-town Milan transfers which yielded the clubs, on paper at least 3.5m [Euros] each time. All fine, except that none of us has ever seen these million-euro footballers play in Serie A, given that they ended up with lower-level clubs Sassuolo, Olbia, Prato, Avellino and Catania.

In January 2007, an inquiry into allegations of false accounting in Serie A football (in part arising out of the *plus-valenza* allegations) was launched, resulting in a request to interview senior executives at both AC Milan and Inter Milan. One issue raised by Milan's public prosecutor was whether Inter Milan would have passed the financial tests necessary to be licensed and therefore be allowed to take part in the 2004/2005 season without improperly adjusting its accounts.[138,139] All the executives interviewed were subsequently cleared of any wrongdoing.[140]

However, the reality is that investigations into alleged financial malpractice at football clubs are commonplace. Agnew recounts how in March 2004, Italy's tax and finance police staged raids on the administrative offices of all Serie A, Serie B and some Serie C sides as well as those of the Lega Calcio and the FIGC. This had in part been prompted by allegations by the owner of the then Serie A club Bologna that some clubs have an unfair advantage because, in Agnew's[141] words:

> ...tax evasion, irregular player wage payment and fraudulent book-keeping leaves them with greater resources to spend on buying the best players.

So prevalent was the culture of tax payment irregularities and a more general culture of late payment that Agnew alleges that the FIGC financial regulator Co.Vi.Soc had no option but to turn a blind eye to many such practices. Virtually all Serie A clubs owe money to the tax authorities.[142]

The fundamental problem with the various mechanisms that have been used to flatter Italian football club accounts is that, of course, they only provide a short-term breathing space for clubs and do not address the core issue of businesses which are making unsustainable losses.

Structural economic weaknesses in Italian football

It is clear that there are a number of structural factors in the economics of the Italian football industry which work against Italian clubs making sustainable profits. The first of these is the decline in Serie A's ability to generate income when compared to its peers as set out in Table 2.

In 1996/1997 Serie A had the second largest turnover of any European league second only to the English Premier League. Ten years on it was only ranked fourth, having been overtaken by Spain and Germany. This relative drop in Serie A's turnover has important implications for the competitiveness of its clubs given the long-established link between expenditure on players' wages and playing success.[144,145] If players' wages are not funded by borrowing then increasing turnover is the only way in which clubs can pay increased wages. In 1996/1997 Serie A's turnover was approximately 80% that of the Premier League; by 2006/2007 this had declined to 51%. This meant that Serie A clubs were now likely to be less competitive in terms of competing and retaining talent in the Europe-wide football labour market. *Ceteris paribus*, this is likely to lead to them being less successful on the field of play in UEFA club competitions, with a consequent impact on clubs' revenue generation. And to complete the vicious cycle, less revenue would make the clubs less competitive still in the player labour market. Table 3 sets outs the comparative information on wages costs for the major leagues over the last ten seasons.

In 1996/1997 Serie A clubs were able to match the English Premier League clubs in terms of overall wages spend on players and indeed in 2000/2001 they exceeded them. But by 2006/2007 their total spend was 50% of that of the Premier League clubs. Indeed it is a testimony to the extraordinary quality of the culture of player

Table 2. Total turnover.

	Turnover (€m)		
	1996/97	2006/07	Increase (%)
England (FA Premier League)	689	2273	230
France (Ligue 1)	393	972	147
Germany (Bundesliga)	524	1379	163
Italy (Serie A)	551	1163	111
Spain (La Liga)	524	1326	153

Source: Deloitte, 2008.[143]

Table 3. Total wage costs for the 'big five' European leagues.

	Wage costs (€m)		
	1996/1997	2006/2007	Increase %
England	324	1,440	344
France	223	619	178
Germany	230	622	170
Italy	324	722	123
Spain	230	822	257

Source: Deloitte, 2008.[146]

development in Italian football that Italian clubs have remained so competitive in European football over the 2001/2002 to 2006/2007 period, as the wage disparity between Serie A and the Premier League clubs started to expand. Considering the 2006/2007 season, the percentage of foreign players playing in Serie A was only 28.9%, compared with 34.3% in La Liga (Spain), 44.8% in the Bundesliga (Germany) and 55.4% in the Premiership (England).[147] The Italian squad that won the 2006 World Cup all played their domestic football in Italy at that time. The only other fully home-based squad was Saudi Arabia.

Returning to income generation, an even starker threat emerges when the turnover figures are segmented. As Table 4 illustrates, in 2006/2007 Serie A was the most dependent of all the major European leagues on income from TV broadcasting contracts, with 63% of total income coming from that source. Should for any reason Serie A become less attractive to TV viewers – for example, due to disenchantment with corruption, financial malpractice or hooliganism – then it would be particularly vulnerable to a downturn in TV revenues.

It is also the case that the performance of Serie A appears rather anaemic when compared with the English Premier League and the Bundesliga in terms of its ability to generate commercial/sponsorship income. While in 2006/2007 the average Serie A club generated nearly 83% of the TV income of an average English Premier League club it generated only 46% of the commercial/sponsorship income; a very low proportion even allowing for the fact that FC Juventus were playing in Serie B that season having been relegated as punishment for its involvement in the *Calciopoli* scandal.

A more fundamental challenge, however, is presented by the decline in attendances. Supporter disillusionment with frequent corruption scandals and increased violence at matches has been cited as a key reason for reduced attendance at the outsized and ageing stadia across the country.[149] Attendances in Serie A have fallen steadily over recent years (see Table 5) and are now well below its peer leagues, and in 2006/2007 actually fell below the average attendance figure of 20,300 spectators registered in season 1964–65.[150,151] From having the highest average league crowd in Europe in the 1997/1998 season Serie A is now fourth after Germany, England and Spain.

Both external (Morrow, 2003)[153] and domestic observers (Baroncelli & Lago, 2006)[154] have observed that, through a mixture of cultural and operational reasons, major Italian clubs were unable or unwilling to exploit their tangible and intangible resources, most notably their stadiums and their brands viz-à-viz merchandising, in a way comparable to the clubs in the English Premier League. They also face a particular problem in relation to the exploitation of merchandising revenues in the form of the particularly entrenched black market in counterfeit merchandise that exists in Italy.[155]

Table 4. Turnover breakdowns for top 5 European leagues 2006/2007.

	England		Germany		Spain		Italy		France	
	€m	%	€m	%	€m	%	€m	%	€m	%
Total turnover	2,273	100	1,379	100	1,326	100	1,163	100	972	100
Television	880	39	480	35	557	42	732	63	565	58
Matchday	802	35	310	22	344	26	156	13	139	14
Sponsorship/ Commercial	591	26	589	43	425	32	275	24	268	28

Source: Deloitte, 2008.[148]

Table 5.   Average league match attendances in Serie A and the English Premier League.

	Average attendance	
	Italy	England
2007/2008	23,000	36,100
2006/2007	18,900	34,400
2005/2006	21,400	33,900
2004/2005	25,000	33,900
2003/2004	25,700	35,000
2002/2003	25,500	35,400
2001/2002	25,900	34,300
2000/2001	29,100	32,800
1999/2000	29,700	30,700
1998/1999	30,700	30,600
1997/1998	31,200	29,200

Source: Deloitte, 2008.[152]

Critically, most Italian clubs do not own their own grounds, or at least do not own the right to control revenues from services provided in the grounds, almost all of which are owned by public authorities.[156] When combined with the declining attendances, this means that Italian clubs derive a much lower revenue from match-day activities (ticket sales, merchandising, hospitality, etc.) because they are severely restricted in leveraging revenue from the additional use of the asset. Deloitte was blunt in its assessment about the impact of this phenomenon in its 2008 *Annual Review of Football Finance*:[157]

> The deteriorating state of Serie A stadia is well documented and continues to hold Italy's clubs back in commercial and financial terms. Whilst the different stadium ownership model often currently in place in Italy … means that clubs have less autonomy over such investment plans, the ownership structure cannot be allowed to be a deterrent to the development of clubs' facilities if their clubs are not to fall further behind their European competitors.

By way of example, Table 6 illustrates that between 2002/2003 and 2006/2007 the average expenditure per attendee at a Serie A club has actually declined. Even in season 2005/2006 when Juventus were still in Serie A, the average spend was still

Table 6.   Matchday revenue per attendee for the 'big five' European leagues.

	Revenue per attendee (€)		
	2002/03	2006/07	% Change
England	40	61	53
France	14	17	21
Germany	19	27	42
Italy	27	22	(19)
Spain	25	35	40

Source: Deloitte, 2008.[158]

only €22. Average match-day expenditure increased in all the other four peer leagues over the period, in the English Premier League by just over 50% (although some might argue that this is a reflection of exploitative ticket-pricing in the Premier League). Premier League game attendees spent on average nearly three times what Serie A fans spent on match-day in 2006/2007.

The problem is recognized at the highest level. The words of the FIGC President Carraro in January 2005 are quoted by Agnew:[159]

> There are stadia in Italy which are simply less than decent, where it's difficult even to find the toilets, where from certain parts of the stand you have difficulty seeing the match … you have got to have a comfortable stadia … in a lot of cases that means taking out the athletics track. There has to be a plus factor about going to the stadium.

As mentioned in the discussion above on how violence at Italian football matches has become a major problem in the twenty-first century, Carraro's comments are laden with irony given that he would have to resign as president of the FIGC as a direct result of the *Calciopoli* scandal for prevaricating when first confronted with the problem (he was also later fined for exercising unfair influence). Nevertheless one might reasonably expect that strategies for addressing the problems enunciated by Carraro should be driven by the leadership of the FIGC and Lega Calcio. In fact, these strategies have not been forthcoming. Although it has to be recognized a similar inability to address the problem was also manifested by the English football authorities when faced with the appalling standards of English football stadia in the 1980s. A solution had to be externally imposed by the UK government following the Taylor Report into the Hillsborough disaster.[160] A *de facto* recognition of the centrality of the problem of inadequate stadia in the business model of Italian football clubs was demonstrated by Juventus' decision to buy the Stadio delle Alpi with a view to demolishing it and building a new club-owned stadium.[161]

TV broadcasting rights and competitive balance

While the fact that Italy's leading football clubs tend to be owned by prominent business and political figures with great influence in wider Italian public and commercial life of itself confers great powers of influence on the clubs they own, it is also the case that these clubs have, as has also been in the case in England and Spain, been able to leverage their greater popularity to acquire a greater share of the commercial income in their respective football markets. Similar to the situation in other countries, since the 1990s there has been a transfer of power away from the traditional football-governing bodies toward major clubs keen to prioritize and manage their own business interests and influence federal policy, particularly in terms of finance.[162] The sale and distribution of television rights has been a central battleground.

Adriano Galliani is a former chief executive of AC Milan (owned by Silvio Berlusconi) and a board member of Mediaset (the media company owned by Berlusconi). Galliani was voted in as president of Lega Calcio in 2002. In this role, he was thus the guardian of the league and its central principle of unity among its member clubs, while at the same time, as CEO of AC Milan and through his role on the executive committee of the G14 group of leading European 'super-clubs', he was the advocate of the interests of Europe's major clubs and his own major club in particular. G14 was at the time raising the threat of a possible breakaway European super-league. He thus did have something of a conflict of interest in his role at Lega Calcio.[163]

His role placed him at the centre of the television rights battleground, where his conflict of interests were revealed starkly. As league president he took on responsibility for negotiations for collective TV rights on behalf of Lega Calcio. The bidding broadcasters were the state-owned RAI network and the Berlusconi-owned Mediaset. The terrestrial highlights were granted to Mediaset[164] (of which, as mentioned above, Galliani was a board member). Given his position as prime minister at the time, questions arose regarding Berlusconi's influence and involvement in several broadcasting tenders. Indeed, following the successful bid in 2005 by Mediaset against Sky Italia for digital-terrestrial rights, the owner of Sky Italia, Rupert Murdoch, lodged a complaint that the Italian government had given illegal financial assistance to encourage the take-up of digital terrestrial TV.[165] Agnew[166] was pointed in his assessment of Galliani's position:

> The Lega [Calcio] president is … Adriano Galliani, one of Berlusconi's closest and most trusted advisers and the acting boss of AC Milan. Galliani's tenure of the Lega presidency represents a 'conflict of interests within the conflict of interests' embodied by his wealthy *padrone*. How, for example, can Galliani adjudicate the allocation of TV rights when one of the contenders is owned by his boss?

And of course, as outlined above, Adriano Galliani[167] would later be banned from Italian football for five months for his role in the match-fixing *Calciopoli* scandal. He would then return as vice president of AC Milan, effectively Silvio Berlusconi's deputy at the club, and in March 2009 was busy negotiating the transfer of David Beckham from LA Galaxy.[168]

The growth of media income can be traced to changes in the Italian broadcast market, specifically the introduction of pay-TV in 1993 and subsequently 'pay per view' television in 1996[169] which, as in most countries, saw the total value of TV broadcasting contracts for football rise. Another factor was that, until season 1999/2000, television rights for Serie A, both public and pay-TV, were negotiated collectively by Lega Calcio on behalf of its clubs.[170] But following an investigation into the marketing of television rights for football matches in 1999 the Italian Competition Authority (ICA) found that the combined sale of television rights for clubs in Serie A and B restricted competition, and was therefore in breach of the Anti-Trust Act.[171] A law was subsequently passed allowing clubs to negotiate their own broadcasting deals, so that bigger clubs could realize their revenue potential fully without subsidizing smaller, less well-supported clubs. As a result, under the new ruling, clubs in Serie A and B were permitted to individually agree deals directly with pay-TV and foreign broadcasters for coverage of their domestic and international matches, although rights for public television coverage continued to be negotiated by Lega Calcio.[172,173]

In 2008 televised football in Italy was provided by three broadcasting companies: Sky Italia, Mediaset and the Telecom Italia company, La7. Sky had contracts with all Serie A teams to cover matches broadcast on satellite television, while digital terrestrial coverage was provided by Mediaset and La 7. The state-owned RAI channels had rights to show highlights of domestic league matches. The ruling allowing clubs to negotiate individual deals had resulted in a huge imbalance in the distribution among Serie A clubs of revenue from TV rights. In an investigation into the football industry the Italian Anti-Trust Commission set out to quantify the financial impact of individual

Table 7. Comparison between Italian and English TV revenue redistributive systems 2001/ 2002.

	Real figures (A)	English Premier League simulation figure (B)	Differential (B)–(A)
Club with the highest TV deal	Juventus €52m	Juventus €32m	–€20m
Club with the lowest TV deal	Piacenza €12m	Piacenza €16m	+€4m

Source: AGCM, 2006.[174]

selling of broadcasting rights compared to collective selling found in countries like England. Comparative figures for the highest (Juventus FC) and lowest (Piacenza Calcio) earning clubs in 2001/2002, one of the early years of the new individual selling regime, are set out in Table 7.

The first-to-last ratio (ratio between the highest and lowest figure), between Juventus and Piacenza was 4.4. Simulating the English Premier League collective selling system in Italian Serie A, both clubs would have received different pay-TV revenue shares, Juventus €32m and Piacenza €16m (B). The differential (B)–(A) would have favoured Piacenza with a surplus of €4m. Juventus, however, would have received 20m less. The first-to-last ratio between Juventus and Piacenza under this distribution system would be 2, while the same ratio in the Premier League between Manchester United and Derby County in the same season was 2.2. In 2002, the first four Premier League Clubs represented together 28% of the total TV revenue deal, while in Italy the first four clubs secured around 47%.[175]

In 2001/2002 Italian Serie A together with La Liga, the Spanish league, had the highest first-to-last ratio among European leagues in respect of television revenues (see Table 8). Notably these were the only leagues which did not operate collective selling of television rights.[176]

The 2008 Deloitte *Annual Review of Football Finance*[177] underlines the impact that individual selling has had in polarizing income distribution. In Italy, AC Milan's total revenue in 2006/2007 was around 17 times of the smallest Serie A teams. In England's Premier League, by contrast, Manchester United's revenue was almost half that, at around eight times that of Wigan Athletic in 2006/2007. During the 2004/2005 season, the top four clubs in Serie A received 52% of the total broadcasting revenue, leaving 48% to be shared among the remaining 16 clubs. Top earners Juventus received more TV revenue than the combined earnings of the bottom nine clubs in Serie A.[178]

The implications of figures like these extend beyond direct financial considerations. In particular, they raise issues of on-field competitiveness, competitive balance and the consequent attraction of the sporting product to spectators and, importantly, broadcasters. As Baroncelli and Lago[179] have observed, in the 1990s competition for the Serie A *scudetto* was dominated by the so-called Seven Sisters – FC Juventus, AC

Table 8. First-to-last ratio in the major football European Leagues (2001/2002).

	France	Germany	UK	Spain	Italy
First-to-last ratio	1.8[a]	2.6[a]	2.3[a]	5.3[b]	6.3[b]

Source: AGCM, 2006.[180]

[a] Collective selling system. [b] Individual selling system.

Milan, FC Internazionale Milan, SS Lazio, AS Roma, AC Parma and ACF Fiorentina
– all of these clubs having the resources to challenge for the Serie A title. One indica-
tion of the decline in competitive balance in Italian football since then is that the seven
quickly became four – FC Juventus, AC Milan, FC Internazionale Milan and AS
Roma – the same clubs which dominated the television earnings league. In short, since
the introduction of the individual selling regime all the evidence suggests that Serie A
has become a much more unbalanced and predictable competition.

It is the received wisdom in the sports economics discipline that the more balanced
a competition, the greater the uncertainty of outcome, then the more attractive the
league will be to spectators and TV viewers (Neale, 1964[181]; El-Hodri & Quirk,
1971[182]). Most North American sports, notably American football's NFL, have
constructed their entire regulatory system on this principle with the application of
various mechanisms for redistribution of collective revenues (e.g. TV broadcasting,
and merchandising income in the case of the NFL) and salary caps in order to control
and attempt to equalize labour spending power by clubs; as it is acknowledged that
playing success is strongly linked to the ability to apply financial resources to hire and
retain the highest performing labour. The extent to which the American theories and
models dependent on closed labour markets can be applied to the open labour market
football of post-Bosman Europe has been questioned by some authors. (Kesenne,
2005[183]; Szymanski, 2003[184], 2004[185]; Szymanski & Kesenne, 2003[186]). In particular, it has been argued that revenue-sharing mechanisms, or a wages cap, depending
on how they are applied, might actually lead to greater imbalance in leagues as they
could simply institutionalize the existing status quo in favour of the clubs with the
highest turnovers and spending power; and because some club owners might simply
use them as an opportunity to take profit at the expense of sporting success (thus creating the need for a minimum salary spend as well as a cap). However, Vrooman
(2007)[187] suggests that the distinction between open and closed markets is irrelevant
because of the *sportsman effect*. This means that where club owners are sportsmen
willing to sacrifice profit in order to win (utility maximizers rather than profit maximizers) then revenue sharing and salary caps should indeed improve competitive
balance. And the experience of European football is that owners do indeed tend to act
to maximize sporting utility. Nevertheless, a particular challenge lies in the fact that
European football does not operate within a hermetic system, but within one which
sees elite clubs seeking to compete in UEFA European competitions as well as in
domestic leagues. Vrooman[188] argues that the *champion effect* (Champions' League
and relegation–promotion effects) has polarized talent and wealth in European football. In the same vein Szymanski[189] argues that the impact of the Champions' League
in terms of the revenue generated and the mechanism of distribution has been to create
'chronic imbalance' in both the competition itself and in its constituent domestic
leagues. This is because clubs which qualify for the Champions League derive a
significant income not open to their non-qualifying competitors in their domestic
leagues thus institutionalizing Champions League qualifiers' domestic financial dominance and by extension their sporting dominances. The fact that the qualification of
Arsenal, Chelsea, Liverpool and Manchester United from the English Premier League
to the Champions League has appeared to become institutionalized in recent years as
they use Champions League revenues to strengthen their position over their other
domestic competitors is an illustration of this effect.

Vrooman (2007)[190] observes that over the last two decades the Italian Serie A has
been the most predetermined in terms of sporting success of the major European

Table 9. Gini Index in the major European football leagues from 2001/2002 to 2005/2006.

Season	Spain	Italy	England	Germany
2001/2002	0.11	0.16	0.17	0.17
2002/2003	0.14	0.17	0.15	0.11
2003/2004	0.13	0.20	0.15	0.16
2004/2005	0.14	0.13	0.17	0.15
2005/2006	0.15	0.20	0.18	0.16
Average	0.130	0.171	0.159	0.148

Source: AGCM, 2006.[191,192]

leagues, and indicates that is significantly influenced by the individual selling arrangements for TV broadcasting in place in Italy. This is supported by analysis by the Italian anti-trust authority in its investigation of the Italian football industry, outlined in Table 9, which uses the Gini Index as a surrogate for changes in competitive balance in Italian football. (The Gini Index – or coefficient – measures the inequality of a distribution. The Gini Index is often used to measure the lesser or greater equity in income distribution. This is a number between 0 and 1, where 0 corresponds to perfect equality, that is the case in which all subjects investigated have the same income, and 1 corresponds to complete inequality i.e. the situation where one person holds the entire income, while all others have a zero income.) Table 9 demonstrates that over the period 2001/2002 to 2005/2006, on average, Italy's Serie A was more unbalanced than top leagues in England, Germany and Spain.

Within this context, the smaller Serie A clubs were, and continue to be, keen to redress the inequality of revenue distribution while simultaneously benefiting from the opportunities which access to increased TV revenues bring. Despite the insistence of smaller Serie A clubs, as well as clubs in Serie B, that television companies should pay more for match coverage, broadcasters have refused to pay higher sums for games they felt would attract too few viewers. In protest against this inequality, smaller clubs threatened to boycott league matches at the start of the 2002/2003 season. The resulting stand-off led to a two-week delay to the start of the season. It took intervention from larger clubs, making up some of the financial shortfall between the sum offered by the television channels and the figure sought by the clubs, for the season to finally go ahead.[193,194]

In January 2006 the smaller clubs initiated moves in the Italian parliament to reintroduce collective selling.[195] While Prime Minister Berlusconi initially seemed sympathetic to the move, the Forza Italia group in the parliament subsequently blocked such a move, ruling *de facto* in favour of Juventus FC, FC Internazionale Milan and of course AC Milan. So enraged was the AFC Fiorentina owner, industrialist Diego Dalle Valle, that he called Berlusconi 'a liar'.

The imbalance, and its perceived impact on competitive balance in top level professional football, has been of sufficient concern to Italy's regulatory bodies that in 2007, the first steps were taken to re-centralize the sale of broadcast rights for Serie A and B clubs. Under the proposal, 50% of revenue was to be shared equally between the Serie A clubs, with part of the remaining sum to be distributed according to audience size and a further smaller sum to be allocated to lower divisions.[196] The return to collective selling was to take effect from 2010 when the existing deals expire.[197] Of course this raises the question as to whether this will further compromise the ability of leading Italian clubs to compete effectively in the Champions' League. Perhaps just as important, it adds even further imperative to the need for them to reform their business management practices in order to drive additional income from match-day (stadium) and commercial enterprises.

Conclusion

To some extent, the future challenges faced by Italian football replicate those faced by the football industries in other European nations. As in other countries in Europe, there is evidence of power being transferred from associations and leagues to clubs, with this redistribution of power being in part a function of the changing economics of professional football in Europe. Arguably, this is less apparent in Italy than in other countries because to some extent this distribution has been masked by the success of the Italian national side. Yet, the impressive results of the national side cloud not only the workings of the club and league structures, but also the political climate within which Italian football operates. In marked contrast, a current polemic in English football centres on the disappointing form of the national team and whether this is influenced by the lack of home-grown talent in league clubs.

The reliance on individual television deals has exacerbated issues of competitive balance within Serie A. It has widened the gap in turnover between the big four clubs and the rest of the league. There is a need to revisit this and the plans to reintroduce a form of collective selling of broadcasting rights in 2010/2011 are welcome, although there is increasing frustration within the lower leagues that the over-riding importance of television monies is undermining the value of their leagues. In addition to this, supporters are losing interest and match day attendances continue to stagnate.

While a coherent pyramid structure appears to remain in place, the system of promotion and relegation has become more a type of 'revolving door' for clubs changing leagues. The emergence of 'super' clubs has led to a more predictable outcome of most matches with promoted clubs gaining entry to the top league for a season – only to face relegation once more at the end of the same season. It appears increasingly likely that only football scandals can alter the positions of the main clubs in Serie A. So, in effect, the football pyramid has been destabilized.

The increasing power of clubs is exacerbated by several factors: the ownership structure of the clubs, the way in which business is done in Italian corporate life – namely through cross shareholding and opaque relationships, the web of personalities and networks of governance and influence. In this regard, Italian football is entirely reflective of Italian corporate culture.

Despite its legal parameters, the existing structure within Italy allows people to go beyond formally accepted levels of involvement. More usually associated with politicians, the durability of key figures in football has become increasingly apparent. At its most extreme, Italian football has become about scandals of influence. Dismissed from one position of authority, it is not uncommon for an individual to immediately take up a new role in a different area.

There also appears to be reluctance on the part of those in positions of authority to face the reality of the current situation in football; i.e. leaving aside any feelings of moral opprobrium or a sense that wrongdoers should be punished, that the health of Italian football has been severely damaged by the series of scandals and the failure to address their root causes, and that this is reflected in declining attendances and a failure of Serie A to keep pace with the commercial successes of its four peer European leagues, in particular the English Premier League. Unwillingness among politicians and regulators to come to terms with, or to take measures to resolve, issues of governance and corruption has led to a sense of their acquiescence with the irregular workings of the game in Italy. Taking cover behind the asserted importance of football and the success of its teams on the field goes some way to explain the willingness to offer *Salva Calcio*, willingness to bend accounting rules and the unwillingness to take on clubs over issues like licensing, unpaid taxes and extreme supporter disruption. Agnew,[198] a harsh critic of the regulation of the Italian industry, poses a key question:

> ...the decisions taken in the summer of 2005, whereby sides like Perugia and Torino were denied promotion to Serie A because of financial irregularities, suggest that FIGC, is finally, beginning to take the problem of fiscal rectitude (or lack of it) seriously. But why was a blind eye turned for so long?

Although keen to gain more power, clubs seem set in more traditional ways of business and are unwilling to modernize. Tied to the mixed economy approach, Italian clubs have sought to increase their individual influence yet continue to rely on direct state aid (through the provision and maintenance of stadia) and indirect support. The 2012 bid to host the UEFA European football championship would have provided much-needed capital to modernize stadia but, ironically, it seems likely that factors such as the frequent tax irregularities reported in Italian football may well have played a part in the decision taken. Without doubt there is a need for clubs to embrace the challenges of modern football business. With this comes the need for modern regulation – including sanctions for misdemeanours – and clear guidelines for strong governance and sound business.

In 1990 Serie A was clearly the dominant league in Europe; the English First Division (now the Premier League) was emerging from the crisis of the Hillsborough disaster and English teams were still banned from competing in European competition following the Heysel stadium disaster in which 37 Juventus fans died during the 1985 European Cup Final with Liverpool (the ban ended at the beginning of the 1990/1991 season). It is instructive to compare the respective strengths and weaknesses of the English Premier League and Serie A in 2008.

The Premier League

Strengths

- Strong reputation for sporting integrity;
- the leading European League in terms of sporting performance achievement;
- modern, safe, stadia operating at near full capacity catering to a differentiated customer base with a large segment of high-spend corporate customers;
- collective selling arrangements for TV rights with rising overall value – critically rising value of overseas rights;
- TV rights, sponsorship and match-day income all important sources of revenue.

Weaknesses

- Top four clubs dominate.
- league not profitable at pre-tax level though clubs have not up to now collapsed into bankruptcy as club owners finance losses (or bankruptcy occurs following relegation e.g. as in the case of Leeds United);

- a tendency toward increasing concentration of media income among top clubs as 50% of the Premier League broadcasting deal is awarded in proportion to final league position (25%) and number of live TV appearances (25%);
- ambivalence about existing 'European' model of the organization of football, e.g. the proposal to play a 39th league game overseas, which may potentially create a rift with other European sports' leagues and associations;
- concerns about overly 'sanitized' stadia atmosphere as traditional fans are excluded through aggressive pricing strategies.

Serie A

Strengths

- Unrivalled historic reputation for sporting excellence internationally;
- Italian football is itself a 'brand' with a truly global reputation, thus providing an excellent platform from which to build commercial revenues;
- very high level of interest among the Italian public.

Weaknesses

- Tarnished reputation for sporting integrity as a result of wholesale match-fixing scandals;
- declining attendances;
- examples of serious crowd disorder as well as some public displays of overt racism by some supporters;
- declining sporting performance achievement;
- old, unsafe stadia operating below capacity and failing to cater for a differentiated customer base;
- third-party ownership of stadia acting as a barrier to investment;
- systemic lack of profitability;
- individual selling of TV rights has increased the financial and sporting domination of a small number of super clubs;
- over-reliance on television revenues;
- wholesale conflicts of interest create barriers to reform;
- an inability and/or unwillingness to make regulatory sanctions stick.

At the start of this article three key questions were asked:

(1) Is it possible for Italian football to prosper in an environment in which there appears to have been significant shortcomings in governance?
(2) If not, what should be the key planks of an agenda for reform?
(3) Is there potential for 'contagion' of negative Italian experience in the rest of the European football market?

On the basis of the evidence, the answer to question 1 must be an emphatic no. The Italian football industry is clearly falling behind its four main European peers in all areas of commercial development, and the performance of Italian club teams looks to have been eclipsed on the basis of their performance in UEFA competitions in 2007/

2008. Only the national team, the *Azzurri*, bucks the trend. Equally clearly, a key reason for this decline is the failure to regulate the Italian industry effectively in the long-term interests of all its stakeholders. The key planks of any reform platform must be:

- the fair and impartial application of financial regulations;
- the re-emphasis of sporting integrity to restore credibility and the public's faith in the uncertainty of sporting outcomes;
- the modernization of stadia and of general management practice;
- a return to more even distribution of income, for example through a collective selling arrangement for broadcasting rights.

In answer to question 3; there is certainly a danger of 'contagion' from negative Italian football experience through the rest of European football, particularly as a different form of oligarchic club owner emerges. In highly competitive sports the pressure to bend the rules is always there. It is the duty and obligation of the regulator to make succumbing to this temptation as difficult as possible and the penalties for doing so a sufficient deterrent. To do otherwise is to undermine the very driver that underpins the underlying value of all aspects of the modern sporting competition – the belief of supporters, sponsors, commercial partners and the public in the integrity of the competition.

The recent history of the Italian football teaches us a lot about the complexity of modern sporting businesses. In particular, it also demonstrates the extraordinary strength that 'brands' such as Italian football embody, a strength which has enabled it to sustain itself through a catalogue of scandal over the last 30 years which might have seen a more conventional industry collapse. However, the conclusion of this case study is that just because it has survived through regulatory neglect thus far does not mean that continued survival, or certainly continued prosperity, is inevitable. A number of self-reinforcing factors have come together to send Italian football into a spiral of decline just as it is confronted with new and dynamic competitors in an era of globalization. Everyone with an interest in the development of a healthy global football industry will share the concern that Italian football is able to meet the governance and regulatory challenge of reform that this presents. In this regard it is perhaps useful to heed the words of the leading business consultants to the football industry, Deloitte, in their 2008 Review of Football Finance[199]:

> ... of all the 'big five' European leagues, it is Serie A whose end of season report would be most likely to read 'could do better/must try harder.' Urgent action is required to address the poor state of Serie A clubs' facilities and the endemic culture of violence and poor safety at matches, before Italian football can hope to reverse the recent decline in both attendances and revenues. On pitch success in a 2006/2007 season which began with a World Cup triumph and ended with a UEFA Champions' League victory, sustained by individual selling, is papering over the cracks. Without serious reform to accompany the return to collective selling, Italy's big clubs will find keeping pace with their major European peers over the next few years very hard going.

Postscript

In April 2009 all but one of the 20 clubs in Serie A voted to breakaway from Serie B to establish an English-style 'Premier League' elite division from the begining of the 2010/2011 season.[200]

Notes

1. Morrow, 'Impression Management in Football Club Financial Reporting', 96–108.
2. Baroncelli and Lago, 'Italian Football', 13–28.
3. AGCM, *Indagine Conoscitiva sul Settore del Calcio Professionistico*, 28.
4. Agnew, *Forza Italia*.
5. Foot, *Calcio*.
6. Jones, *The Dark Heart of Italy*.
7. Agnew, *Forza Italia*.
8. Foot, *Calcio*, updated edition.
9. Jones, *The Dark Heart of Italy*.
10. Kuper, 'Azzurri's Quest Consoles Nation Rocked by Scandals'.
11. Ghirelli, *Storia del calico italiano*.
12. Foot, *Calcio*, updated edition.
13. Federazione Italiana Giuoco Calcio (FIGC), *History*, 2007. http://www.figc.it/en/3149/2077/HpSezioneConMenuSX.shtml. Accessed March 10, 2009.
14. Lega Calcio, *Rapporto 2007*.
15. Dunford and Greco, *After the Three Italies*.
16. Istat, *Rilevazione sulle forze di lavoro* (*Labour Force Survey*).
17. Ridley, 'Maradona Hand in North–South Divide – Italy v Argentina'.
18. Foot, *Calcio*, updated edition, 389.
19. De Biasi, '*Ultra*-Political: Football Culture in Italy', 115–27.
20. Ibid.
21. Semino and Masci, 'Politics is Football: Metaphor in the Discourse of Silvio Berlusconi in Italy', 243–69.
22. Agnew, *Forza Italia*, 120.
23. Ibid., 114.
24. Ibid., 101–2.
25. Jones, *The Dark Heart of Italy*, 125–6.
26. Ibid., 187.
27. *Reuters UK*, 'UPDATE 1 – Berlusconi Loses Libel Suit Against the *Economist*'.
28. For a detailed description of the organization and functions of the FIGC view its website at http://www.figc.it/
29. Squillaci, 'Risorse, il Coni Premia il Calico (perdente)'.
30. Federazione Italiana Giuoco Calcio, 2007. http://www.figc.it/en/90/3087/Struttura.shtml. Accessed March 24, 2009.
31. Levante, *Creative Accounting in Italian Football Clubs*, 8.
32. Agnew, *Forza Italia*.
33. Foot, *Calcio*.
34. Jones, *The Dark Heart of Italy*.
35. Hewitt, *Sporting Justice*, 67–71.
36. Jones, *The Dark Heart of Italy*, 23.
37. Foot, *Calcio*, 244–53.
38. Foot, *Calcio*.
39. Jones, *The Dark Heart of Italy*, 79.
40. Ibid.
41. Ibid., 69–70.
42. Ibid., 69.
43. Foot, *Calcio*, 255.
44. Ibid.
45. Jones, *The Dark Heart of Italy*, 70–1.
46. Burke, 'Paradiso to Inferno'.
47. Agnew, *Forza Italia*, 63–93.
48. Agnew, *Forza Italia*, 89.
49. Agnew, *Forza Italia*, 217–49.
50. Foot, *Calcio*, 266–9.
51. Jones, *The Dark Heart of Italy*, 72–4.
52. Gianluca Vialli comprehensively refutes these implications in his co-authored 2007 book on English and Italian football. Vialli and Marcotti, *The Italian Job*, 358–61.
53. Agnew, *Forza Italia*, 235.
54. Ibid., 233.

55. Jones, *The Dark Heart of Italy*, 83.
56. Foot, *Calcio*, 268.
57. Agnew, *Forza Italia*, 229.
58. Foot, *Calcio*, 268.
59. Agnew, *Forza Italia*, 231.
60. Ibid., 227–8.
61. Ibid., 249.
62. Ibid., 242–4.
63. Ibid., 249.
64. Jones, *The Dark Heart of Italy*, 74.
65. Agnew, *Forza Italia*, 238.
66. Jones, *The Dark Heart of Italy*, 71–2.
67. Ibid.
68. Agnew, *Forza Italia*, 263–5.
69. Ibid., 251–65.
70. Foot, *Calcio*, updated edition, 282–3.
71. Ibid., 282.
72. Agnew, *Forza Italia*, 197.
73. Foot, *Calcio*, updated edition, 283–302. Foot provides a detailed account of the *Calciopoli* scandal.
74. Hewitt, *Sporting Justice*, 67–71. Hewitt provides a succinct summary of the key elements of the *Calciopoli* scandal.
75. Burke, 'Paradiso to Inferno'. Burke gives a full account of the *Calciopoli* scandal, in particular the role of Luciano Moggi.
76. Jones, *The Dark Heart of Italy*, 271–2.
77. Ibid., 272–3.
78. Burke, 'Paradiso to Inferno'.
79. Ibid.
80. Sparre, 'Fallen Italian Football President can Continue in the IOC'.
81. Foot, *Calcio*, updated edition, 289.
82. *USA Today*, 'Galliani's Match-Fixing Penalty Reduced by 4 months'.
83. Foot, *Calcio*, updated edition, 264.
84. BBC Sport, 'Italian Football's Tangled Web'.
85. Foot, *Calcio*, updated edition, 287.
86. *Reuters UK*, 'UPDATE 3 – Soccer – Former Juve Chief Moggi Jailed for 18 Months'.
87. Agnew, *Forza Italia*, 267–80.
88. Guschwan, 'Riot in the Curve'. Guschwan provides an insightful assessment of the historical development of Italian fan culture.
89. Foot, *Calcio* updated edition. Foot offers an assessment of the development of *ultra* fan culture.
90. Agnew, *Forza Italia*, 275.
91. Ibid., 276–7.
92. Jones, *The Dark Heart of Italy*, 81.
93. Agnew, *Forza Italia*, 295–6.
94. Guschwan, 'Riot in the Curve'.
95. *BBC Sport*, 'Italian Fans Face Stadium Lockout'.
96. Fraser, 'Doors Locked for Many Italy Games'.
97. *Reuters.com*, 'Italy Matches to go Ahead, Even Without Fans'.
98. For details of the activities of L'Osservatorio Nazionale sulle Manifestazioni Sportive' see: http://www.osservatoriosport.interno.it/
99. *BBC News*, 'Officer "Rues" Killing S.S. Lazio Fan'.
100. Kennedy, 'Italian Football Violence Resurfaces'.
101. Deloitte, *Annual Review of Football Finance*, 15, 2008.
102. Inquiry by the Rt. Hon. Lord Justice Taylor. *The Hillsborough Stadium Disaster: Final Report*. Inquiry by the Rt. Hon. Lord Justice Taylor. *The Hillsborough Stadium Disaster: Interim Report*.
103. Deloitte, *Annual Review of Football Finance*, 24, 2008.
104. Guschwan, 'Riot in the Curve'.
105. Agnew, *Forza Italia*, 278.
106. Foot, *Calcio*, updated edition, 536, 545.

107. Fraser, 'Juventus Under Cloud of Suspicion'.
108. Jones, *The Dark Heart of Italy*, 68.
109. Bianchi, Bianco, and Enriques 'Pyramidical Groups and the Separation Between Ownership and Control in Italy', 154–88.
110. Morrow, *The People's Game?*, 135.
111. Jones, *The Dark Heart of Italy*, 76.
112. Jones, *The Dark Heart of Italy*, 256–7.
113. *Corriere della Sera*, 'La GEA dei Figli di Papa' Sempre al Centro dei Sospetti'.
114. AGCM, *Indagine Conoscitiva sul Settore del Calcio Professionistico*, 118–25.
115. Marcoliguori Blog. http://marcoliguori.blogspot.com/search/label/gea. Accessed March 30, 2009.
116. *Corriere della Sera*, 'Il Vero Padrone Del Calcio Italiano? Uno Banca'.
117. AGCM, *Indagine Conoscitiva sul Settore del Calcio Professionistico*, 118–25.
118. Foot, *Calcio*, 283–92.
119. Jones, *The Dark Heart of Italy*, 273–4.
120. Collins, 'Rune Hauge, International Man of Mystery'.
121. Smith, and LeJeune, *Football*, Para. 2.1.
122. Inquiry by the Rt. Hon. Lord Justice Taylor, *The Hillsborough Stadium Disaster: Final Report*. Inquiry by the Rt. Hon. Lord Justice Taylor, *The Hillsborough Stadium Disaster: Interim Report*.
123. Deloitte, *Annual Review of Football Finance*, 17, 2008.
124. Ibid., 11–21.
125. Ibid., 18.
126. Ibid.
127. Moerland, 'Corporate Ownership and Control Structures', 443–64.
128. Morrow, *The People's Game?*, 123–6.
129. Foot, *Calcio*, updated edition, 543.
130. Morrow, 'Impression Management in Football Club Financial Reporting', 96–108.
131. Ibid., 105.
132. *ANSA*, 'Soccer: S.S. Lazio Stays Afloat Thanks to Tax Deal'.
133. *Agence France Presse*, 'Saving S.S. Lazio Prevented Fan Violence, Says Berlusconi'.
134. *ANSA*, 'Soccer: S.S. Lazio Stays Afloat Thanks to Tax Deal'.
135. euFootball.BIZ, 'S.S. Lazio President Sent to Prison'.
136. Foot, *Calcio*, 537–8.
137. Agnew, *Forza Italia*, 287–8.
138. Calandra, 'Milan and Inter Executives Could Face False Accounting Trial'.
139. *euFootball.BIZ*, 'Inquiry into False Accounting in Inter and Milan'.
140. Jacobelli, 'Plusvalenze, Ecco Perchè Milan e Inter Sono Stati Prosciolto'.
141. Agnew, *Forza Italia*, 287.
142. Ibid., 288–9.
143. Deloitte, *Annual Review of Football Finance*, 12, 2008.
144. Szymanski, and Kuypers, *Winners and Losers*, Chapter 5.
145. Deloitte, *Annual Review of Football Finance*, 37, 2008.
146. Ibid., 17.
147. Poli, and Ravenel, *Annual Review of the European Football Players' Labour Market*, 38.
148. Deloitte, *Annual Review of Football Finance*, 14, 2008.
149. Lawton, 'Football: The Beautiful … and the Damned'.
150. Lega Calcio Centro Studi, *Rapporto 2005*.
151. Details of trends in attendances at Italian football can be found on the Lega Calcio website. http://www.lega-calcio.it/it/Lega-Calcio/Bacheca/Regolamenti/Dati-statistici-su-Incassi-e-Spettatori.page Accessed March 24, 2009.
152. Deloitte, *Annual Review of Football Finance*, 15, 2008.
153. Morrow, *The People's Game?*, 120–1.
154. Baroncelli, and Lago, 'Italian Football', 16.
155. Ibid.
156. Ibid.
157. Deloitte, *Annual Review of Football Finance*, 15, 2008.
158. Ibid., 16.
159. Agnew, *Forza Italia*, 290.

160. Inquiry by the Rt. Hon. Lord Justice Taylor, *The Hillsborough Stadium Disaster: Final Report*. Inquiry by the Rt. Hon. Lord Justice Taylor, *The Hillsborough Stadium Disaster: Interim Report*.
161. Agnew, *Forza Italia*, 290.
162. Porro, and Russo, P. (2004). 'Italian Football between Conflict and State Aid', 219–34. This article provides an extensive analysis of how the power of Lega Calcio and the FIGC has been eroded by the leading clubs in the context of the Italian market for the broadcasting of domestic football.
163. Ibid., 226.
164. Agnew, *Forza Italia*, 127.
165. Gratton, and Solberg, *The Economics of Sports Broadcasting*, 195.
166. Agnew, *Forza Italia*, 286.
167. *USA Today*, 'Galliani's Match-Fixing Penalty Reduced by 4 Months'.
168. *BBC Sport*, 'Beckham to Part Fund Milan Switch'.
169. Lago, 'The State of the Italian Football Industry', 463–73.
170. Ibid..
171. Tonazzi, 'Competition Policy and the Commercialization of Sport Broadcasting Rights', 17–34.
172. Lago, 'The State of the Italian Football Industry', 463–73.
173. Baroncelli, and Lago, 'Italian Football', 18.
174. AGCM, *Indagine Conoscitiva sul Settore del Calcio Professionistico*, 50–1.
175. Ibid., 51.
176. Ibid., 58.
177. Deloitte, *Annual Review of Football Finance*, 13, 2008.
178. Gratton and Solberg, *The Economics of Sports Broadcasting*, 161.
179. Baroncelli and Lago, 'Italian Football', 22.
180. AGCM, *Indagine Conoscitiva sul Settore del Calcio Professionistico*, 5.
181. Neale, 'The Peculiar Economics of Professional Sports', 1–14.
182. El-Hodiri and Quirk, 'An Economic Model of a Professional Sport League', 1302–19.
183. Kesenne, 'Revenue Sharing and Competitive Balance', 98–106.
184. Szymanski, 'The Economic Design of Sporting Contests', 1137–87.
185. Szymanski, 'Professional Team Sports are Only a Game', 111–26.
186. Szymanski and Kesenne, 'Competitive Balance and Gate Revenue Sharing in Team Sports', 165–77.
187. Vrooman, 'Theory of the Beautiful Game', 314–54.
188. Ibid.
189. Szymanski, 'The Champions League and the Coase Theorem', 355–73.
190. Vrooman, 'Theory of the Beautiful Game', 315.
191. AGCM, *Indagine Conoscitiva sul Settore del Calcio Professionistico*, 59.
192. Montanari and Silvestri, 'Ieri, Moggi e Domani'.
193. Dougal and Garcia-Bennett, 'Two Week Time Delay to Italian Season as Clubs Dig in Heels'.
194. Tynan, '"Big Six" Clubs Pay Out to Ensure Italian Season Begins'.
195. Agnew, *Forza Italia*, 128.
196. *Corriere della Sera*, 'Diritti tv, la serie A trova l'accordo'.
197. Deloitte, *Annual Review of Football Finance*, 16, 2008.
198. Agnew, *Forza Italia*, 291.
199. Deloitte, *Annual Review of Football Finance*, 21, 2008.
200. *BBC Sport*, 'Serie A to Form Breakaway League'.

References

AGCM. *Indagine Conoscitiva sul Settore del Calcio Professionistico,* ed. Autorita' Garante della Concorrenza e del Mercato, 2006. http://www.agcm.it/AGCM_ITA/DSAP/DSAP_IC.NSF/0/602911f6ec387433c125725a003febbb/$FILE/IC27-testo_conclusivo.pdf. Accessed March 24, 2009.

Agence France Presse. 'Saving S.S. Lazio Prevented Fan Violence, Says Berlusconi', *Agence France Presse,* March 31, 2005 (in English).

Agnew, P. *Forza Italia.* London: Random House, 2007.

ANSA. 'Soccer: S.S. Lazio Stays Afloat Thanks to Tax Deal'. *ANSA* (English Media Service), March 29, 2005.

Baroncelli, A., and U. Lago. 'Italian Football', *The Journal of Sports Economics* 7, no. 1 (2006): 13–28.

BBC News. 'Officer "Rues" Killing S.S. Lazio Fan', *BBC News*, November 12, 2007. http://news.bbc.co.uk/1/hi/world/europe/7090170.stm. Accessed March 10, 2009.

BBC Sport. 'Italian Football's Tangled Web', *BBC Sport*, January 14, 2006. http://news.bbc.co.uk/sport1/hi/football/europe/4989484.stm. Accessed March 10, 2009.

BBC Sport. 'Catania Lose Stadium Ban Appeal', *BBC Sport*, February 22, 2007. http://news.bbc.co.uk/sport1/hi/football/europe/6361463.stm. Accessed March 11, 2009.

BBC Sport. 'Italian Fans Face Stadium Lockout', *BBC Sport*, February 5, 2007. http://news.bbc.co.uk/sport1/hi/football/6327655.stm. Accessed March 11, 2009.

BBC Sport. 'Beckham to Part Fund Milan Switch', *BBC Sport*, March 8, 2009. http://news.bbc.co.uk/sport1/hi/football/europe/7931186.stm. Accessed March 30, 2009.

BBC Sport. 'Serie A to form breakaway league', *BBC Sport*, April 30, 2009. http://news.bbc.co.uk/sport1/hi/football/europe/8027857.stm. Accessed June 6, 2010.

Bianchi, M., M. Bianco, and L. Enriques. 'Pyramidical Groups and the Separation Between Ownership and Control in Italy'. In *The Control of Corporate Europe,* ed. F. Barca, and M. Becht, 154–88. Oxford: Oxford University Press, 2001.

Burke, J. 'Paradiso to Inferno', *The Observer Sport Monthly,* July 30, 2006. http://www.guardian.co.uk/sport/2006/jul/30/football.features. Accessed March 10, 2009.

Calandra, R. 'Milan and Inter Executives Could Face False Accounting Trial', *Il Sole 24 Ore,* September 25, 2007.

Collins, R. 'Rune Hauge, International Man of Mystery', *The Guardian,* March 18, 2000. http://www.guardian.co.uk/football/2000/mar/18/newsstory.sport1. Accessed March 16, 2009.

Corriere della Sera. 'Il Vero Padrone del Calcio Italiano? Uno Banca', *Corriere della Sera,* April 27, 2003. http://archiviostorico.corriere.it/2003/aprile/27/vero_padrone_del_calcio_italiano_co_0_030427008.shtml. Accessed March 30, 2009.

Corriere della Sera. 'La GEA dei Figli di Papa' Sempre al Centro dei Sospetti', *Corriere della Sera,* March 24, 2005. http://archiviostorico.corriere.it/2005/aprile/01/Gea_dei_figli _ papa_sempre_co_9_050401716.shtml. Accessed March 30, 2009.

Corriere della Sera. 'Diritti tv, La Serie A Trova L'Accordo', *Corriere della Sera,* October 30, 2007. http://www.corriere.it/sport/07_ottobre_30/diritti_tv_calcio.shtml. Accessed March 16, 2009.

De Biasi, R. '*Ultra*-Political: Football Culture in Italy'. In *Football, Nationality and the State,* ed. V. Duke, and L. Crolley, 115–27. Harlow: Longman, 1996.

Deloitte. *Annual Review of Football Finance.* Manchester: Deloitte, 2008.

Dougal, S., and C. Garcia-Bennett. 'Two Week Time Delay to Italian Season as Clubs Dig in Heels', *The Independent,* August 21, 2002. http://www.independent.co.uk/sport/football/european/twoweek-delay-to-italian-season-as-clubs-dig-in-heels-640513.html. Accessed March 16, 2009.

Dunford, M., and L. Greco. *After the Three Italies. Wealth, Inequality and Industrial Change.* Oxford: Blackwell, 2006.

El-Hodiri, M., and J. Quirk. 'An Economic Model of a Professional Sport League', *Journal of Political Economy* 79 (1971): 1302–19.

euFootball.BIZ. 'Inquiry into False Accounting in Inter and Milan', *eufinal.BIZ,* January 19, 2007. http://www.eufootball.biz/Legal/3608-190107-Inquiry-false-accounting-Inter-Milan.html. Accessed January 19, 2007.

euFootball.BIZ. 'S.S. Lazio President Sent to Prison', *euFootball.BIZ,* March 5, 2007. http://www.eufootball.biz/Clubs/6818-S.S. Lazio_president_prison.html. Accessed March 25, 2009.

Foot, J. *Calcio: A History of Italian Football.* London: Fourth Estate, 2006.

Foot, J. *Calcio: A History of Italian Football.* London: Harper Perennial, updated edition, 2007.

Fraser, C. 'Juventus Under Cloud of Suspicion', *BBC News*, May 12, 2006. http://news.bbc.co.uk/1/hi/world/europe/4766503.stm. Accessed March 11, 2009.

Fraser, C. 'Doors Locked for Many Italy Games', *BBC News*, February 10, 2007. http://news.bbc.co.uk/1/hi/world/europe/6349051.stmn. Accessed March 22, 2009.

Ghirelli, A. *Storia del Calico Italiano.* Turin: Einaudi, 1990.

Gratton, C., and H.A. Solberg. *The Economics of Sports Broadcasting*. Abingdon: Routledge, 2007.

Guschwan, M. 'Riot in the Curve: Soccer Fans in Twenty-first Century Italy', *Soccer & Society* 8, no. 2/3 (2007): 250–66.

Hewitt, I. *Sporting Justice: 101 Sporting Encounters with the Law*. Cheltenham: SB Sport Books, 2008.

Istat, *Rilevazione sulle forze di lavoro (Labour Force Survey)*. Rome: Istat, September 2007. http://www.istat.it/salastampa/comunicati/in_calendario/forzelav/20070920_00/testointe-grale.pdf. Accessed March 10, 2009.

Jacobelli, X. 'Plusvalenze, Ecco Perchè Milan e Inter Sono Stati Prosciolto: "I Loro Bilanci Erano in Regola"' *Quotidano.net*, February 20, 2008. http://club.quotidianonet. ilsole24ore.com/?q=node/1145. Accessed March 25, 2009.

Jones, T. *The Dark Heart of Italy*. London: Faber & Faber, 2007.

Kennedy, F. 'Italian Football Violence Resurfaces', *BBC News*, November 12, 2007. http://news.bbc.co.uk/1/hi/world/europe/7090833.stm. Accessed March 30, 2009.

Kesenne, S. 'Revenue Sharing and Competitive Balance: Does the Invariance Proposition Hold?', *Journal of Sports Economics* 6, no. 1 (2005): 98–106.

Kuper, S. 'Azzurri's Quest Consoles Nation Rocked by Scandals'. *Financial Times*, July 7, 2006. http://www.ft.com/cms/s/0/97e3f396-0ele-11db-a385-0000779e2340.html. Accessed March 10, 2009.

Lago, U. 'The State of the Italian Football Industry'. In *Handbook on the Economics of Sport*, ed. W. Andreff, and S. Szymanski, 463–73. Cheltenham: Edward Elgar, 2007.

Lawton, J. 'Football: The Beautiful ... and the Damned'. *The Independent*, January 28, 2006. http://www.independent.co.uk/sport/football/news-and-comment/the-beautiful-and-the-damned-524836.html. Accessed March 10, 2009.

Lega Calcio. *Rapporto 2007: Analisi Economico Finanziaria 1998–2006*. Milan: Lega Calcio, 2007.

Lega Calcio Centro Studi. *Rapporto 2005: Analisi del trend degli spettatori allo stadio e degli ascolti televisivi della Serie A Tim e della Serie B Tim negli ultimi anni*. Milan: Lega Calcio, 2005.

Levante, M. 'Creative Accounting in Italian Football Clubs: Ethical Issues and the Impact of International Accounting Standards (IAS) on Listed Clubs', paper presented at the 5th International Conference on Sports and Culture: Economic, Management and Marketing Aspects, Athens, Greece, 2005.

Moerland, P. 'Corporate Ownership and Control Structures: An International Comparison', *Review of Industrial Organisations* 10 (1995): 443–64.

Montanari, F., and G. Silvestri. 'Ieri, Moggi e Domani', www.lavoce.info, May 18, 2006. http://www.lavoce.info/articoli/pagina2184.html. Accessed March 24, 2009.

Morrow, S. *The People's Game? Football, Finance and Society*. Basingstoke: Palgrave, 2003.

Morrow, S. 'Impression Management in Football Club Financial Reporting', *International Journal of Sports Finance* 1, no. 2 (2006): 96–108.

Neale, W. 'The Peculiar Economics of Professional Sports; A Contribution to the Theory of the Firm in Sporting Competition and in Market Competition', *Quarterly Journal of Economics* 78, no. 1 (1964): 1–14.

Poli, R., and L. Ravenel. *Annual Review of the European Football Players' Labour Market*. Neuchatel: CIES Editions, 2007.

Porro, N., and P. Russo. 'Italian Football Between Conflict and State Aid'. In *Italian Politics: Italy Between Europeanization and Domestic Politics*, ed. S. Fabbrini, and V. Della Sala, 219–34. New York: Berghahn Books.

Reuters.com. 'Italy Matches to Go Ahead, Even Without Fans', *Reuters.com*, February 9, 2007. http://www.reuters.com/article/sportsNews/idUSL08452067620070209. Accessed March 22, 2009.

Reuters UK. 'UPDATE 1 – Berlusconi Loses Libel Suit Against the *Economist*', *Reuters.com*, September 5, 2008. http://uk.reuters.com/article/rbssTechMediaTelecomNews/idUKL521441520080905. Accessed March 10, 2009.

Reuters UK. 'UPDATE 3 – Soccer – Former Juve Chief Moggi Jailed for 18 Months', *Reuters.com*, January 8, 2009. http://uk.reuters.com/article/footballNews/idUKL855507420090108. Accessed March 10, 2010.

Ridley, I. 'Maradona Hand in North–South Divide – Italy v Argentina', *The Guardian*, July 3, 1990.

Semino, E., and M. Masci. 'Politics is Football: Metaphor in the Discourse of Silvio Berlusconi in Italy', *Discourse & Society*, 7, no. 2 (1996): 243–69.

Smith, J., and M. LeJeune. *Football: It's Values, Finances and Reputation*. London: The Football Association, 1998.

Sparre, K. 'Fallen Italian Football President Can Continue in the IOC', www.playthegame.org, January 31, 2007. http://www.playthegame.org/news/detailed/fallen-italian-football-president-can-continue-in-the-ioc.html. Accessed March 30, 2009.

Squillaci, L. 'Risorse, il Coni Premia il Calico (Perdente)', *24 Ore*, August 23, 2008.

Szymanski, S. 'The Economic Design of Sporting Contests', *Journal of Economic Literature* 41, no. 4 (2003): 1137–87.

Szymanski, S. 'Professional Team Sports are Only a Game: Walrasian Fixed-supply Conjecture Model, Contest-Nash Equilibrium, and the Invariance Principle', *Journal of Sports Economics* 5, no. 2 (2004): 111–26.

Szymanski, S. 'The Champions League and the Coase Theorem', *Scottish Journal of Political Economy* 54, no. 3 (2007): 355–73.

Szymanski, S., and S. Kesenne. 'Competitive Balance and Gate Revenue Sharing in Team Sports'. *Journal of Industrial Economics* 52, no. 1 (2003): 165–77.

Szymanski, S., and T. Kuypers. *Winners and Losers: The business Strategy of Football*. London: Penguin, 1999.

Rt. Hon. Lord Justice Taylor. *The Hillsborough Stadium Disaster: Final Report*. Cm 962. London: HMSO, 1990.

Rt. Hon. Lord Justice Taylor. *The Hillsborough Stadium Disaster: Interim Report*. Cm 765. London: HMSO, 1989.

Tonazzi, A. 'Competition Policy and the Commercialization of Sport Broadcasting Rights', *International Journal of the Economics of Business* 10, no. 1 (2003): 17–34.

Tynan, G. '"Big Six" Clubs Pay Out to Ensure Italian Season Begins', *The Independent*, September 11, 2002. http://findarticles.com/p/articles/mi_qn4158/is_20020911/ai_n12640357. Accessed March 30, 2009.

USA Today. 'Galliani's Match-fixing Penalty Reduced by 4 Months', *USA Today*, December 18, 2006. http://www.usatoday.com/sports/soccer/europe/2006-12-18-galliani-penalty-reduced_x.htm. Accessed March 17, 2009.

Vialli, G., and G. Marcotti. *The Italian Job: A Journey to the Heart of Two Great Football Cultures*. London: Bantam Books, 2007.

Vrooman, J. 'Theory of the Beautiful Game: The Unification of European Football', *Scottish Journal of Political Economy* 54, no. 3 (2007): 314–54.

Websites

Federazione Italiana Giuoco Calcio. http://www.figc.it/index_en.shtml

Lega Calcio. www.lega-calcio.it

Marcoliguori Blog. http://marcoliguori.blogspot.com/search/label/gea

L'Osservatorio Nazionale sulle Manifestazioni Sportive. http://www.osservatoriosport.interno.it/

Governance and the Gaelic Athletic Association: time to move beyond the amateur ideal?

David Hassan

School of Sports Studies, University of Ulster at Jordanstown, Newtownabbey, UK

The Gaelic Athletic Association (GAA) is Ireland's largest sporting organization. It has a membership of almost 1 million people and a presence in every part of the island. It has advanced an amateur ideal for the 125 years of its existence, albeit in recent years there has been a considerable growth in the professional administration of Gaelic games activity in the country. This article deals with the question of corporate governance within the GAA, an issue that to date has never received any form of academic coverage. It argues that the current approach to governance in the association is outdated, unwieldy and inefficient. An argument for the adoption of a stewardship model, with the appointment of a professional board of directors, is outlined throughout the course of this article. This is seemingly all the more pressing when one considers the growing number of stakeholders who would wish to have a say about the way the GAA manages its affairs. Indeed it is notable that many of the association's fiercest critics on this matter have emerged from within its own ranks. As these are the same individuals on whom the GAA has relied to secure its current position of strength, their growing levels of dissent should be of concern to those in positions of authority within the organization.

Introduction

It appears that issues of governance are becoming part of everyday discussions surrounding sport.[1] That said, the accent is rarely on examples of 'good' sport governance. Instead, some of those who control modern-day sport are viewed with suspicion by the public at large. Individuals are thought to lack the proper skills to execute their responsibilities or, worse still, in the view of some commentators, are deliberately corrupt.[2] However, not all of the blame can necessarily be placed at the feet of the individuals concerned. Katwala (2000) argues persuasively that the structures of many governing bodies are inadequate for the demands of modern-day sport as they were developed in a different, that is to say amateur, era. It is an assertion supported by a number of others, among them Forster (2006) and Sugden (2002). Regardless of whether the fault lies with the individual or the structure in which they operate, what is notable is the relative silence among a range of others, academics included, about the way sport is being managed. What work has taken place has tended to focus on certain (typically association football) clubs or on global sporting organizations, such as the International Olympic Committee (IOC) or Fédération Internationale de Football Association (FIFA). Research on individual national governing bodies (NGB) of sport is rare; Bairner's (2004) insightful analysis of the situation in Northern Ireland being something of an exception.[3] The reasons for this level of neglect are unclear. For some, NGBs have lost such control over sport in their jurisdictions that they have become virtual bystanders amid its relentless commercialization. Undeniably, as Sugden and Tomlinson (1998) and Jennings (2006) have demonstrated, sport and big money have become convenient bedfellows. The argument follows that control over sport is now the result of negotiation and conditional upon the input of a range of interested stakeholders.[4] In many cases, the net result is that the well-being of the sport itself is compromised.

Of course, such an analysis overlooks the capacity of individual countries to respond differently to the forces of capitalism.[5] In cases where sport is firmly located within the national psyche and has a cultural resonance that extends beyond that which may be considered 'normal', the ability of national bodies to exercise resistance is increased. Notwithstanding this, even in such countries, those charged with directing sport cannot exist in splendid isolation. They actively court big business, negotiate with various arms of the media and market their activities often in the naïve belief that they still retain autonomy over their sport. The reality is, however, 'that when they act, they do so as one element of a collective corporate decision-making network'.[6] While it is easy to appreciate that for certain NGBs a financial imperative renders this process almost inevitable, the case of the Gaelic Athletic Association (GAA) is something of an exception. The GAA is the largest sporting organization in Ireland, with almost 1 million members, and promotes a range of indigenous games of which Gaelic football and hurling are the most popular. Although comparatively small as a NGB, this essentially amateur organization is financially sound. Its operating profits, £19m in 2009, result from a form of cooperative management that belies much of the cynicism surrounding modern-day sport.[7] It has a presence in every community on the island of Ireland and commands a level of altruism and selfless commitment by its members that is, in many ways, exceptional.

It is ironic therefore that the focus of this article is on corporate governance within the GAA. The suggestion that its management system is outdated in light of the challenges it faces is made. The result of this is that the association is not being run as efficiently or effectively as it should be. By way of context, the article begins with an overview of some of the more significant developments that have taken place concerning the management of the GAA during the past decade. Throughout this period the GAA has sought to realign its operating strategy to respond to the changing environment in which it finds itself. However, its success in doing so has been limited. Ostensibly, this process has involved a move away from a benign, community-led body to a modern, commercially aware sporting organization. In order to guide this transformation, the GAA undertook a strategic review of its activities in 2002. An analysis of its findings is central to the early part of this article. The argument is made that many of the recommendations contained within the document, specifically those relating to the issue of corporate governance, have not been properly enacted. The fact that this was the first strategic review commissioned by the GAA since the McNamee report of 1972 supports the assertion that many of the proposals contained within it were well overdue. However, of the 55 recommendations within the most recent review, only 15 were passed at a special congress of the association held in October 2002. Even then most of the 'radical' proposals concerning the effective management of the organization were roundly defeated.

Consequently, a call for the introduction of a more professional approach to sport governance by the GAA is a constant theme of this article. This is to replace an outdated and strategically inept administrative model, with which the organization has persisted long after its effectiveness has been lost. The administrative approach is ill-equipped to respond to the changing context in which the GAA now operates. Election to a new streamlined board of directors should be based on merit and replace the existing executive arm of the association which is unwieldy, unnecessarily bureaucratic and, for the most part, ill-equipped to deal with the issues the organization now faces. In this regard, the GAA has increasingly had to engage with a range of internal and external stakeholders, each demanding a level of input into how the organization is run. Therefore, by way of conclusion, the point is made that as the GAA enters a period of unprecedented opportunity it must prove responsive to the demands placed upon it and thereby ensure its continued relevancy in an evolving Irish society.

The 'place' of the GAA in Irish life

The formation of the GAA in 1884 was integrally connected to a wider campaign for Irish sovereignty unfolding in Ireland at that time. It was also an important aspect in the promotion of a distinctively Irish culture, which had first been suggested by Michael Cusack, a school teacher of some note in late eighteenth-century Ireland.[8] The All Ireland senior football and hurling championships began in 1887, but the first finals were not played until the beginning of 1888.[9] The formation of the competitions marked an important period in the early life of the GAA – from a system of localized club competitions operating independent of each other, to a dual system in which leading players from each county could compete against each other at a national level. To begin with only five county teams took part in the hurling championship and eight in the football championship, but the popularity of both quickly grew.[10] Since then, the emergence of the All Ireland championships has fuelled a greater, arguably disproportionate, level of interest in the elite aspect of Gaelic sports to the possible detriment of the local game. That said, the All Ireland senior football and hurling championships remain two of the most prized competitions in Irish sport.[11] Both provide benchmarks for participating teams, are key components of broadcasting schedules and central to the marketing campaigns of corporate Ireland. Critically, as platforms for the leading exponents of Gaelic football and hurling, and with an historical backdrop spanning over 120 years, both competitions have proved immensely successful at driving and maintaining the profile of Gaelic sports in an increasingly congested sports marketplace.[12]

For almost 117 years, the All Ireland senior championships operated on a strict knock-out basis.[13] These games took place at provincial level and at neutral venues, in many cases attracting large crowds. By the turn of the new millennium, the ever-increasing role of television and the demands of participating teams for a series of games, rather than the potential of only one, led to a review of what had become an established format.[14] The knock-out system, and the risk that leading counties could be eliminated after only one match, became unacceptable to players, television executives and the GAA itself, the latter ever more mindful of its commercial responsibilities. Proposals aimed at transforming the competitions had been raised at various points in the late 1990s but the appeal of the established system still held sway among the GAA's traditionalists. However, in due course, the GAA took action to reconsider the commercial and sporting aspects of its two main intercounty competitions. As a result, in 2001 the All Ireland senior football and hurling championships were transformed to facilitate the re-entry of teams into the competitions, who previously would have been eliminated under the 'old' system.

The formation of this new qualifying arrangement has frequently been cited as a strategy to increase profits for the GAA.[15] Although this has been denied, the transformation of both competitions into lucrative sources of revenue for the association has consolidated its image as a cash-rich organization and its position at the leading edge of sport in Ireland. Since the turn of the millennium, the GAA has recorded improved year-on-year profitability with overall revenue standing at £56.1 million in 2009.[16] Notwithstanding this, a number of wider environmental transformations have triggered challenges to traditional modes of governance in the GAA, particularly in relation to the continued threat of global sporting pastimes for the nation's youth, the potential loss of free-to-air coverage of Gaelic games by the national broadcaster Radio Telefis Eireann (RTE) and the ever-present concern that the amateur status of the GAA may be gradually eroded. Nevertheless, impressive levels of revenue growth have led to incremental change within the organization in which the GAA's management board, its Central Council, has sought to adopt an ever more professional and commercial approach to the administration of Gaelic sports in Ireland.

Simultaneously, the games' elite performers have assumed a more strident approach to their perceived exploitation, operating as they do under a strict amateur code preventing them from benefiting financially from their talents. The Gaelic Players Association (GPA), effectively a players union, has sought greater commercial freedom for its members but has an uneasy relationship with the GAA, which is wary of its ultimate aspiration. On the one hand, the GAA emphasizes the importance of its amateur ethos and points to the many administrators and members throughout Ireland that give their time free of charge. On the other hand, the GPA, whose constituency is dominated by the games' leading stars, emphasizes the critical role of the players in the appeal of the GAA, the ever-increasing revenue from matches and the levels of expensive, bureaucratic management overseeing games played by committed amateur sportsmen.[17] Individual counties and provincial councils – those aspects of the organization with responsibility for Gaelic games in each of the four provinces on the island of Ireland – have also sought to retain a degree of flexibility, particularly in relation to the negotiation of individual television deals. The Ulster council of the GAA has an exclusive deal with the British Broadcasting Corporation (BBC) to show 'live' games from its Ulster Senior Football Championships (as well as an extensive edited package) and is intent on retaining this despite ongoing negotiations by the GAA's central operation to arrange a deal involving all four provincial championships.

This process, indeed the entire unpacking of the GAA's *modus operandi*, has been assisted by wider political and societal changes throughout Ireland in which a capitalist ideology has become evermore dominant. Furthermore, the increasing affluence of the GAA, a major beneficiary of public funding in both Northern Ireland and the Republic of Ireland, has spawned considerable external political unrest, in particular from political parties in the Republic of Ireland who have questioned ongoing investment in an organization which, compared with other sporting codes in Ireland, is very wealthy indeed. In an attempt to offset such dissenting voices the GAA voted in 2005 to temporarily suspend Rule 42 of its constitution, which had previously prevented so-called 'foreign' games from being played at its grounds. The move allowed the Republic of Ireland soccer team and the Irish rugby side to play home international games at Croke Park, the GAA's foremost stadium. This ruling favoured those who believed it was high time the GAA moved away from its position of perceived self-importance and faced up to the realities of modern-day Ireland. However, the decision also proved financially very lucrative for the GAA, which received in excess of £17.7m from the Irish Rugby Football Union and the Football Association of Ireland for the hire of Croke Park during 2009.[18] At the same time, it shone a light on the management activities of the GAA's hierarchy, which until then had remained very much in the background.

The GAA Strategic Review and internal governance

In its broadest sense, corporate governance deals with two issues; the philosophy of accountability evidenced towards stakeholders and the presence of a management framework that ensures the effective and efficient supervision of the organization.[19] Thus its principle aim is to ensure that high standards of corporate behaviour are upheld and the activities an organization engages in are ethical and transparent. Consequently, corporate governance describes all the influences affecting how an organization conducts it business, including those for appointing the controllers and regulators involved in organizing the production and sale of goods and services.[20] Of course, viewed in these terms, corporate governance includes all types of businesses whether they are officially incorporated or otherwise. The GAA, as an unincorporated entity, is not mandated to abide with the provisions of the Turnbull Report, which is the established model of best practice in this area.[21] Nevertheless, it could be argued that many examples of good practice contained within the code can and should be adopted by all large organizations.

Those behind the GAA's Strategic Review in 2002 were clearly concerned at the way in which the organization was being managed, which was at best inefficient, and made specific recommendations on how it might undergo much needed transformation. It recommended that 'Coiste Bainisti (the management committee of the GAA) should prepare its proposals in respect of governance, and these should be set out in a document formally approved by Central Council'.[22] The GAA's management committee look after the day-to-day running of the association. It is at this level that rules and regulations governing the affairs of the GAA are ratified and, if appropriate, implemented. It is also considered good practice under these arrangements to appoint an audit committee to monitor the implementation of such proposals. In most cases the audit committee would also contain an independent person, someone with the requisite expertise, to provide additional assurances to the network of stakeholders, not least the GAA membership, of the practices of the organization. What is more, if the correct person is appointed, their commercial expertise can prove invaluable when advising the newly constituted management personnel regarding certain aspects of GAA activity.[23]

The strategic review report went further in providing detailed recommendations on how the difficult matters of remuneration and performance were to be handled within the GAA. Because the GAA is an organization founded upon its amateur ethos, the issue of finance has always been one it has experienced difficulty with. Indeed the question of commerce reflects a clear distinction between the GAA's central operation and its membership 'on the ground'. A view exists that the former has access to considerable amounts of money, whereas the latter is comparatively less well off. The review body was intent on reflecting the concerns of many grassroots members regarding an apparent self-regulating, relatively autonomous body in which the issue of accountability has never been made entirely transparent. Instead, drawing upon examples of best practice in the corporate and semi-state sectors, the review body made specific reference to the remuneration of executive officers at the central level and the need for these to be kept under continual review by a separate committee. This committee may also be involved in compiling criteria for evaluating 'performance' for the ever-growing body of full-time employees within the GAA. The inference was clear; that any GAA policy on governance was either unfit for purpose or that one simply did not exist. The mechanisms through which the wider GAA membership, not to mention its commercial stakeholders, are integrated into the decision-making process, are equally outdated. One general meeting each year, referred to as the GAA's Annual Congress, constitutes the only occasion when those who govern the association can be held to account.[24] Even then, much of the discussion that takes place at this meeting is preordained as delegates are obliged to forward motions for debate, many of which are deferred or ruled out of order, often on account of some technical minutia.

In detailing the proposed benefits of the appointment of a properly empowered audit committee to examine and hold to account the activities of those paid to manage the GAA, the strategic review details how 'it would increase public (especially members') confidence in its (the GAA's) financial reporting'.[25] In 2009, the GAA reported profits of £19m, a figure that had increased year on year over the previous decade.[26] It is clear that the GAA has the capacity to earn considerable amounts of revenue, albeit it is at pains to stress that 78% of any such income is returned to the various elements of the GAA hierarchy, including county boards and clubs. Nevertheless, the lack of a balanced and understandable assessment of Central Council's financial position and prospects was a final concern for those charged with conducting a strategic review of its activities. The lack of commercial awareness was equally unsettling for the committee who recommended that the GAA's annual report 'should outline the (Central) Council's responsibility for the preparation of the financial statements and include a representation on the applicability of the 'Going Concern' basis for the preparation of the financial statements, with supporting assumptions and qualifications, as necessary'.[27] It is against this backdrop that wider concerns about the GAA's capacity to cope properly with its increasing commercial workload are being raised. 'Nobody can blame the GAA for maximizing its financial returns which have come about from money well spent on developing grounds, coaching, etc., over many years. But lots of GAA people are worried about the emphasis being placed on making more and more money.... Big money and amateur sport have had a volatile relationship the world over and it's hard to see how it would be any different within the GAA'.[28]

What was ultimately being proposed by the strategic review body was a form of governance that reflects best practise in managing large organizations, which prioritizes efficiency and foregrounds transparent and effective processes of financial management. To this end the stewardship model sees managers work effectively for an organization with the expressed aim of maximizing return for the shareholders or members.[29] Built around the suggestion that managers wish ultimately to work for the betterment of the organization, Donaldson and Davis (1994) argue that they should be freed from an essentially subservient role to assume a position on a board of directors, where they can control the direction of the business much more productively. This process can be assisted by the presence on the board of external regulators, whose role is to ensure that the fiduciary duty of the board is carried out to the satisfaction of its stakeholders. This remains valid in the case of not-for-profit organizations, who occasionally believe that their responsibilities in respect of the organization's membership need not be as resolutely adhered to.

Stewardship theory is the bedrock upon which United Kingdom (UK) company law is based. It differs from the simple finance model because an individual must behave as if he/she was the principal of the organization and not merely an agent, which it has been suggested can lead to difficulties.[30] Of course the willingness of an individual to act as a selfless steward is tied quite closely to the cultural expectations present within the respective business field. In some settings, it is possible that managers would be willing to assume such a role yet in a great many others this may not be the case. The particular cultural norms and values underpinning the activities of the GAA though make this model, as suggested by the strategic review body, an ideal one for the effective regulation and strategic future of the association. One of the reasons why the strategic review body recommended the stewardship model of governance was because of the changing nature of the environment in which the GAA now operates. In essence this is one in which the GAA's capacity to effectively manage its own affairs is under increased scrutiny.

Governance and the GAA in Ireland

The structure of GAA governance is important to an understanding of the stakeholder network of Gaelic games activity in Ireland. Essentially, this is comprised of a hierarchical pyramid in which representatives of the 32 county boards that together regulate the GAA at a national level form the membership of the central regulating authority, the all-powerful GAA Central Council. As such, there exists a potential conflict of interests whereby a select group of people emerge from a greater membership body only, in turn, to seek to exercise authority over this broader grouping. Although the structures of the national associations vary, they are largely based on wide representation of individuals, counties and provincial bodies at the various levels of the games, including those from higher education colleges and overseas delegates. Each of the four provincial bodies, Ulster, Munster, Leinster and Connacht, organizes club and county games within their own geographical area (and have their own staffing structures), while the aforementioned GAA management committee look after national competitions, including the All Ireland championships, the interprovincial competitions and other all-Ireland series. The hierarchical integration of the elite and the grassroots of the GAA through a single system ensure that everything from the laws of the game to the organization of leagues and championships operates within one framework. The GAA's Central Council, management committee and provincial councils effectively enjoy a monopoly position controlling the regulation and organization of Gaelic games activity. There is a single governing body at county level, a single council in each province sanctioned by the GAA, and a single national authority. The rules of the GAA prevent Gaelic games from taking place outside their own structures on a competitive basis, and ensure that leagues and clubs are, theoretically, subordinate to the provincial and national organizations.

This subordination is intended to recognize that in a multi-organizational context, in which clubs and counties compete across levels and across defined regulatory areas, and with interdependence between those levels in terms of the development, well-being and provision of players and finance from the intercounty games right down to the grassroots, there should be a body that looks at the overall interests of the games at all levels. Thus, the provincial and national associations are routinely composed of different forms of representative combinations of GAA figures across the various levels. These are typically male, middle-aged and imbued with the guiding ethos and principles of a GAA, which are often located in the past. The structures also reflect the belief that there is a responsibility at the top end of the game to redistribute revenue to other areas of the pyramid. According to the GAA's strategic review document, 'the continued voluntary efforts and commitment of thousands of people who play, mentor, coach or administer in every parish and every community through-out the country, remains a distinguishing feature of the Gaelic Athletic Association; its clubs have developed into a source of both personal and community pride and identity'.[31] Within the GAA there remains a strongly held belief that the elite game should continue to make a contribution to supporting other levels of the pyramid. According to the aforementioned strategic review, within the section entitled 'Enhancing Community Identity', the authors remark how 'The GAA continues to attract support from all sectors and social classes of the Irish community (both in Ireland and overseas), many of whom are attracted by its ideals and the cultural aspects of its activities, as well as by the unique Irishness of its essentially indigenous games'.[32]

However, this hierarchical system of authority has come under increasing pressure, mirroring developments in wider policy-making arenas. 'Governance' has been redefined as 'a change in the meaning of government, referring to a new process of governing'.[33] It is argued that this manifests itself through decision-making networks rather than direct control and an increase in the number of actors in the policy-making process. Henry and Lee (2004) have similarly referred to 'systematic governance' in which the 'old hierarchical model of the governance of sport, the top-down system, has given way to a complex web of interrelationships between stakeholders in which different groups exert power in different ways and in different contexts by drawing on alliances with other stakeholders'.[34] Yet, at the same time, the GAA has come under intense criticism from within its own ranks concerning the way in which it manages its affairs. As far back as November 2002, former president of the GAA Mr Peter Quinn, himself a very successful businessman, commented that:

> the GAA has huge strengths and assets but we (the GAA) are not using them as effectively as we should be. We are not well managed; it is as simple as that. In fact, we wouldn't survive if we were a business, so unless we change our management structures we will have serious difficulties.[35]

An even more forceful series of criticisms followed in 2007 as Quinn again expressed his frustration at an apparent malaise within the organization where, he suggested, a 'civil service mentality' existed and a lack of strategic thinking regarding the future of the GAA was evident.[36] He was not alone in expressing his concerns about the bureaucratic, administrative approach to running the affairs of the GAA seemingly evident among the current regime. The then chairman of the Derry County Board, Mr Seamus McCloy, a self-made millionaire business tycoon, suggested in December 2006 that

> Central Council's managerial ability is virtually negligible. We (the GAA) operate in an inefficient, inexpert and unprofessional way. Our organisational structures, systems and operations are out-of-date for the modern GAA. This carbuncle has to be lanced. A

professional board, under the direction of a chief executive, should be appointed to manage our affairs at Croke Park.[37]

Therefore two separate, but nonetheless related, concerns about the GAA emerged during the early years of the new millennium. On the one hand, there were the issues, present within a range of other sport governing bodies, about the way the GAA was dealing with an increased number of stakeholders who wished to have some say on how it was being managed. On the other hand, criticism about the GAA's internal structures and, by implication, the competencies of those in positions of authority, came from leading figures within the GAA itself. However, the conclusion was ultimately the same – the GAA in its current guise was ill-prepared to respond to the challenges it faced unless it demonstrated a willingness to change.

In this respect, the concept of 'network' governance provides an appropriate starting point from which to assess the changing nature of control within the GAA. Within the context of elite-level competition (the All Ireland senior championships), the GAA has had to re-evaluate its relationships with stakeholders who are both part of the GAA sphere (its clubs, wider membership and various levels of management) and external stakeholders with the power to influence (such as the GPA, institutions of the state, the increasing media interest in its affairs and wider developments in Irish life). If control within the GAA occurs through a network of influence, then it is important to understand how that network operates as the breakdown of influence will necessarily impact upon the achievement of 'good governance' in the running of the GAA. In the context of the management of the association, this relates directly to the administration of revenue (including its maximization), the role of non-salaried members (specifically its elite players and managers) and the strategic direction of the GAA in an evolving Irish society where, among other concerns, a changing work–life balance and the appeal of global sports are prime considerations. An understanding of the GAA governance network can be gleaned through analysis of the different dimensions of power and the ebb and flow of the association's transition from a wholly amateur body to the management of one in which the primary means of revenue generation (the players) appear to fund a over inflated, inefficient and complacent central operation.

Internal and external influence and the control of the GAA's elite competitions

The GAA network can be broken down into what can be termed an 'internal' and 'external' network.[38] The 'internal network' consists of the established GAA structures, through which stakeholders can influence policy. The 'external network' implies the means through which stakeholders influence the policy of the GAA by engaging in activity outside of established GAA structures.

The clearest example of the influence of external networks can be seen in the challenge to the GAA's policy on its treatment of players by the GPA, which emerged in September 1999 through a campaign for better conditions and regard for the games' leading performers. The redevelopment of Croke Park into an 82,000 capacity stadium provided further evidence of the financial potential of the GAA. This coupled with the exponential growth in salaried employees of the association confirmed the view that the GAA was cash rich and yet its stance on the nonpayment of players remained intact. A body of elite performers became increasingly dissatisfied at the level of income accrued by the GAA through its foremost competitions, and also the manner in which it was distributed. The GPA exploited this situation by bringing together some of the leading hurlers and Gaelic footballers in order to campaign for, as they saw it, proper recognition for the players as the primary source of entertainment and revenue for the association. In a departure from the egalitarian ethos that formed the fabric of much GAA-related activity up until that point, the GPA was unashamedly elitist in its ambitions and determined to exact proper recognition for its membership. Despite this, the GPA was hampered in its formative years by a lack of credibility and its exclusive (indeed continued) concern with the well-being of its male members and the commensurate neglect of any such interest in the affairs of leading female Gaelic games players. Indeed, its inability to properly convey its message on a number of levels did little to allay the view that it was a militant trade union intent on threatening the very basis upon which the GAA had been founded and which had proved its bedrock throughout what by then was its 115 years in existence. However, the GPA was able to point to the considerable support it enjoyed among the games' elite and its capacity to attract significant sponsorship from corporate Ireland. This emergence of the GPA was the first attempt to seriously challenge the hegemony of the GAA in the treatment of players and offer a voice to athletes from some of the more marginalized parts of Ireland who felt disenchanted with the organization on account of their maltreatment.

In the context of environmental transformation, by acting outside the established GAA structures, a network including the games' leading players, an entrepreneurial businessman in the form of the GPA's founder Donal O'Neil, and the capacity of the player's body to attract leading companies in Ireland to fund its activities succeeded in generating an alternative context for elite Gaelic sports in Ireland. The initial result was to pressure the GAA into a reformulation of the rules governing player sponsorship and endorsements, increasing the rights of individual athletes to receive financial reward for, albeit limited, commercial activity. However, in March 2008 the GAA's Central Council endorsed a decision by the Irish Sports Council (acting on behalf of the Irish government) to permit the payment of grants to elite players. The sum, approximately €2000, was to cover legitimate expenses incurred by intercounty players during the course of the playing season. Despite the limited monetary reward, the decision divided opinion within the GAA community, with some members resolutely opposed to such a move, branding it 'pay for play' and thus in clear breach of Rule 11 of the GAA's constitution governing the amateur status of the association. At the time of writing, emotions remain high, with a groundswell of opposition from the organization's grassroots members ever present.

The intervention of the GPA therefore constituted one important contributory factor in the consequent re-evaluation of the GAA's formal relationship with its stakeholder network. Its actions inadvertently led to an awakening among the GAA itself of the potential for increased revenue contained within a properly organized commercial strategy. In the latter months of 2007, for example, the GAA was involved in negotiating new terms for three major sources of income – television rights, sponsorship of competitions and stadium advertising. Its decision to bring to an end the practice of permitting a single sponsor to be associated with the All-Ireland football or hurling championships was significant. Instead it decided to have three sponsors associated in a broader fashion with both competitions in the same way as the UEFA

Champions League format, which has proved remarkably successful. According to one commentator 'It is expected that the revenue from this approach will increase the value of the hurling and football championship sponsorship from the present euro 2 million per year to around euro 6 million'.[39] Regarding television rights, a similar fragmentation policy is in the pipeline where the sum of the new parts will greatly exceed the present system under which the national broadcaster RTE still retains the rights to 'live' coverage of all games played in the All Ireland series. A number of television stations have been bidding for various sections of the GAA's competitive structures, which is likely to prove beneficial for the GAA and its loyal viewers.

Nevertheless, divisions within the GAA (and among elements of the GPA) may act as an obstacle to radical change, and may be one reason why the latter has so far been unable to transform latent power into sizeable political gains. Elite players need a successful and united GAA, and the need for consensus among a sufficient number of GAA members and delegates means that changes to directives pertaining to the remuneration of players will require broad support. Of course, on a range of issues the GPA has legitimate grounds for protest. Any situation where the primary means of revenue production are inadequately compensated for their efforts is likely to create resentment and quite possibly lead to a withdrawal of their services. The players have common concerns such as dealing with a congested fixture programme, meaning an off-season is considered a luxury rather than a permanent arrangement, a failure to be adequately compensated for unavoidable absence from their full-time employment and the negotiation of commercial contracts. The fact that the players help drive revenue production for the GAA, which ultimately helps subsidize the activities of the GAA on a national level, has led to demands for more direct integration into the decision-making structures of the governing body. To this end, the GAA has recently expanded its Central Council to incorporate a representative from the GPA. Conversely, there is distrust within the GAA about the GPA's motives, fearing its agenda is to create an elitist arm of the association. Although the GPA denies this, given its present consti-tution and similar capacity to attract commercial sponsorship, it would be a natural development were the organization to pursue this at a national level.

In essence then, any balanced analysis of the regulation and governance of the GAA under its current arrangements suggests that while its grassroots membership will play a major role in any future developments, the GAA's hierarchy itself is under-mined by the nature of its own composition. The level of exclusivity and the lack of defined and coherent membership criteria pose problems of legitimacy and credibility. Positions of authority are held for considerable periods and even in those cases where arrangements of this nature are expressly prohibited, such difficulties are overcome by simply rotating portfolios. The GAA makes much play out of its democratic credentials but in reality the reigns of power are held by a small group of influential personalities, albeit they rely on the passive consent of a much larger group to carry out their duties. It is unlikely that such an arrangement can continue to prove sustain-able going forward. In turn, the argument that this situation should be reversed and a professional board of directors put in place has gained considerable support amongst the GAA's broader constituency.

The continuing role of the GAA in the stakeholder network

The existence of various stakeholders with power encourages caution and leads to the view that it is unlikely that any single actor will have a monopoly on change in the period ahead. The GAA, through a policy of limited dialogue and a convoluted series of 'select committees', has so far managed developments by integrating players, media and corporate Ireland into the existing system, yet at the same time withholding genuine decision-making power. It remains questionable whether this strategy is sustainable in the long-term, but by opting for dialogue the GAA has positioned itself in direct and regular contact with key stakeholders. The GAA's continued commercial and sporting control of the All Ireland championships means that the organization retains its central role in the regulation of the sport in Ireland. Nevertheless, the latent market power of the players is evident. That being so, the inclination of stakeholders to operate (but increase their influence) within the established structures, means that market power is offset by the realities of modern-day sport governance. The GAA has gradually attempted to come to terms with this transition, albeit it has had sporadic success in doing so. Its principle difficulty is managing a vibrant, professional and modern sporting body within the confines of an historically determined and fundamentally amateur context.

The level of stakeholder influence is further clouded by legal uncertainty regarding the rules of governing bodies in a self-regulatory framework. While stakeholders are largely inclined to operate within the system, they have also succeeded in altering the system through recourse to outside bodies. The full workings of NGBs and their lack of political and legal standing has occasionally been exposed and the GAA has proved as susceptible to this as any other organization. It must remain mindful of the fact that although at one level it is imbued with the right to regulate Gaelic games activity, the full extent of this capacity set against the law of the land often results in its autonomy being compromised. It is not beyond the realms of possibility that as the GAA continues to move ever-increasingly in the direction of a full-fledged commercial sports body that it may require a more defined appreciation of its legal and political shortcomings. It is for this reason that a move away from a long-standing administrative approach to managing its affairs is long overdue. Indeed the imposition of a professional board of directors offers the opportunity to at least ensure that the GAA safeguards its current position within an increasingly congested sport and entertainment marketplace.

Conclusion

In many ways the GAA is a unique sporting organization. For its entire existence of some 125 years the association has expressed its strong belief in the amateur ideal and rejected any movement towards professionalism. While it remained a modest, community-based organization such an approach proved to be very effective and it benefited enormously from considerable levels of volunteerism and financial altruism. Yet, as the GAA has developed into a fully fledged, professional sporting organization it has encountered difficulty in retaining support for its policy on amateurism. As its central and salaried operation grew exponentially, it continued to employ a straightforward administrative model of governance, one that lacked any proper strategic underpinning or financial acumen. Whereas in the past this was almost part of the GAA's intrinsic charm, as its central bureaucracy grew so too did calls for the adoption of a more professional operating strategy on the part of the association. These issues were laid bare following the GAA's own strategic review, published in 2002. A catalogue of issues requiring immediate attention were outlined, with the need for a more efficient and effective form of governance foremost among these. The recommendation of this article, a view supported by those charged with the GAA's own review, is that a stewardship model of governance should be adopted by the association. This would involve a streamlining of the GAA's Central Council, to be replaced by a much smaller board of directors who would be appointed on merit and not merely on a representative basis. This imperative is made all the more real when one considers the growing body of internal and external stakeholders the GAA is attempting to engage with. Some of these stakeholders are intent on challenging the GAA's traditional *modus operandi*, and indeed have negotiated partial acceptance of some of their demands. Finally, what is noticeable (and presumably concerning for the association) is that some of the GAA's fiercest critics have emerged from within its own ranks. It exists as a reminder that even the most benign and erstwhile organizations eventually encounter problems as their mode of governance becomes outdated and ineffective in the face of demands placed upon it from modern-day sport.

Notes

1. On international governance within association football, for example, see Jennings, *Foul*; Sugden and Tomlinson, *FIFA and the Contest for World Football*; and Sugden and Tomlinson, *Great Balls of Fire*.
2. For example, see A. Jennings, *Foul*.
3. Bairner 'Creating a Soccer Strategy for Northern Ireland', 27–42. In this article, Bairner outlines and critically engages with attempts on behalf of local government and football authorities in Northern Ireland to deal with a crisis within senior soccer in the country. He argues persuasively that issues that emerge at a 'local' level and are apparent within all national governing bodies of sport exist as meaningful barriers to progress for those wishing to chart a better future for their sport.
4. Ibid.
5. Ibid.
6. Ibid., 28.
7. GAA, *Annual Report, 2010*.
8. Mandle, *The Gaelic Athletic Association and Irish Nationalist Politics, 1884–1924*.
9. DeBurca, *The GAA: A History*.
10. Ibid.; Sullivan, *Story of the GAA*.
11. Cronin, *Sport and Nationalism in Ireland*.
12. Meenaghan, 'Ambush Marketing', 305–22.
13. DeBurca, *The GAA: A History*.
14. GAA, *Annual Report, 2000*.
15. For example, see McGee, 'GAA is Getting Rich Quick But What of its Poor Relations', 60.
16. *GAA, Annual Report, 2010*.
17. For a balanced and informed overview of this debate, see Crossan, 'GPA Strike Could Split Up the Game's One Big Soul', 49.
18. *GAA, Annual Report, 2010*.
19. McNamee and Fleming, 'Ethics Audits and Corporate Governance', 425–37.
20. For extensive coverage of this, see Turnbull, 'Corporate Governance', 180–205.
21. See *GAA Strategic Review*.
22. Ibid., 161.
23. *GAA Strategic Review*.
24. The only exception to this would be in the case of a 'Special Congress' called to discuss salient, often controversial issues (e.g. the removal of Rule 21).
25. *GAA Strategic Review*, 163.
26. *GAA, Annual Report, 2010*.
27. *GAA Strategic Review*, 163.
28. McGee, 'GAA is Getting Rich Quick But What of its Poor Relations', 60.
29. Donaldson and Davis, 'Boards and Company Performance', 151–60.
30. Ibid., 153.
31. *GAA Strategic Review*, 10.

32. Ibid.
33. Rhodes, 'The New Governance', 652–3.
34. Henry and Lee, 'Governance and Ethics in Sport', 27.
35. Quoted in 'GAA Must Embrace Change', *The Kingdom*, November 14, 2002, 14.
36. Quoted in 'Business "Strung Up in Red Tape Bias" – Quinn Attacks the 'Non-risk-taking Dead Hand', www.irishconsultants.ie/news. Accessed July 19, 2007.
37. Quoted in 'Croke Quiet on McCloy Criticism', www.bbc.co.uk/sport/northern ireland/gaelic_games. Accessed December 12, 2006.
38. For a similar analysis of 'network' governance within the sphere of association football, see Holt, 'The Ownership and Control of Elite Club Competition in European Football', 50–67.
39. McGee, 'GAA is Getting Rich Quick But What of its Poor Relations', 60; Heaney, 'Rocketing Profits Lead to Record Investment' places this figure at 'Euro 29.1 millions (approx. £20 millions) over the next three years' (62).

References

Bairner, A. 'Creating a Soccer Strategy for Northern Ireland: Reflections on Football Governance in Small European Countries', *Soccer & Society* 5, no. 1 (2004): 27–42.

Cronin, M. *Sport and Nationalism in Ireland: Gaelic Games, Soccer and Irish Identity Since 1884*. Dublin: Four Courts, 1999.

Crossan, B. 'GPA Strike Could Split Up the Game's One Big Soul', *The Irish News*, October 5, 2007, 49.

DeBurca, M. *The GAA: A History*. Dublin: Gill and MacMillan, 2000.

Donaldson, L., and J.H. Davis, 'Boards and Company Performance – Research Challenges the Conventional Wisdom', *Corporate Governance: An International Review* 2, no. 3 (1994): 151–60.

Forster, J. 'Global Sports Organisations and Their Governance', *Corporate Governance* 6, no. 1 (2006): 72–84.

GAA, *Annual Report, 2000*. Dublin: GAA, 2000.

GAA, *Strategic Review*. GAA: Dublin, 2002.

GAA, *Annual Report, 2010*. Dublin: GAA, 2010.

Henry, I., and P.C. Lee. 'Governance and Ethics in Sport'. In *The Business of Sport Management*, ed. S. Chadwick and J. Beech. Harlow: FT Prentice Hall, 2004.

Holt, M. 'The Ownership and Control of Elite Club Competition in European Football', *Soccer & Society* 8, no. 1 (2007): 50–67.

Jennings, A. *Foul*. London: HarperSport, 2006.

Katwala, S. *Democratising Global Sport*. London: The Foreign Policy Centre, 2000.

Mandle, W.F. *The Gaelic Athletic Association and Irish Nationalist Politics, 1884–1924*. Dublin: Gill and MacMillan, 1987.

Meenaghan, T. 'Ambush Marketing: Corporate Strategy and Consumer Reaction', *Psychology and Marketing* 15, no. 4 (1998): 305–22.

McGee, E. 'GAA is Getting Rich Quick But What of its Poor Relations', *Irish Independent*, September 8, 2007, 60.

McNamee, M., and S. Fleming, 'Ethics Audits and Corporate Governance: The Case of Public Sector Sports Organizations', *Journal of Business Ethics* 73 (2007): 425–37.

O'Sullivan, T. *Story of the GAA*. Dublin: unspecified publisher, 1916.

Rhodes, R.A.W. 'The New Governance: Governing without Government', *Political Studies* 44, no. 4 (1996): 652–3.

Sugden, J. 'Network Football'. In *Power Games*, ed. J. Sugden and A. Tomlinson. London: Routledge, 2002.

Sugden, J., and A. Tomlinson. *FIFA and the Contest for World Football*. Oxford: Polity, 1998.

Sugden, J., and A. Tomlinson, *Great Balls of Fire. How Big Money is Hijacking World Football* Edinburgh: Mainstream, 1999.

Turnbull, S. 'Corporate Governance: Its Scope, Concerns and Theories', *Corporate Governance: An International Review* 5, no. 4 (1997): 180–205.

Who owns England's game? American professional sporting influences and foreign ownership in the Premier League

John Nauright[a] and John Ramfjord[b]

[a]Academy of International Sport, School of Recreation, Health, and Tourism, George Mason University, Manassas, USA; [b]Athletic Department, Georgia Southern University, Statesboro, USA

Changes to the organization of, and commercialism in, the Barclay's Premier League in England have made clubs attractive to international investors. Recently, in particular, there has been a rapid increase in American ownership of Premier League teams with Aston Villa, Liverpool and Manchester United owned by Americans and a large minority shareholder at Arsenal is American. Beyond directorship/ownership issues, North American organizational and marketing structures of professional sport have increased their influence within the Premier League. These include a focus on diverse revenue streams including media rights, luxury seating, commodification and branding of clubs and their heritage, and diversified services as well as differing patterns of club ownership and administration. Although these have merged with English traditions within professional football, there is no doubt that North American influences have begun to change the nature of marketing within the game and have also made leading English clubs attractive to North American and other international investors. The result of the increasing 'Americanization' of English professional football (soccer) marketing and management strategies has clashed with English traditions of organization as well as supporters' consumption of the game itself.

Introduction

Since 2002, there has been a dramatic increase in the number of foreign-owned clubs in the Premier League in England. The process appears to be accelerating with virtually all of the large market and well-known clubs being targeted by international investors most notably from the USA and Russia. In February 2007, Liverpool FC's shares were bought by George Gillett, Jr and Tom Hicks, valuing the club at £218.9m[1] and Manchester City was acquired in November 2007 by exiled former Thai Prime Minister Thaksin Shinawatra, who incidentally had failed in an earlier attempt to purchase Liverpool FC. In 2006, Sunderland was taken over by an Irish group led by former player Niall Quinn. Sunderland subsequently won the Football League Championship and promotion back to the Premier League for the 2007/2008 season. As of the beginning of 2008, the total number of Premier League clubs with foreign owners stood at 10, while Arsenal, Birmingham City and Everton also had large blocks of shares held in international hands. Put simply, fully one half of the League's teams were in foreign hands. In addition, Football League Championship team Leicester City was owned by Serbian-born American Milan Mandaric, himself a former owner of Portsmouth FC. In the lower divisions, Americans are involved as leading investors or directors at Oldham Athletic and Millwall football clubs. Of the so-called 'big four' clubs in English football, Arsenal, Chelsea, Liverpool and Manchester United, two are owned by Americans (Liverpool and Manchester United) and one by a Russian (Chelsea), while the fourth has been subjected to attempted acquisition by both a Russian and an American investor (Arsenal). Of the top seven clubs in the Premier League in early March 2008, only Everton was not under foreign control and even there, Robert Earl, the American owner of Planet Hollywood, had invested heavily.[2] This wave of international ownership, primarily, though not exclusively, American and Russian in origin, is a relatively new phenomenon in English football. This investment has been predicated on the enhanced revenue streams in the game generated by its reorganization in the 1990s, expansion of pan-European competitions and media coverage, and the concomitant global marketing possibilities that have ensued. American presence in England's Premiership is based on potential investors' belief that the Premier League offers a sound business investment for them in a league with ownership and financing structures they recognize and a culture that is understandable to them at a time when the growth of several professional sports brands in the USA has levelled off.[3] Our purpose is to examine the factors that have made the Premier League and its teams attractive to foreign investment and how the League and its teams have been influenced by North American models of management and marketing. More than other leagues in Europe, the Premier League is structured similarly enough now to North American professional sports leagues that investors from across the Atlantic can see the potential benefits for them of team ownership.

Background

In order to understand this phenomenon, it is important to appreciate the economic shifts in professional sport that have occurred in North America and Britain over the past several decades. While the histories of professional sport have been very different, in recent times similarities have increased greatly. As Julian Ammirante points out, historically football clubs in Britain and on the European Continent lost money and were more philanthropic in nature. Club directors were involved with teams to promote a sense of civic pride or to raise awareness of other enterprises in which they were engaged.[4] Richard Giulianotti reinforces this notion stating that 'Until recently, the major shareholders did not expect to profit greatly from football, though their social status was enhanced by their public influence over a major popular cultural institution'.[5] Low-cost entry to matches meant that most anyone could afford to attend and fans identified with the team as an extension of themselves. In North America, professional sports such as baseball and ice hockey were largely outgrowths of middle and upper class social institutions. In England, by contrast, football clubs were largely supported by the working class and many were outgrowths of social institutions aimed at social control of the growing urban population. Even in the late 1990s, Aston Villa's regular supporter base was 48% working class.[6] Additionally, in North America 'professional sport was always more business-like, not least in the sense that teams in the early twentieth century moved around, going to other communities (and arenas) where their owners thought they could operate more profitably'.[7] The closed nature of professional sporting leagues in North America meant that the number of cities that could host teams was always fewer than the number of cities who wanted them and zonal market protections meant that multiple teams in metropolitan areas in the same sport were rare. Indeed, today only New York, Chicago and Los Angeles sustain two teams in any of the four main professional sports leagues.[8] The National Hockey League (NHL) kept its number of teams restricted to six until 1967 though other leagues were less extreme. Professional sports leagues in North America now command hundreds of millions of dollars in up-front fees to join their leagues when they do occasionally expand. Team relocation was rampant in the 1980s and 1990s as owners sought to extract the maximum revenues in tax-free support from local and state governments eager to play in the 'big league' while building new stadiums for team owners.[9] With no prospects for promotion or relegation professional franchises in North America have relied on a greater need for competitive balance to ensure healthy competition.

Although there has been growth in the value of major professional sports teams in the USA, the trend of expansion of market share domestically has slowed. Even so, the New York Jets were sold in 1999 for $635m and the National Football League (NFL) was able to demand a $700m entry fee for the new Houston Texans franchise in 2002. Mark Rosentraub argues that the inflation in team values is linked to leagues having 'restrained the supply of these valuable assets'.[10] Yet, there is also evidence that values have gone up progressively in British football where the promotion–relegation system has allowed a much larger number of professional teams to exist.[11] For example, Doug Ellis invested £500,000 in Aston Villa in 1982 and received £23m for his shares when they were sold in 2006.[12] Similarly in Scotland, David Murray's £6m investment in Glasgow Rangers realized him nearly £100m by the late 1990s.[13]

In the USA, domestic market value in most professional sports leagues began to slow after 2000 with only the NFL showing sustained growth. The reason for this was a series of labour disputes in each league, the diversification of the sporting landscape, with sports such as NASCAR auto racing and new competitions such as X-Games generating widespread interest, and greater competition from other components of the entertainment industries.[14] As a result, leagues such as the NFL and the National Basketball Association (NBA), and teams such as the Boston Red Sox and New York Yankees in Major League Baseball (MLB), have turned to international markets, Japan and China respectively in particular, for expansion since the mid-1990s.[15]

A brief history of the genesis of the Premier League is also needed to explain recent foreign interest. The English professional game reached an all time low during the 1980s. This was a decade that included a ban on English clubs participating in European competitions following the deaths in 1986 of 39 fans at the Heysel stadium, Belgium prior to a European Cup final featuring Juventus and Liverpool. The English First Division lagged behind other large European leagues in overall popularity and its ability to attract leading players to play for its club sides. Indeed, many leading English players used the First Division as a stepping stone to more lucrative contracts in Germany, Italy and Spain. As a response to this situation and the reluctance of the Football Association (FA) to think in real market terms, the top clubs formed a breakaway league (though one endorsed by the FA), the English Premier League in 1992. This league replaced the old First Division and was able to negotiate separate television contracts so that each of the clubs could have more money to compete with continental European clubs for talent. Television would eventually cement the stature of the Premier League as one of the top leagues in the world. With the parallel development of BSkyB satellite television and its Sky Sports network controlled by Rupert Murdoch's News Corporation, the amount of each television contract grew significantly with each renewal.[16] Unlike other European leagues which felt that football should be available to the public for free, the Premiership had their games on pay television or a pay-per-view basis.[17]

In this respect, the Premier League began slowly to adopt marketing strategies that were commonplace in North America, revenue streams based on a diverse range of sources beyond gate money, and focused on the selling of television rights as the key single source of revenue. The Premier League has struggled, however, with the issue of competitive balance as Manchester United (9), Arsenal (3) and Chelsea (2) have been League Champions every year except one (Blackburn Rovers in 1994/1995) over the first 15 seasons of the League's existence. Only Liverpool, Aston Villa and Newcastle United among the other clubs in the Premier League have finished as high as second. Compare this with Major League Baseball where seven different teams claimed the World Series Championship in the eight years from 2000 to 2007 or the NFL where seven different teams won the nine Super Bowls between 2000 and 2008. The television contract with Sky distributes revenue on the basis of final league position and number of matches aired, so although all Premier League teams share in television revenues, the nature of the contract has served the larger clubs better overall. This approach is similar to the MLB contract in North America whereby national television rights are shared between teams but local television rights are allowed to be negotiated by teams individually. Thus, large market teams like the New York Yankees and New York Mets are advantaged significantly over small market teams such as the Tampa Bay Devil Rays or Kansas City Royals, despite attempts to distribute revenues more equally among teams since 2003 with luxury taxes and percentage of profits shared.[18]

Increased revenue streams enabled each of the clubs in the Premier League to have more money to spend on better talent. Coupled with the 1996 Bosman ruling which opened up the European Union labour market to greater player mobility, diversified revenue streams have allowed leading English clubs to compete for the best talent in Europe and world wide.[19] Indeed post-Bosman European football began to resemble its American sporting counterparts more closely as a form of minor league system emerged with large clubs like Manchester United directly investing in smaller clubs in other countries. Manchester United used Belgium's less-restrictive labour regulations to its advantage by securing agreement with Standard Liege to allow it to bring non-European players through Belgium and then on to United.[20] Additionally, new television deals, approaching American ones in scale, led to a large influx of cash for the clubs in the Premier League. In 1997 the Premier League television rights were sold for over £647m for four years and in 2002 for £1.6 billion for four years.[21] Despite this economic boost, however, there has been a highly uneven performance by Premier League teams with pre-tax profits running in the red for many clubs, although Manchester United (up to 2005) and Arsenal were the only consistent positive performers.[22] So there must be two motivations behind new investment. The first is the promise of profits from ever-increasing television contracts both domestically and internationally. The second is the related increase in the value of leading clubs due to increases in television money and global marketing possibilities.

Foreign ownership and English football

The expansion of foreign ownership in English football has been little short of an explosion, given that prior to 1997 there were no foreign owners in the English game. Egyptian Mohamed Al Fayed bought Fulham in May 1997 as he expanded his presence in the English and London markets with marquee purchases such as Harrods' department store. English clubs began to see new possibilities to raise revenues through public trading as early as 1983, but it was a long time before outsiders viewed clubs as a good investment. Indeed as Michael Wulziner points out:

> Since 1983, when Tottenham Hotspur became Europe's first publically traded football club, English professional clubs have been targets of speculation and the subjects of wild fantasies of profitability. But for years it was only the British business elites who were buying the major share packages, including racehorse owners, the heirs of fortune, construction magnates, theater impresarios and diamond dealers. Some of these original shareholders have since sold off their football assets and done so at substantial profits.[23]

It took five years after the inception of the Premier League for the first foreign owner to appear and then another six years for the next when Russian businessman Roman Abramovich bought a controlling interest in Chelsea in June 2003. Since 2003, there has been a rapid expansion of foreign ownership due in part to Abramovich's perceived success at Chelsea. There was one other significant early attempt at foreign ownership in this period that pre-dated Abramovich. The jewel in the crown of English, and possibly world, sport, Manchester United was the focus of a planned takeover by Australian-American Rupert Murdoch in 1998 who offered £625m for a controlling interest in the club. This was blocked by the United Kingdom Competition Commission on the grounds that it would limit competiveness in English soccer. The link between media rights and club ownership by media owners was a strategy that Murdoch and others began to employ in the 1990s (though Ted Turner had done this in the 1980s with the Atlanta Braves of Major League Baseball [MLB] and Atlanta Hawks of the National Basketball Association [NBA] as he entered the national cable television market in the USA showing the teams' games on his TBS Superstation). Murdoch through his News Corporation expanded his direct ownership in clubs internationally, with acquisitions such as the Los Angeles Dodgers in American base-ball (later sold) and the Brisbane Broncos and Canberra Raiders in rugby league in Australia, as well as minority interests in other clubs such as the National Hockey League's New York Rangers. Thus, Manchester United seemed a natural target for Murdoch. Foreign interest waned as Murdoch's attempt was blocked, only to be revived by Abramovich and a new sense among American professional sports team owners that the international market was perhaps more important long-term than the domestic market in the USA. Evidence of this international awareness has accelerated since 2000 and can be seen in ventures such as the global marketing partnership signed between Manchester United and the New York Yankees in 2001.[24] The success of this partnership, the growing awareness of soccer's cultural and economic power internationally, began to focus more American attention on global possibilities of soccer for investment, particularly in relation to Premier League teams listed on the Stock Exchange with shares available for purchase.

American businessmen appear to be comfortable investing in the Premier League. There are two reasons for this, first is the gradual shift to a recognizable American-style business model for professional sports in England and second is the amount of money generated by leading football clubs. With strong performances in the European Champions League along with the new television contract for the Premier League, there are English clubs that will make close to £50m in television revenues alone for the 2007/2008 season. In winning the Champions League in 2005, Liverpool netted well over £20m in television revenues from UEFA. That same year Chelsea reached the semi-finals and made £19m. UEFA divides the television revenues by the share of the European television market, thus England and Germany with the largest television markets get a larger percentage of the payouts. In the 2006 final Arsenal lost to Barcelona, but received £23m compared with Barcelona's £21.5m for their efforts. English clubs continue to reap the benefits from the Champions League, which was evident in the 2007 tournament. Runners up Liverpool took home €32.22m, while Chelsea received the highest payout for an English club with €34.66m.[25] So with the prospect of lucrative television deals, four Champions League places for English teams and a record of European success, certain Premier League football clubs have become, and should continue to be, attractive investment targets in international sport.

Thus the owner of the Tampa Bay Buccaneers in the NFL, Malcolm Glazer, bought controlling interest in Manchester United in May 2005 to the dismay of many fans. Glazer was soundly booed by large sections of the team's support when he first arrived at Old Trafford, though the League Championship in 2006 helped ease some fans' concerns. In 2006, three more clubs were acquired by foreign owners: Portsmouth was bought by Russian Alexandre Gaydamak (from Serbian-American Milan Mandaric), and Icelanders Bjorgolfur Gudmundsson and Eggert Magnusson purchased West Ham. American investment continued as Cleveland Browns (NFL) owner Randy Lerner took controlling interest at Aston Villa.[26] In distinct contrast to Glazer's reception, Lerner was treated as a conquering hero at Villa Park as, in the eye's of the team's loyal followers, Lerner's intention to make money available to secure better players and modernize club operations stood in stark contrast to years of stagnation under previous owner Doug Ellis. Following on in 2007, George Gillett, Jr and Tom Hicks purchased a controlling stake in Liverpool. Hicks heads the company that owns the Texas Rangers in MLB and the Dallas Stars in the NHL while Gillett owns the Montreal Canadiens, the most storied franchise in the history of professional ice hockey. Gillett also owns one of leading auto racing teams in NASCAR in the USA. Thaksin Shinawatra's purchase of Manchester City brought the total number of Premier League clubs with foreign owners to 10 (Niall Quinn headed an Irish owner-ship group at Sunderland).

Another possible takeover, and a fourth American one, was ongoing at the time of writing at Arsenal. The power struggle continues there as Stan Kroenke, head of the group that owns the St. Louis Rams of the NFL, the Denver Nuggets of the NBA, the Colorado Avalanche in the NHL, and the Colorado Rapids in Major League Soccer in the USA among other teams, tried for most of 2007 to purchase a majority stake in the club. In the USA, Kroenke's group also owns the cable sports network that broadcasts all of his sports franchises' games, a strategy for cross-ownership that Murdoch hoped to achieve with the acquisition of Manchester United.[27] At the same time that Kroenke had been purchasing bulk shares in Arsenal, Uzbek billionaire Alisher Usmanov had been doing the same in an attempt to rival Roman Abramovich.[28] Kroenke and Usmanov's acquisition of large number of shares prompted the Arsenal Board to agree not to sell any more shares until April 2009 at least in an effort to stall the takeover bids. It needs to be noted that most of the foreign-owned teams were purchased after they were in the Premier League. Fulham was purchased while they were in a lower division and were subsequently promoted in the 2001/2002 season. Portsmouth was also promoted with a foreign owner, Milan Mandaric, and was sold again in 2005. Chelsea was the first team to be bought while in the Premier League in 2003 and that began a process that brought new international attention to leading clubs.

There was a convergence of several forces in the early 2000s that precipitated American, as well as other foreign, investment in English soccer. First was the increasing international market for selling licensed products and television broadcasts of games. Second, economic structure and possibility of direct ownership meant that American owners could take a controlling interest in a club and run it much like an American sporting franchise. This is not possible to do at membership-based clubs such as FC Barcelona or in Germany where only minority holdings are allowed. Third, there was a possibility of cross-marketing sporting brands and other products in large-scale investment portfolios. In 2006, not long after Lerner took control at Villa, support for his Cleveland Browns NFL team in Birmingham and surrounding areas increased and a supporters club formed as a member club of Browns Backers World-wide, as officially reported by the Cleveland Browns.[29] More directly, Aston Villa has benefited from the way in which the Cleveland Browns organization is run, down to shared medical treatment for players. Villa striker Luke Moore reporting on his trip to Cleveland for an operation:

> I've been over to Cleveland quite a lot and I'm familiar with their set-up. I've met Mr. Lerner on a few occasions and ... I can tell, just by looking at the Browns, what he wants to incorporate over here. You just know he's going to be successful. My operation was done by their expert in shoulder injuries, Dr Miniaci and his team. Touch wood, I haven't had a problem with the injury, despite getting a few bangs on it in the reserves. I was treated superbly in Cleveland – it was so impressive. They took me back for a week's rehab and it was great. Mr Lerner wants to take a lot of the way his players are treated at the Browns and bring that over to Villa. They are looked after.[30]

In North America, the owners of professional franchises run the leagues, agree on media rights and whether to allow expansion within their leagues. Membership is stable from year to year unless owners agree to allow an expansion team into the league. In the four main professional team sports, only the Green Bay Packers are publicly owned. While league offices and commissioners run the leagues, the owners have the final say in governance. While some owners have over the years invested in more than one professional franchise, the profitability of leagues and franchises other than the National Football League and its teams since 2000 has been less attractive to owners seeking to expand their sporting empires within the USA. As a result, there have been three new avenues for expansion of revenues among team owners. The first involves expansion of media and marketing interests internationally such as with the global marketing partnership between the Yankees and Manchester United, the open-ing of a series of regional offices by the NBA in Asia, the partnership between the Yankees and the Chinese Baseball Federation, and the now failed attempt of the NFL to create a viable American football competition in Europe among others. The second involves investment in sports teams as part of an owner or company's entertainment and real estate portfolios. Related to this is a third area that involves emerging interest in sports team ownership overseas. A good example of this development is Tom Hicks, who, as of the time of writing, owned Southwest Sports Group, a subsidiary of Hicks Inc., which holds a 50% stake in Liverpool FC and also owns the Texas Rangers in MLB, the Dallas Stars in the NHL and Mesquite Championship Rodeo.

Features of American professional sport and impact on the Premier League

While it is clear that American sports leagues and team owners are beginning to look internationally to enhance their revenue streams, it is less clear as to whether the features that distinguish American professional sports leagues and their operations have had, as yet, a huge impact internationally. The NFL learned an expensive lesson in its failed NFL Europe experiment that it is not easy to overwrite American sporting practices onto an international landscape. Having said that, there are features of American professional sporting practice and business organization that are making an impact on sport globally. These include, diversified revenue streams from television rights and sponsorships, forms of revenue sharing, entertainment activities linked to sport and flexible scheduling, among others. It has been harder to sustain an American level of competitive balance in European leagues, however, due to both the existence of the promotion–relegation system and the lure of riches in pan-European competition. For clubs like Glasgow Celtic or Ajax Amsterdam, it makes little sense to argue for domestic competitive balance but to focus on European success. Even in more relatively competitively balanced leagues, there is a pull towards Europe among leading clubs at the expense of greater competitive balance.[31]

American sports economists James Quirk and Rodney Fort caution, however, that the perception that North American sports franchises are highly profitable is an exaggeration. Indeed, they argue that 'with just a handful of exceptions, pro team sport does not appear to be a terribly profitable business'.[32] It is difficult to assess closely the profitability of most American franchises, however, since nearly all are privately held with limited public access to records and owners are able to depreciate player contracts for tax purposes. Rosentraub counters that 'where unprofitable teams exist it is usually a result of the failure of the leagues to share revenues or local mismanagement' rather than a lack of profitability.[33] Indeed, the health and relative competitive balance in the NFL is largely attributable to its revenue-sharing programme where national television contract money is distributed equally among its franchises. This allows for small market teams such as the Green Bay Packers to remain competitive with teams in much larger markets. Annual player drafts in which the weakest performing teams select new players first also assist in maintaining relative competitive balance. This system works in North America due to the key role of universities operating as developmental leagues for the pro leagues. In England, such a system might be possible if Premier League clubs formed a separate relegation-proof league in which the lower leagues became their 'minor' leagues much in the way that the Minor Leagues operate in MLB. In the case of MLB, minor league clubs are classed by level according to the strength of the players and clubs are affiliates or 'farm teams' for the MLB teams and are usually located in smaller markets. While this is currently unlikely in Britain, it is not completely far-fetched. Since the Bosman ruling, major European clubs have used smaller ones in other EU member states as feeder clubs such as the aforementioned arrangement between Manchester United and Belgian club Standard Liege.

Some have argued that American influences on English professional football are increasing rapidly and perhaps irreversibly. Vic Duke, in a provocative 2002 article, states that there has been a process of McDonaldization and Disneyization of professional football in England in recent times. He explains how the traditional British sport model has begun to change to resemble a more American business model. As Duke puts it, 'Some commentators link the changes to wider processes of globalisation, whereas others point to the progressive Americanisation of English sport'.[34] He continues in pointing out differences between the British and American models of sport:

> The American model of sport is more commercially oriented than the traditional English structure with key roles for advertising, sponsorship and particularly television. The primary function of sports team franchises is profit making. Sport is viewed as a branch

of the entertainment industry, which results in a different relationship between spectator and team; the discerning consumer replaces the committed fan.[35]

It is important to reiterate aspects of the traditional British model of sport as we begin to compare it with the American model. Traditionally, fan culture in Britain was centred around community-based clubs. There is a deep tradition with this type of support for football clubs, it started during the industrial revolution; more importantly, it started when workers in the factories were given half days off on Saturday.[36] This began the traditional Saturday lunchtime at the pub followed by the afternoon football match. It helped to unite and generate civic pride in the local football club. Contrast this against the newly television driven match times on a typical weekend of football in England which Duke points out:

> All leading English spectator sports (for team games) have experienced the alteration of fixtures to suit the needs of the new paymasters, television. Gone is the traditional sporting Saturday when all the football matches would kick off at three pm. Televised games are now regularly moved to Friday evening or Sunday lunchtime or Sunday afternoon or Monday evening.[37]

So as the Premier League model continues to shift from the traditional British model to the American model, matches occur at various times during weekends as well as mid-week as pay television searches for content that will attract viewers to sign up. As clubs move to new stadiums and increase the number of luxury boxes, the average ticket price to a match has skyrocketed. A match ticket had become a valued commodity so clubs can keep raising the price until they start to see a diminishing return. Not unlike American sport teams, English football clubs have begun to focus on corporate hospitality with raised ticket prices, renovated stadiums, and luxury suites and corporate boxes. For example, as of 2007 Manchester United had a total of 8000 corporate seats out of its 76,000 capacity.[38] The more affluent the crowd, the more revenue a club can generate, not only from ticket prices, but also from merchandise, concessions and even parking. Just as the American sports franchises during the 1980s and 1990s began to make these changes the British sports teams have begun to follow the corporate hospitality approach from 2000 onwards.

As early as the late 1980s, the FA promoted the conversion of 'going to a match' on a Saturday afternoon to 'integrated leisure experiences'.[39] The FA envisaged that, in the style of North American professional sports, attendees at football matches could be attracted by a festive atmosphere in which entertainment beyond the match itself would be attractive to families and a more diverse audience. At a surface level this approach appears to have taken hold in England. Attendances increased as the game's image improved and stadia were transformed post-Taylor into sites for family entertainment.

Potential implications and pitfalls of the 'American' model

It is clear that there are several areas of conflict between traditional English footballing culture, organization and administration and the ways in which American professional sports leagues operate. While fans and teams may be protected via the role of the FA as the ultimate governing body for football in England, there are certainly tensions between the goals of clubs like Manchester United and Lincoln

City, for example. The former aims to be a leading global brand competing for European championships, whereas the latter hopes perhaps for a good season that might lead to promotion to a higher league within the English game and hopefully to sustain a high enough attendance to remain in business from season to season. Indeed, for clubs like Manchester United, Arsenal and Chelsea, European success is far more important than domestic competitions such as the FA Cup. The latter is nice to win, but the former puts real money in the bank from television rights and global exposure. For the four English teams playing in the Champions League each season the potential return can nearly double their television income earned domestically. It is possible for leading teams to earn substantial sums from success in the Premier League, however. The latest television contract for the English Premier totalled $4 billion over three years, an amount only rivaled by the NFL in the USA among domestic professional sports leagues internationally. With this new contract it was possible for the champion of the 2007/2008 season to earn £50m. Compare this with the £30m Chelsea received upon winning the Premier League in the 2005/2006 season. That same amount will be made by the bottom finisher in the 2007/2008 season.[40]

Coda: a note on the Liverpool and the Champions League dilemma

A specific example of the tensions created by leveraging a takeover through borrowing against future earnings has become evident at Liverpool during the 2007/2008 season. Liverpool spent much of the season just inside or outside the cut-off for the last European Champions League place for the 2008/2009 season despite a strong performance in the Champions League. Knowing that the American owners of the club had leveraged their takeover based on Champions League qualification until the new stadium was complete in 2011 or 2012, Dubai International Capital made a buyout offer of £200m in early 2008. Gillett was immediately interested in selling his share based upon the healthy return he could make, though Hicks was determined not to sell. The dilemma is clear, if Liverpool do not qualify it would create a cash flow problem by 2009 when the debt they created has to be serviced with interest at an estimated £28m a year. Thus, Champions League qualification is essential to sustaining profitability in the short-term.[41] This has left the fans in a position of supporting investment from Dubai International Capital as a means of securing long-term success of the club, since it is clear that Gillett wanted out soon after buying in, and concerns over the Hicks strategy worried many supporters. Hostility to American owners appears greater than for others due to the widely held perception – rightly or wrongly held – that Americans do not really know or care about football but that investment in English clubs is purely for profit taking and not long-term club development.

Fan responses to new ownership and markets

While the situations of American ownership, and fan responses to those owners, are quite different at Manchester United, Aston Villa and Liverpool, it is clear that there is an uneasy relationship between soccer supporters in England and the spate of foreign owners now infiltrating 'their' game, as Liverpool's 2008 ownership issues demonstrated. A glance at senior managerial positions from the national team through the Premier League down to players suggest that the English game has been fully globalized and is well on the way to commercialization that resembles many of the aspects evident in North American professional sport. Yet, although supporters generally have been sceptical about foreign investment, the responses have by no means been uniform even within clubs. While many Manchester United supporters decried the Glazer takeover of the club, and subsequent relocation of some of the club's operations to the USA, matches continue to sell out and global revenues have expanded. Others, however, established a new soccer club, Football Club United of Manchester (FCUM), which has begun to work its way up the league structures. The club attracts an average attendance of some 3000 supporters, many of whom became disillusioned with the situation at Manchester United following the Glazer takeover.[42] For these supporters, the Glazer takeover was the last straw in a series of changes at Manchester United since the mid-1990s. As Hamil points out:

> Ever higher ticket prices forcing traditional supporters out of the ground, rampant commercialism, and an increasingly anaemic atmosphere at United's Old Trafford ground borne out of too many in attendance with no real emotional investment in the outcome. All contributed to a sense that Manchester United was no longer the club they grew up with.... It was now simply a speculative asset in the portfolio of a family of entertainment industry entrepreneurs.[43]

Additionally, the Independent Manchester United Supporters' Association, who successfully helped fight off the failed Murdoch takeover, has argued to the government that there should be a more equitable distribution of cash among Premier League clubs to enhance competition between Premier league teams, even though this would obviously disadvantage their own club in the process.[44]

Manchester City capitalized on its local rival's global focus and branding to position itself as the true local team of Manchester using a clever campaign launched in October 2005 entitled 'Our City' which used signs and slogans such as 'This is Our City' and 'Réal Manchester'. At the same time, Manchester City also developed a highly sophisticated programme that collected data on fans and their purchases at the club and included the personalization of season ticket mailouts by placing the surnames of supporters on a Manchester City jersey. Fans of Manchester City embraced this branding of the club. However, with the purchase of the club by Thaksin Shinawatra with his globally focused strategy, the branding of Man City evolved. With significant investment, the appointment of former England manager Sven Goran Ericksson (who subsequently left the club at the end of the 2007/2008 season) and on field success, the overwhelming majority of City fans adapted to the new focus as a trade off to success after many years of struggle.[45]

Conclusion

Who owns English football in the twenty-first century? It is clear that a new marketing class of owners and directors have moved into a sport that for more than a century prided itself on local affinities and are changing and further globalizing the Premier League and its clubs. These owners, along with the influx of television money and increasingly diversified revenue streams, have led clubs to pursue a much more professionalized operational model in the marketing and management of clubs. This model is aligned ever more closely to those apparent in North American professional sports leagues where fans are viewed as loyal consumers more than hard core supporters. While the structures of leagues differ between North America and England, it is clear that the trend is towards a globalized business model that began in North America and is sweeping the world as investors seek to maximize profits in diversified sport, entertainment, leisure, media and property portfolios. At times fans resist, and seek alternative means of expression and entertainment, at other times, fans welcome the infusion of capital that might make their club competitive and successful both in England and in Europe. Traditional supporter cultures come under threat at the same time as global branding has enhanced international support for leading clubs.

Fears of foreign investment ruining the traditional game persist. Some are tied up with xenophobia, while others are genuine concerns about the future of the game, particularly as performances of the English national team has not lived up to the performances that should be expected with English club success in the Champions League. At the start of the 2006/2007 season in the Premier League the big fear from foreign investment was that football clubs might be used for money-laundering and that criminals could be buying and using clubs to hide illegal sources of income.[46] These fears only surfaced after Chelsea started that season as the two-time defending Premier League Champions. Abramovich was accused of accumulating his vast fortune through questionable means and the perception was that Chelsea simply 'bought' their titles with his money. By 2007, many concerns surrounded questions that the new foreign owners, particularly the Americans, were only in it for the money rather than the long-term good of the club.

Foreign investment is such a touchy issue that Michel Platini, president of UEFA, the governing body of football in Europe, sent a letter in 2007 to the leaders of each of the member associations of UEFA urging them to be wary of foreign investment in their domestic football leagues.[47] Ironically, Platini praised the once maligned Chelsea owner Roman Abramovich because in Platini's eyes he demonstrated a genuine love for his football club and he had spent money to improve the club. Platini neglected to mention that part of the Gillett/Hicks investment included funding for the new stadium for Liverpool so the club can keep up with the other top clubs in England. While the debate continues over the impact of foreign ownership, it is clear that Duke and other analysts are correct to suggest that we are seeing a convergence of organizational and managerial structures between the North American model of professional sport and those in the Premier League in England that is likely to continue well into the future.

Notes

1. BBC Sport, 'US Pair Agree to Liverpool Takeover'.
2. These clubs were Arsenal, Manchester United, Chelsea, Liverpool, Everton, Aston Villa and Manchester City. For a brief discussion of Earl's and other investments in the Premier League, see Mackenzie, 'Football Takeover Trends'.
3. For a recent discussion of this in relation to major professional sports leagues and NASCAR, see Brown, 'Exceptionalist America', 1106–35.
4. Ammirante, 'Globalization in Professional Sport', 237–61.
5. Giulianotti, *Football*, 87.
6. Duke, 'Local Tradition Versus Globalization', 13.
7. Ammirante, 'Globalization in Professional Sport', 243.
8. New York Yankees and New York Mets, Chicago Cubs and Chicago White Sox, and Los Angeles Dodgers and Anaheim Angels in MLB; New York Giants and New York Jets in the NFL; New York Knicks and New Jersey Nets, and Los Angeles Lakers and Los Angeles Clippers in the NBA; New York Rangers and New York Islanders in the NHL. In MLB and the NFL the teams play in different leagues/conferences.
9. For an excellent discussion of this phenomenon, see Rosentraub, *Major League Losers*.
10. Rosentraub, 'Private Control of a Civic Asset', 109.

11. In this assumption we exclude minor league baseball teams, which, while they are professional, are subsidiaries of Major League Baseball teams.
12. Mackenzie, 'Football Takeover Trends'.
13. Giulianotti, *Football: A Sociology of the Global Game*, 99.
14. See Brown, 'Exceptionalist America'.
15. For discussions of this phenomenon, see Burton, 'Does the National Football League's Current Economic Model Threaten the Long Term Growth of Professional Football Globally?', 5–17; Means and Nauright, 'Going Global', 40–50.
16. Duffy, 'Football May be Ill, but Don't Blame Bosman', 277–89.
17. See Ammirante, 'Globalization in Professional Sport'; Bonn, 'Premiership Shares 900m TV Windfall'.
18. For further discussion of this, see Rosentraub, 'Playing with the Big Boys', 143–62.
19. McArdle, 'They're Playing R. Song'.
20. Ibid.
21. Duffy, 'Football May Be Ill, but Don't Blame Bosman'.
22. Hamil, 'Manchester United', 114–34.
23. Wulzinger, 'The Great Foreign Takeover'.
24. Ammirante, 'Globalization in Professional Sport', 244.
25. Payout figures sourced at UEFA.com in March 2007: http://www.uefa.com/uefa/keytopics/kind=16384/newsid=559777.html.
26. Gauge and Maindment, 'The Most Valuable Soccer Teams'.
27. Holmes, 'Stan Kroenke Targets Arsenal'.
28. BBC News, 'Foreign Cash Can Boost Arsenal'.
29. Villa Backers Club Formed (2006). http://www.clevelandbrowns.com/article.php?id=5656. Accessed February 12, 2008.
30. Moore, 'Aston Villa's Future'.
31. In Scotland the League Championship has been an exclusive competition between the two giant clubs of Glasgow Celtic and Glasgow Rangers while in the Netherlands, only PSV Eindhoven, Ajax and Feyenoord have won championships during the past quarter century. An examination of the Premier League suggests that there has been less competitive balance than before its formation.
32. Quirk and Fort, 'Hard Ball', 9.
33. Rosentraub, 'Private Control of a Civic Asset', 109.
34. Duke, 'Local Tradition Versus Globalization', 5.
35. Ibid.
36. The best discussion of this is still Tony Mason's account in *Association Football and English Society 1863–1914*.
37. Duke, 'Local Tradition Versus Globalization', 13.
38. Hamil, 'Manchester United', 128.
39. Football Association, *Blueprint for the Future of Football*, cited in Nauright, 'Global Games', 1331.
40. J. Chaffin, 'No Title', 21.
41. G. Moore, 'DIC Aims to Force Liverpool Sale with Final Offer'.
42. Hamil, 'Manchester United', 131–2.
43. Ibid., 132.
44. S. Brennan, 'Put "Fair" Back into Football'.
45. For a full discussion of the campaign, see Edensor and Millington, '"This is Our City" 172–93.
46. Wulzinger, 'The Great Foreign Takeover'.
47. Reuters, 'Platini Seeks EU Help Over Foreign Owners'.

References

Ammirante, J. 'Globalization in Professional Sport: Comparisons and Contrasts Between Hockey and European Football'. In *Artifical Ice: Hockey, Culture, and Commerce,* ed. D. Whitson and R. Gruneau, 237–61. Toronto: Garamond, 2006.

BBC News. 'Foreign Cash Can Boost Arsenal', BBC News, August 31, 2007. http://news.bbc.co.uk/2/hi/business/6971124.stm. Accessed February 12, 2008.

BBC Sport. 'US Pair Agree to Liverpool Takeover', BBC Sport. http://news.bbc.co.uk/sport2/hi/football/teams/l/liverpool/6323037.stm. Accessed December 12, 2007.

Bonn, D. 'Premiership Shares 900m TV Windfall', *The Telegraph,* January 18, 2007. http://www.telegraph.co.uk/news/main.jhtml?xml+/news/2007/01/18. Accessed November 26, 2007.

Brennan, S. 'Put "Fair" Back into Football: Reds Fans in "Rich Man Poor Man" Campaign', *Manchester Evening News,* November 15, 2006.

Brown, S.F. 'Exceptionalist America: American Sports Fans' Reaction to Internationalization', *International Journal of the History of Sport* 22, no. 6 (2005): 1106–35.

Burton, R. 'Does the National Football League's Current Economic Model Threaten the Long Term Growth of Professional Football Globally?', *Football Studies* 2, no. 2 (1999): 5–17.

Chaffin, J. 'No Title', *Financial Times,* February 5, 2007, 21.

Duffy, W. 'Football May be Ill, but Don't Blame Bosman'. In *The Business of Sports,* ed. S. Rosner, and K. Shropshire, 277–89. Subury, MA: Jones and Bartlett, 2004.

Duke, V. 'Local Tradition Versus Globalization: Resistance to the McDonaldisation and Disneyisation of Professional Football in England', *Football Studies* 5, no. 1 (2002): 13.

Edensor T., and S. Millington, '"This is Our City": Branding Football and Local Embeddedness', *Global Networks* 8, no. 2 (2008): 172–93.

Gauge, J., and P. Maindment, 'The Most Valuable Soccer Teams', *The Telegraph,* January 18, 2007. http://www.forbes.com/2006/03128/soccer-manchester-madrid-cz. Acccessed March 25, 2007.

Giulianotti, R. *Football: A Sociology of the Global Game.* Cambridge: Polity, 1999.

Hamil, S. 'Manchester United: The Commercial Development of a Global Football Brand', In *International Cases in the Business of Sport,* ed. S. Chadwick, and D. Arthur 114–34. London: Butterworth-Heinemann.

Holmes, L. 'Stan Kroenke Targets Arsenal', April 22, 2007. http://english-premier-league.suite101.com/article.cfm/american_kroenke_targets_arsenal. Accessed March 1, 2008.

Mackenzie, A. 'Football Takeover Trends', BBC Sport, February 6, 2007. http://news.bbc.co.uk/sport2/hi/football/eng_prem/6179569.stm. Accessed January 22, 2008.

Mason, T. *Association Football and English Society 1863–1914.* Brighton: Harvester, 1980.

McArdle, D. 'They're Playing R. Song: Football and the European Union after *Bosman*', *Football Studies* 3, no. 2 (2000): 42–66.

Means, J., and J. Nauright, 'Going Global: The NBA Sets Its Sights on Africa', *International Journal of Sport Marketing and Sponsorship* 9, no. 1 (2007): 40–50.

Moore, G. 'DIC Aims to Force Liverpool Sale with Final Offer'. http://www.independent.co.uk/sport/football/premier-league/dic-aims-to-force-liverpool-sale-with-final-offer-791198.html. Accessed March 8, 2008.

Moore, L. 'Aston Villa's Future', 2007. http://www.topblogarea.com/rss/Aston-Villa.htm. Accessed February 28, 2008.

Nauright, J. 'Global Games: Culture, Political Economy and Sport in the Globalised World of the 21st Century', *Third World Quarterly* 25, no. 7 (2004): 1325–1336.

Quirk, J.P., and R. D. Fort, 'Hard Ball: The Abuse of Power in Pro Team Sports', In *The Business of Sports,* ed. S.R. Rosner, and K. Shropshire, 9. Sudbury, MA: Jones and Bartlett, 2004.

Reuters, 'Platini Seeks EU Help Over Foreign Owners', Reuters, September 19, 2007. http://uk.reuters.com/article/sportsNews/idUKL1986611020070919. Accessed October 5, 2007

Rosentraub, M. *Major League Losers: The Real Costs of Sports and Who's Paying for It.* New York: Basic Books, 1999.

Rosentraub, M. 'Private Control of a Civic Asset: The Winners and Losers from North America's Experience with Four Major Leagues in Professional Team Sport'. In *The Commericalisation of Sport,* ed. T. Slack, 109. London: Routledge, 2004.

Rosentraub, M. 'Playing with the Big Boys: Smaller Markets, Competitive Balance, and the Hope for a Championship Team'. In *Artifical Ice: Hockey, Culture, and Commerce,* ed. D. Whitson and R. Gruneau, 143–62. Toronto: Garamond, 2006.

Wulzinger, M. 'The Great Foreign Takeover: English Premier League Changing Hands', *Spiegel,* October 23, 2006. http://www.spiegle.de/international/Spiegel/0,1518,444999,00.html. Accessed November 25, 2007.

'Club versus country' in rugby union: tensions in an exceptional New Zealand system

Camilla Obel

School of Sociology and Anthropology, University of Canterbury, Christchurch, New Zealand

In contrast to the global reach and popularity of the association game, rugby union enjoys the position of being the national sport of New Zealand. This position is sustained by an exceptional model of governance with central control by the national administration. It was established before the turn of the twentieth century and has remained New Zealand's governance model in the new professional era. A comparative discussion of the different organizational structures in the northern and southern hemispheres shows how the sport is vulnerable to the contrasting governance systems characterized as 'club – versus – country'. Drawing on Leifer's account of the transformation of the major leagues in North America, the article investigates how the tension between hierarchical control by a central authority and the drive for local autonomy by clubs is resolved. It details the early establishment of local and national amateur rugby union competitions in New Zealand and argues that these 'professional-like' competitions represented a strategic compromise by the NZRU. In the global professional era, the NZRU has retained central control over the sport and players through the establishment of NZRU contracts to players and coaches in the five New Zealand Super 14 teams. While the wealthy English clubs exercise a considerable degree of control relative to the English RFU on the issue of player releases for national representation, the current tension in the New Zealand system resides in the saturation of the local player/coach labour market and the ability of players and coaches to exit for better-paying contracts in the northern hemisphere.

Introduction

Despite the existence of amateur regulations in rugby union until 1996, the worldwide governance of the sport has been characterized by contrasting systems. This article provides a discussion of the governance systems in New Zealand in the amateur and professional periods and contrasts these developments with those in England. The article begins by explaining the exceptional New Zealand system of popular amateurism. This included successful local and national competitions and a strong national team governed by a national administration with central control and authority which helped secure rugby union as the national game. In contrast to this goal of producing successful national teams, the establishment of an English system in the late nineteenth century was characterized by a concern with clubs both before and after the split and the establishment of the professional game of rugby league in 1895. While clubs in England had direct representation on the national body (the RFU), clubs in New Zealand were governed by provincial unions whose representatives together formed the national body, the New Zealand Rugby Football Union (now the New Zealand Rugby Union; NZRU[1]). This delegated system of governance, whose authority is based on its legitimacy as the elected body, formed part of the sport's early hierarchical structure and it has extended beyond the amateur period to the current professional era where governance has been further delegated to a reduced board. This article traces the tensions in the New Zealand system, highlighting that competitive amateur competitions were sanctioned by the NZRU as a solution to the provincial unions' desire for local autonomy despite international concern that these competitions were a form of professionalism. It goes on to explain how organizational tensions in the professional period are provoked by players' and coaches' mobility. The current solution, in the form of the transnational Super 12/14 competition with a central contracting structure, a national player-transfer system and the nonselection of overseas-based players and coaches, has been introduced to combat the vulnerable, peripheral position of the New Zealand game relative to the economic power of the clubs in the northern hemisphere.

The (elusive) national goal of All Black success

Until a couple of decades ago, concern with commercial matters was frowned upon throughout much of the rugby union world. While debates about player transfers and transfer fees, distribution of media sponsorship and the growing gap between the richest and poorest clubs have occupied fans and administrators of association football worldwide for decades, among rugby union followers a concern with how to finance the sport, distribute income and expand markets was generally discouraged. That said, there were rumours of 'shamateurism', of players being paid 'under-hand', and some voiced concerns about what they saw as an overemphasis on competitiveness, both of which were said to be counter to the principles of amateurism. Much of this criticism came from the northern hemisphere and was directed at developments in the southern hemisphere. Not surprisingly, the concept of a Rugby World Cup (RWC) was promoted by the national administrations of Australia and New Zealand. As predicted, the inaugural tournament in 1987 ignited audience interest and the income-generating possibilities in the sport, but it also highlighted problems with how to manage this income.

In the case of New Zealand, the RWC was crucial in reconfirming the position of rugby union as the nation's most popular game, a position that had been challenged in the 1970s and 1980s when the NZRU had maintained contact with the South African rugby authorities despite international condemnation and internal protest.[2] Despite the enormous interest and national investment in maintaining New Zealand as the number one country in the sport, winning the Rugby World Cup has remained elusive. The shock exit of the national New Zealand 'All Black' team in the quarter-final knockout round of the 2007 RWC again ignited the debate over the different playing styles and governance structures of the game in the northern and southern hemispheres. The northern hemisphere traditional stronghold of the sport in the UK accuses the southern hemisphere game in New Zealand, Australia, South Africa and the Pacific nations of playing a kind of hybrid game of rugby union and rugby league that favours running with the ball and try scoring.[3] By contrast, the southern hemisphere rugby nations reject the northern hemisphere rugby style as outmoded and boring, with too much emphasis on forward play and kicking. Underlying this debate is a contrast in organizational and economic structures that shape the game in two contrasting directions.

This article traces some of the organizational strategies pursued by the NZRU and highlights how these strategies were central to preserving rugby union as the national sport in New Zealand and in securing the international strength of the All Black team. This discussion, which emphasizes struggles for control between the national union and provincial unions, and between players and the NZRU, draws on a comparison with the organizational struggles in the UK, particularly England. These struggles for control, characterized as club versus country, emphasize the battles between club owners and national administrators for control over competitions and the availability of players for national teams. This article begins by showing how the popularity of the amateur game in New Zealand was secured through the early establishment of inter-provincial competitions with teams attached to provincial centres throughout the country. This argument, emphasizing organizational strategies, differs from the local accounts of the centrality of the national men's All Black team as a result of its early northern hemisphere tours, popularly regarded as iconic moments in the nation's history, and for establishing a sense of national identification.[4] It also questions, rather than takes for granted, amateurism as an explanation for the organization of the sport. It does so by drawing on an argument about professional leagues as a model of organizing popular support for sports.[5] New Zealand 'amateur leagues' show both similarities to and differences from the professional leagues in the North American and European contexts. A key feature of the New Zealand governance model of rugby union is the centralized control exerted by the national administration.

The article extends the observation about leagues and control by the national administration to show how in the current professional era, the governance model of rugby union in New Zealand, in contrast to that in the northern hemisphere, continues to rely on a high degree of control exercised by a central administration. This has ensured that the national All Black team has continued to be the focus of the competitive infrastructure where player mobility is firmly regulated and subordinated to the 'nation' such that the club versus country relationship favours 'country' while ensuring 'club' (in this case provincial unions and in particular those hosting Super 14 teams) welfare. There are two aspects of the reconfigured professional game that pose a threat to the previously stable and successful New Zealand game: the dominance of northern hemisphere clubs relative to their national unions affects the availability of players for these national teams – and this has the knock-on effect of lowering the appeal of test matches involving the All Black team; and northern hemisphere clubs' financial strength acts as a pull for southern hemisphere players and coaches seeking better remuneration. Both of these factors threaten to undo the position of rugby union as the national game in New Zealand.

Explaining amateur rugby's popular appeal

Rugby union established itself as the national, popular game in New Zealand before the turn of the twentieth century. This 'exceptional'[6] position was enjoyed in only a few other nations, including Wales, the Pacific nations and among the dominant, minority white community in South Africa. In these countries, a kind of popular amateurism evolved which included the careful managing of competitions overseen and centrally controlled by a national union. Thus, contrary to common perceptions about amateurism as fostering exclusivity and a rejection of market solutions for securing games' popularity, in New Zealand, rugby union came to enjoy popular support before the turn of the twentieth century due to organizational strategies involving a high degree of centralized control in return for fostering the spread of the game through local and national competitions.

Contrary to Markovits and Hellerman's claim that '[rugby] union had no leagues',[7] it was exactly the carefully managed competitive structures that fostered rugby union's popularity in New Zealand as it did in Wales, and in the north of England.[8] Rugby union's popularity in New Zealand was fostered through the development of club and interprovincial matches which from the late 1880s attracted gatherings, equal to the size of professional First Division soccer crowds in England,[9] eager to watch the most skilled local players perform against other regions' best players. Despite the claim that 'Welsh rugby was watched by larger numbers of spectators than anywhere outside of the North of England',[10] it did not take long before provincial teams in New Zealand could match 'the lustrous Swansea side of the early 1900s [which] regularly drew crowds of 20,000 home and away'.[11] In fact, the New Zealand challenge competition, the Ranfurly Shield introduced in 1902, gained a reputation as 'the goose that lays the Golden Egg' and 'the greatest money spinner ever in the Rugby world'.[12]

Drawing on Eric Leifer's observations concerning the organization of 'leagues' in the North American context, together with aspects of the two early New Zealand representative All Black players, David Gallaher's and John William Stead's account of the early colonial organization of rugby union in New Zealand,[13] an argument can be made that the popularity of amateur interprovincial rugby union competitions in New Zealand rested on the adoption of aspects central to the organization of professional competitions. The establishment of domestic, amateur rugby union competitions served to cultivate and secure 'enduring or regular publics'.[14] This observation provides an explanation, different from previous ones that emphasize the role of the All Black team as a focal point for national identification, which explains how, given the growing popularity of rugby league in Australia and New Zealand in the early part of the twentieth century[15] and the very few international matches involving the All Black team, the union game maintained its position as the national, popular game in New Zealand.[16] Rather than professionalism, introduced in 1996, representing a radical change in organizational strategies, these early centralized strategies for cultivating and maintaining the game's popularity and strength have continued into the professional era.

Drawing on Leifer's comparative historical and economic sociological account of the transformation of the major leagues in North America, this article investigates how the tension, characteristic of all team sport, between hierarchical control and the drive for local autonomy is resolved. This tension was at the heart of the conflict that split the game in 1895[17] and it has been at the forefront in disputes over the introduction and organization of professional rugby union a century later. In the century of amateur rugby union, both local and international disputes, relating to the contrasting goals of competitive outcomes and the employment of an amateur ethos, have characterized the sport. Today, the disputes no longer concern amateur goals; rather 'clubs' and 'nations' confront each other over the regulation of player mobility.

Leifer's organizational analysis of the four professional major leagues shows that success in cultivating enduring local publics for professional teams in the period before World War I rested on the organization of leagues and the attachment of teams to cities. After World War II, he shows that national publics were cultivated through the attachment of leagues to national television broadcasters. Leifer's central insight is that in order for owners to achieve financial viability they had to give up their local autonomy, change their view of winning as being the most effective way of ensuring financial prosperity, and agree to affiliate into a centrally organized league. He therefore shifts attention for the explanation of the game and the generation of identification to the organizers of leagues and the support for teams. The focus becomes not the game in general, but relations between teams.

According to Leifer, the central organization of a limited number of teams into leagues involved in closed circuit home-and-away pennant races was the first step towards solving some of the owners' collective problems. The control over players' movement and the allocation of teams to large cities was the second. These mechanisms enabled the attachment and cultivation of regular local support for city-based teams, ensuring individual team's survival and the overall viability and prosperity of the leagues. Later the introduction of air travel and national television broadcasting created the opportunity for leagues to cultivate national audiences. For Leifer, the significance of these developments is that they represented a shift in organizing professional sports from a focus on 'gathering crowds for matches to creating publics'.[18]

Although it is useful to think with Leifer's argument concerning how to cultivate support for sports, amateur rugby union in New Zealand did not require all of the organizational features of North American professional sports leagues. Yet, national administrators' desire to cultivate and maintain the game's popularity and to strengthen the All Black team, while maintaining ties with the four national unions in the United Kingdom and Ireland, the 'Home Unions', required centralized authority to regulate local relations. Provincial rugby unions (rather than 'clubs') were not business-like 'franchises', as in the case of teams in the North American professional leagues, but rather reflected European soccer clubs, about which Whitson notes that they were 'part of non-profit, multi-sport "clubs" managed by boards composed by local business people' and attached to 'civically rooted, less entrepreneurial structures'.[19] Although both clubs and provincial unions in New Zealand and England were based on the amateur ethos, their organizational goal differed and therefore also their versions of amateurism. From the grassroots to the national level the overriding goal was competitiveness culminating in a strengthened All Black team.[20] By contrast, from club level and through to the RFU, volunteerism characterized English rugby and clubs were 'friendly institutions' hosting 'slightly chaotic parties'.[21]

Despite these differences in the institutionalization of sport both among and between professional and amateur sports, which relate to the ownership of teams, the focus on financial gain and the contracting of players, Leifer's analysis provides a way of explaining the success of the New Zealand amateur rugby union competitions. More significantly, the adoption of some of the organizational features of professional competitions meant that rugby union organizers would not only face some of the problems and opportunities affecting professional sports, but that they would also become embroiled in both domestic and international disputes over professionalism. The NZRU's solution to these disputes was to deny professionalism while at the same time ceding power to provincial unions to pursue competitions that utilized the same means as professional competitions to generate income and spectator support. In doing so, the NZRU controlled the suspicion from the Home Unions that it was pursuing professional competitions. For provincial unions, in particular the larger city-based unions, it meant that interprovincial competitions proved to be very popular with local and later national audiences providing these unions with, first, high gate-takings, later sponsorship income and, most recently, the ability to contract star players. For the NZRU, these competitions provided the vital foundation for the production of All Black players.

Organizational efficiency in a centrally governed system

Disputes over what it meant to be an amateur athlete and how amateur competitions should be organized occupied national rugby union administrators for more than a century. These conflicts most famously included the early internal rupture of the game as a result of the development of cups and league competitions in the north of England whose popularity and inclusion of working class and entrepreneurial communities encouraged the introduction of payment to players and ultimately resulted in the split and the establishment of the 'northern' professional, rugby league game. Externally, early relations between the Home Unions were similarly characterized by tension over the need to surrender national authority to a supranational body and the desire to protect national interests. Thus, the English RFU initially refused to join the newly established International Rugby Board (IRB) in 1887 until it had been granted a dominant position and its point system for scoring adopted, and in 1897 the Welsh RFU withdraw briefly from the IRB following the dispute over the 'testimonial' to the famous Welsh player Arthur Gould.[22] In the case of New Zealand, it was the sending and receiving of national teams that provoked the establishment of the 'NZRFU' in 1892. The first national team assembled in New Zealand to tour Australia in 1884 consisted of players selected from only some of the existing provincial unions, including Otago, Canterbury, Wellington and Auckland. This tour and later the northern hemisphere tour by the privately organized 'Native' team in 1888 provoked tension between provincial administrators and was potentially more damaging for those administrators eager to foster international relations with the Home Unions.[23] Once formed, the national body quickly sought to subordinate provincial unions, control local competitions and punish any infringements of the amateur principles.

The New Zealand centralized organization in the amateur period, in which the tensions between 'clubs' and 'country' were resolved through the subordinating of provincial unions, served two national purposes: the cultivation of popular and strong competitions that could produce competitive national teams, and protection against professionalism. This organization required that local, district-based clubs were subordinated to provincial unions, which in turn were governed by the national union. The efficient relations between these three levels are explained in this description by Gallaher and Stead:

> There is no unnecessary piece of governmental machinery, and the whole fits together with splendid exactness. The New Zealand Rugby Union being the chief authority, it has immediately below it the various provincial Unions, each province having its own union in the same way as with English counties, but a province is very much bigger and a more unwieldy thing than the English county, Auckland, for instance, being more than four hundred miles from one end to the other. In each province there are several country Unions, subservient directly to the provincial Union, and through it to the head body. After the provincial and the country Unions come the clubs.[24]

This development contrasted with the English RFU's inability to contain club matches as exclusively 'friendlies' and the English clubs' autonomous establishment, as the northern English county cup and league developments showed. Gallaher and Stead described those developments as 'promiscuous'. They point out that the establishment of provincial unions, affiliated to the national union, with authority to control not only the location of local clubs, but also their management, was the crucial means of ensuring both protection against professionalism and the viability of clubs and competitions:

> ...in Auckland, which we are particularly considering, there are several clubs called by the names of the respective districts of the town from which they draw their players. Clubs are not organised promiscuously in New Zealand as they are in Britain, [...] The Union decides what clubs there shall be, and supervises their management. In doing so it particularly desires to ensure the thoroughness and effectiveness of the working of each club, the equality of all of them so far as conditions and opportunities are concerned, the maintenance of strict amateurism throughout, the prevention of one club being completely overshadowed by another by reason of superior financial resources, or by any social or other non-financial inducement that it might offer to players to belong to it, and too easily facilitates for changing clubs.[25]

The success of this extraordinary system of 'organizational efficiency' might be exaggerated in these accounts but they nevertheless highlight that centralized power and local subordination characterized the New Zealand rugby governance model. This organizational efficiency contrasted with the English 'amateur' organization as referred to by Malin and Malcolm, Sheard and White, who suggest volunteers resisted overly organized and formalized competitions because they feared that such formalization would lead to over-serious play, violence, professionalism and spectatorism.[26] Not surprisingly, there were expressions of local resistance by New Zealand provincial unions and clubs and concessions granted by the national union throughout the amateur period. Until the 1970s, most New Zealand amateur, interprovincial rugby union matches were played as 'friendlies' or as a challenge a provincial team issued to another team. These matches were not subject to the kind of rationalization and calculation that characterized professional competitions with teams organized into divisions or leagues, match victories translated into points and teams' standing throughout the season measured. However, those organizers keen to popularize amateur rugby union matches did introduce cup and league competitions.

As in the north of England and Wales, the New Zealand game became organized to encompass and encourage both player and spectator involvement from the late nineteenth century. In both New Zealand and Wales, a kind of democratic or popular amateurism was encouraged as a way of popularizing the game.[27] While administrators in New Zealand did not allow payment to players (until much later in the 1980s and through sanctioned promotional company structures – see below), they did hire coaches, charge money at the gate, provide tour allowances to All Black players and encourage players to train and improve their skills.

In contrast to the southern English clubs, only some of which charged spectators for admission to club matches,[28] all provincial unions in New Zealand began to charge spectators for admission to matches against visiting provincial teams and to club matches before the turn of the twentieth century. Additionally, Gallaher and Stead explain that each club had several teams which participated in graded cup and league competitions:

> Each club runs three fifteens, and the same arrangements in every respect are made for the seconds and thirds as for the firsts. The Union offers three Cups for competition by the district clubs on what in Britain is known as the League system, one Cup being allotted to each grade of players in the various clubs ... the competition in each case is strictly limited to players of the proper class.[29]

This grading of players into first-, second- and third-graded club competitions restricted players to only the competition-grade to which he was 'classed'. The provincial union committee decided any promotion of players and a player could not play in the grade from which he was promoted. This ensured that the lower grades were as competitive and 'scarcely inferior in point of interest to those of the grade above'. While the residential regulations encouraged balanced competitions and thus 'spectatorism', clubs were prohibited from owning their venues and the provincial unions seized the gate-takings from all club and interprovincial matches staged at the provincial union stadium, thus 'keeping pure amateurism'.[30]

This promotion of spectatorism through cups and leagues raised the Home Unions' suspicion of 'veiled professionalism' in the colony[31] and placed the national administration in New Zealand in a precarious position between the Home Unions and its own provincial unions. The problem that the NZRU faced was that its dedication to the All Black team required a form of decentralization which promoted highly competitive and graded domestic competitions capable of ensuring that the NZRU got 'all football worth out of the youth of the nation [which] is necessary if it aspires to hold its own, or a little more, in competition with its contemporaries'.[32]

Amateur friendlies and local cups and leagues

Despite the fact that *interprovincial* matches were friendlies and not formalized to the same extent as the local, graded club competitions, consistent with the NZRU's and some provincial delegates' desire to resist competition structures involving the 'grading of union against union in merit tables or leagues',[33] they did generate large spectator interest. At the beginning of the twentieth century a total of around 50 interprovincial friendlies were played and between the two World Wars up to 100 matches were staged annually.[34] While the number of friendlies grew, and regional cup competitions were established between 1906 and 1965 involving two-thirds of all provincial unions, interprovincial friendlies eventually became incorporated into national, interprovincial competitions, the Ranfurly Shield and the National Provincial Championship (NPC), established three-quarters of a century apart.

The NZRU's agreement to introduce the Ranfurly Shield in 1902 represented the first move towards involving city-based provincial teams in a national competition. The amateur rules of the competition required that the Shield be contested in 'challenge matches' – 'the New Zealand Union seeing to it that they [the Shield holders] are not over done by challenges'.[35] This meant that the competition involved only half a dozen provincial teams in the few matches staged each year.[36] Despite these restrictions, the amateur competition was highly successful with local spectators. Crowds of 20,000 spectators for Ranfurly Shield matches were not unusual from the 1920s onwards. This competition became the most significant revenue-generating means for provincial unions enabling a few, the largest city-based unions, Auckland, Wellington and Canterbury, to claim a powerful position vis-à-vis the NZRU. But, more significantly, the success of Ranfurly Shield matches was critical for the continued popularity of rugby union in the first half of the century when few All Black matches took place. However, this popularity may have contributed to the Home Unions' suspicion of 'professionalism' and their reluctance to tour New Zealand – after the Anglo-Welsh tour in 1908 a British team did not tour New Zealand until 1930, and this 'snub' is likely to have influenced the NZRU to restrict the number of the annual challenge matches.

Overall, the financial benefits of the competition favoured only a few unions but its popularity helped foster and promote the game. In the period between 1902 and 1999 only 14 unions successfully defended the Shield, the Auckland and Canterbury unions dominated the Shield and only the Wellington union came close to achieving the success of these two large city-based unions. Despite the uneven benefits of the Shield competition, favouring the major provincial unions, these unions promoted the idea of a national 'league' in the 1960s. Similar development occurred in the northern hemisphere where gate-taking clubs in England and Scotland campaigned for the introduction of national club competitions. Yet, it was not until 1987 that all-inclusive national club competitions with merit tables were introduced in England.[37] In both hemispheres the introduction of televised sport and the broadcasting of the rival rugby league code likely boosted the position of the major gate-taking clubs in England and the larger provincial unions in New Zealand, both in favour of national competitions.

Following Leifer's argument, the introduction of these national competitions represented a shift from gathering crowds for matches to creating enduring publics. The later establishment of the television-sponsored transnational Super 12 competition and the European club competition facilitated the establishment of enduring mediated national and transnational publics. In New Zealand, the introduction of the NPC with two, and later three divisions (and most recently, two 'leagues' – see below), represented a collective strategy to increase income for all teams involved as opposed to the previous individual strategy of creating winning teams to ensure local financial prosperity.

While the NZRU retained control over the NPC competition and issued rules to regulate it and the Ranfurly Shield, according to the provincial rugby union administrator Barry Smith, the provincial unions arranged matches at 'intensely fought out' annual NZRU meetings known as the 'Woolsale'.[38] As a result, the first NPC season spanned from May until mid-October in an effort to accommodate the provinces' seasonal obligations. A consequence of the decentralized match arrangement was that the championship could be won before the end of the season, resulting in low spectator attendance at the end-of-season matches. It was not until 1985/1986 that changes to the NPC increased the uncertainty of the championship outcomes. The NPC became national and changes to the points scoring made teams benefit from close matches. These changes introduced an 'ordered performance inequality', ensuring that more teams remained contenders for the championship facilitating a season-long local interest in the competition.

Coinciding with these changes, the first *live* interprovincial match was broadcast on public television in 1986.[39] The introduction of play-offs in 1992, which coincided with guaranteed live television coverage of the NPC, and the central organization of the draw were attempts to attract, for the first time, a *national* television public for live play-off matches. Significantly, these competition changes came at a time when the NZRU was forced to compete for viewers with rugby league. From 1989, the Australian Rugby League Winfield Cup competition began to be broadcast live on a weekly basis to New Zealand viewers.[40] This generated viewer interest in New Zealand and increased the income for the Australian rugby league clubs, which began offering several high-profile New Zealand rugby union players high-paying professional salaries to switch to play rugby league for their clubs. By 1995, and coinciding with the third RWC, this threat escalated as a result of media sponsorship 'wars' in both rugby codes. Tumult in rugby league was caused by a News Corporation proposal for a new Super League structure involving both the Australian and English rugby league premier competitions and which provoked a sharp rise in player contract offers to both established rugby league and star rugby union players.[41] In rugby union, the Kerry Packer sponsored global World Rugby Corporation was ultimately unsuccessful in luring away the control of the game from the national unions. Backed by a News Corporation sponsorship deal worth US$555m over 10 years, the national unions in South Africa, Australia and New Zealand (SANZAR) were successful in retaining control of the game and their players by offering professional contracts in return for introducing new competitions in the form of the transnational Super 12 and the Tri Nations competitions.[42]

A century after the first split in the rugby 'football' code the union game faced a new challenge in the form of professional player contracts and increased player mobility. Yet, this challenge which was provoked by media-sponsorship interest in both the rugby codes emerged as a result of the spectator interest and popularity of the local and emerging transnational competitions. Thus, Markovits and Hellerman's claim that 'Various cup competitions at the club level were only introduced in the 1970s, the period in which Union, too, began a process of overt professionalization',[43] neglects the early conflicts surrounding the establishment of cup and league competitions in the north of England and in Wales and uses the, later, English organization of the game as the model of explaining this particular amateur 'football' version. In doing so, they also completely neglect the popular organizational model of amateur rugby union that developed in New Zealand and in Wales.

Tensions in a centralized system: success, failure and uneven global regulations

In 1995, professional contracts replaced amateur eligibility regulations as the principle for allocating sporting opportunities for rugby union players. In the northern shemisphere, clubs controlled these contracts, much like the situation in soccer. In the southern hemisphere, national unions controlled contracts and introduced a national player-transfer system regulating provincial unions' player contracting and players' national mobility. The establishment of a new News Corporation-sponsored 'television league' – the Super 12 transnational SANZAR competition involving newly formed teams in New Zealand (5) and provincial teams from South Africa (4) and Australia (3), became controlled by the national unions in these countries. In contrast to this centralized control, in the northern hemisphere premier clubs, backed by wealthy new owners, dominated the 'open market' system. These contrasting systems created a global context in which player mobility was relatively unregulated. As a consequence of this, national unions in the southern hemisphere became increasing vulnerable to the economic power in the north where the wealthy clubs began contracting southern hemisphere players and coaches. While the shift to professional contracts introduced player labour markets and increasing global mobility, regulations in the amateur era did not completely exclude player mobility. Rather, as McGovern has shown with respect to soccer player-migration patterns, rugby player migration in the new professional era is shaped by tradition, early contact and social networks.[44]

Until 1995, player labour markets did not exist and players were tightly regulated. Player mobility was constrained through residence rules which required players to be resident in their province and a member of a local club for at least three weeks prior to selection for their provincial team, while amateur regulations prohibited players from accepting money in return for any service relating to rugby, in particular a move to the highest bidder.[45] The few players who transferred between provincial unions within New Zealand officially did so because of work commitments and, later, increasingly to take advantage of educational opportunities. However, public speculation suggested that this form of mobility was underhand, or a form of shamateurism, which had produced a 'black market' where players moved to a new province in return for money or a 'rugby job'. This pattern of mobility was dependent on local sponsorship of clubs in both New Zealand and Europe. While accusations of shamateurism increased, this form of player mobility did not provoke a tension between individual players and the national team. Players such as Murray Mexted, Andy Haden and John Kirwan,[46] based overseas in the off-season, were not excluded from All Black selection, as is the case in the new professional game, as long as they were able to return home for trials and selection procedures.

'Rugby jobs' paved the way for indirect player payment provoked by the establishment of promotional companies by star players. Companies, such as John Kirwan's Forza Promotions in 1987 and Wayne Smith's Tryline in 1989, were copied by provincial unions and the NZRU in the early 1990s. All Black Promotions, formed in 1994, received sponsorship from the Union's major sponsors, Steinlager, Coca Cola, Ford and Philips, and paid All Black players a fee of approximately NZ$50,000 for promotional services for sponsors in 1995 leading up to the RWC and including the end of year/season northern hemisphere tour. Similar promotional companies were formed in the northern hemisphere, and while the NZRU's player payment was reported by be greater than these, star players in the northern hemisphere were expected to be able to earn as much as £50,000 a year through individual sponsorship deals.[47] These forms of payment were considered crucial in the southern hemisphere where the rival rugby league code threatened to lure away the best international players with attractive contracts. Thus, prior to the introduction of 'fully' professional contracts, player payments were characterized by an uneven distribution dependent upon both the local and national administrators' attitude to player retention and welfare and the size of their respective sponsorship markets.

In contrast to the form of player mobility in the amateur period, which did not threaten the strength of the New Zealand game and the All Black team, the introduction of professional player labour markets has produced tension between elite players' power to move and the NZRU's efforts to secure the national team. The professional player labour market is geared to the highest bidder and the mobility of players and teams is the condition for the way the game is organized now. The NZRU's solution to this threat was to introduce centralized contracts for New Zealand players and coaches and thereby create an exceptional player/coach labour market subordinated to the national team. The NZRU justified this system of contracting, requiring players to participate in initially as many as five different teams and competitions, on the basis that it strengthened New Zealand teams. This exceptional player labour market consolidated the NZRU's paternalistic control over its constituent members, provincial unions, coaches and players. In contrast to the early organizational form in which producing a strong national team was secured through the development of and central control over local and national competitions, the solution to protecting the All Black team in the professional era required the creation of new teams to participate in a transnational competition. The centralized contracts and the initial lack of an effective players' association ensured the lowest payment to New Zealand Super 12 players as well as highly differentiated, longer term, individually negotiated player contracts.[48] It enabled the NZRU Super 12 selectors (including the Super 12 coaches) to control the drafting of players into the five Super 12 teams and to dictate the teams' composition, ensuring the establishment of five 'NZRU' teams, which would test and develop promising and established All Black players.

The Super 12 competition, restructured from the earlier Super 10 competition,[49] was introduced in the traditional southern hemisphere 'pre-season' running between February and May and culminating in the Tri Nations series in June–July. The Super 12 and Tri Nations competitions thus fitted in with existing international and domestic competitions, but importantly added a minimum of 11 matches to the workloads of the country's best 150 players. It culminated in a Tri Nations series consisting of home-and-away matches between the three national representative sides in South Africa, New Zealand and Australia. The Super 12 competition included a play-off format similar to that introduced in the NPC in 1992. In the Tri Nations series, score-differentials were used to determine a winner in the event of a 'dead heat'. This latter competition regulation was changed to include an additional round with play-offs, while the Super 12 competitions was expanded to 14 teams (one new team from Australia and South Africa) after the renegotiation of the sponsorship deal between SANZAR and News Corporation in 2005.

To encourage the cultivation of local publics, the five New Zealand Super 12/14 teams were allocated to existing provincial unions. Rather than franchises, as in the North American cartel model of major leagues with franchises, these unions acted as 'caretakers' of the Super 12/14 teams, which were made up predominantly of players from within the 'region'. The regions were constructed by the NZRU by dividing the 27 first, second and third division provincial unions into five regions and 'attaching' a Super 12/14 team to the largest first division union within each region. By contrast, the selection of four South African provincial teams to participate in the Super 12/14 competition followed the promotion–qualification procedures for the earlier Super 10 competition to which the top four provincial unions in the domestic Currie Cup qualified. However, by 1998, the four South African Super 12/14 teams (with a fifth added in 2006) became regional as in New Zealand, with the best players selected from across all the 14 provincial unions. In Australia, the three (and now four with the inclusion of Western Australia) state representative teams, New South Wales, Queensland and Australian Capital Territory were automatically included in the competition.

This new 'television league' consisting of mostly new 'franchises' in a closed league structure represented the adoption of fully professional league structures with teams guaranteed inclusion season after season irrespective of performance and with no promotion–relegation system between this transnational league and national competitions. Yet, while this competition represents an adoption of 'fully professional' competition structures, the New Zealand organizational model of professional rugby union shows a high degree of continuity with the central control during the amateur period that sought to secure the national team through strong domestic competitions. The aim of securing the game as national and strengthening the All Black team today requires participation in a transnational league and players' involvement is controlled by the NZRU through the central contracting of the best 150 players and 5 coaches. This situation breaks with the tradition of securing professional teams' independence and the NZRU is in the exceptional situation of being the only buyer of rugby talent to the new competition.

To protect the local game against the effects of a professional player labour market, the NZRU swiftly sought Commerce Commission approval for the introduction of a player transfer system to take effect in 1997.[50] The transfer system included a three-tiered structure: a maximum of five transfers to a provincial union of which a maximum of three of these can be Super 12/14 players or above; a transfer fee cap set centrally limiting the fee a provincial union can demand for the release of a player, the maximum being NZ$100,000 for a current All Black player; and a transfer window of one month per year.[51] The introduction of a national transfer system and an All Black and coaching selection policy that precluded overseas-based player and coaches from selection in 1996, further sought to prevent the effects of a global professional player and coach labour market from exposing the economic inequality between provincial unions and the weakness of the smaller New Zealand market relative to the economic strength in the northern hemisphere.

Not surprisingly, New Zealand provincial unions reacted differently to the new professional regulations, governance structures and competitions. Added to their concerns over the introduction of a professional competition with new teams, was the change in governance structures which followed changes in amateur sports both nationally and internationally.[52] While the governance of both the provincial unions and the NZRU in the amateur period consisted of elected representatives from, respectively, the clubs and the provinces into unions and the national council, in the new professional era these bodies have been replaced with boards consisting of fewer members, some of whom are elected for their business expertise and sponsorship connections. Yet, despite this 'professionalization' of the governance of the game, the influence of the provincial unions was demonstrated in the new 'downsized' NZRU board in 1995. The new board shrank from being a 19-member council dominated by zone representatives to a 9-member board, again dominated by provincial or more accurately regional representatives and with only two independent members with business connections, despite recommendations in the Boston Consulting Report for greater delegation to a professional management team.[53]

Despite this show of power by the provincial unions, those unions not hosting Super 12/14 teams were concerned that the existing national competitions would diminish in popularity and thus damage their financial prospects, whereas those hosting Super 12/14 'franchises' were concerned that they would not control 'their' teams. The solutions to these tensions were to grant the provincial unions hosting Super 12/14 teams the gate-takings for their home games, which they were required to share with the other provincial unions in their region. Also, and after much deliberation, the NPC was revamped in 2006 into a two-league competition without promotion–relegation, effectively expanding the previous first division NPC group of provincial teams from 9 to 14 in the new Air NZ Cup competition, and separating it from the AA Heartland Championship involving the bottom 12 provincial teams. Lastly, the NZRU has introduced a salary cap for provincial teams which, it has argued, is a means to protect the smaller and less financially secure provincial unions and limit the wealthier provincial union from creating 'super' teams.[54] From 2006, provincial unions' 'A' team's total salary package cannot exceed NZ$2m. The cap includes provincial contracts and notional values for players depending on their ranking, less a discount for the most senior players including current All Black players and eight-year provincial veterans.

Despite these regulations in the national market, financial and competitive differences between provincial unions have intensified rather than decreased. The ability of provincial unions to strengthen their representative teams with 'imported' players has enabled the wealthiest to dominate the domestic player transfer market. The establishment of the five regional Super 12/14 teams as NZRU franchises subordinated to the All Black team, and their allocation to the five largest city-based unions has formally institutionalized the strength of these unions. In addition, by creating 'farm systems', through the establishment of rugby academies recruiting younger players directly from school competitions, these unions have created a new income source from the new transfer market and contributed to a weakening of the links between schools, clubs and provincial unions. This new flow to and development of player talent by these unions are critical for their maintenance of a Super 12/14 'franchise'.

The centralized contracting of players in New Zealand and the establishment of new teams to participate in a transnational league contrasted with the contracting of players by elite clubs in the northern hemisphere and reconfirmed their strength relative to the national unions. While professionalism was ushered in in the southern hemisphere by the national unions in the form of a transnational 'league' competition, the English RFU instituted a moratorium on player contracting in the first season of professional rugby union, although not all of the clubs respected it, as the case of Sir John Hall's purchase of Newcastle-Gosforth Rugby Club and subsequent contracting of players showed. The emergence of financial investments in English rugby union clubs began to characterize the field of northern hemisphere rugby and, not surprisingly, the greater sporting and economic opportunities offered by these clubs encouraged increasing migration of players and coaches to the northern hemisphere.[55] The leading English clubs formed the English Professional Rugby Union Clubs (EPRUC now Premiership Rugby) as a joint venture or oligarchy in December 1995 and this powerful group has since then been a key actor in negotiations over the new governance model in English rugby union.[56] While the introduction of professional contracts was met with concern by the northern hemisphere unions in 1995, leading to the English and Scottish national unions banning their top clubs from participating in the new European Cup,[57] northern hemisphere clubs' power relative to their national unions was highlighted several times in the first decade of professional rugby union. Despite the English and Scottish unions agreeing to join the European Cup in the 1996/1997 season, disputes between the RFU and the leading clubs continued and escalated to the point where premier clubs resisted releasing players for international duties and threatened to withdraw from the European Cup, a threat they acted upon in the 1998/1999 season.[58] The Premiership clubs' power relative to the RFU increased following an agreement between it and the Professional Rugby Players' Association. Attempts at establishing agreement between the Premiership clubs, the Professional Rugby Players' Association and the RFU included, first, the 1996 Mayfair Agreement, the 1998 Leicester agreement, the 2001 long-form agreement and the 2004 eliteplayer scheme, all of which offered brief periods of 'peace' between the elite English clubs and the RFU on matters including promotion and relegation between the top two divisions, and the release of players for internationals including the Six Nations, tours and tests.[59] In the midst of these negotiations divisions between the clubs increased as a result of the forming of the Premiership in 1998 and disagreements over the exact workings of the promotion–relegation structures. Most recently, in 2007 a new eight-year, £100m agreement between the Premiership clubs and the RFU looks likely to be ratified. It involves resolutions on international player release periods, financial compensation to the clubs, promotion and relegation to be guaranteed for the duration of the agreement, season structure, the establishment of a Professional Game Board (PGB) to run the professional game, and the streamlining of the England squad structure.[60]

Future uncertainty in a professional game

Despite the tensions in the northern hemisphere game, both clubs and national teams have continued to attract players and coaches from the southern hemisphere who perform in new transnational or expanded international competitions. Thus, while the game of rugby union continues to be one played by nations, its global span now exceeds the former 'orderly' Commonwealth community and New Zealand's place in it has become increasingly uncertain. As New Zealand's exceptionalism is celebrated in the new global game, its dominance is threatened. New Zealand's dominance in the professional era was initially achieved through Super 12/14 teams but, in the new era the All Black team's advantage is no longer assured, as it was in the amateur period, through the adoption of organizational aspects of professional sports. In the context of a professional game, organizational solutions at club and national levels, as Leifer has pointed out, no longer guarantee success. Success, as the global media companies understand it, is now measured by the success of the global game. The respective positions of nations and clubs within the game are therefore necessarily uncertain. The All Black team is not guaranteed a place among the top three rugby nations, as the recent 2007 RWC result shows, and this has increased the pressure on the NZRU to develop new strategies to further protect the national game and halt the All Black team's loss of ground to opposition in bigger overseas markets. The continued exceptionalism and dominance of New Zealand rugby is therefore threatened in the new global game.

Notes

1. The NZRFU dropped 'football' in its name in 2006. I use the new shorter abbreviation.
2. R. Thompson, *Retreat from Apartheid*; Fougere, 'Barbed Wire and Riot Squads'; S. Thompson, 'Challenging the Hegemony'; Nauright, 'Race, Rugby and Politics'; Richards, *Dancing on our Bones*.
3. Torres and Hager 'Competitive Sport, Evaluation Systems'.
4. Richardson, 'Rugby, Race and Empire'; Sinclair, *A Destiny Apart*; Phillips, *A Man's Country?*; Nauright, 'Sport, Manhood and Empire'; Zavos, *Ka mate! Ka mate!*; Fougere, 'Sport, Culture and Identity'; Perry, 'Cinderella and the Silver Mercedes'.
5. Leifer, *Making the Majors*.
6. The term 'exceptional' is drawn from the argument about the absence of soccer in the North American sports space in Markovits and Hellerman, *Offside. Soccer and American Exceptionalism*. Here the term is used to explain the different institutionalization of the game of rugby union.
7. Markovits and Hellerman, *Offside. Soccer and American Exceptionalism*, 29.
8. Dunning and Sheard, *Barbarians, Gentlemen and Players*; Collins, *Rugby's Great Split*.
9. Vamplew, *Pay up and Play up the Game*, 63.
10. Williams, 'Rugby Union', 315.
11. Ibid., 316.
12. Carman, *Ranfurly Shield Rugby*, 225, 238.
13. Gallaher and Stead. *The Complete Rugby Footballer*; Palenski, Chester, and McMillan, *The Encyclopaedia of New Zealand Rugby*, 2–3. David Gallaher was the captain of the All Black team that toured the northern hemisphere in 1905 and captained all tests except for the one against Ireland, due to injury, which was captained by John William ('Billy') Stead. Gallaher retired from playing after the tour and served as the sole Auckland selector between 1906 and 1916 and as New Zealand selector between 1907 and 1914.
14. This section draws on the work by Leifer, *Making the Majors*. Leifer distinguishes between enduring publics and infrequent crowds of the North American major leagues. He argues that the large number of people who daily pay attention to major league sports either by attending or viewing games on television or by reading the sports pages in the daily newspaper, listening to sports radio or buying major league products constitute a sports public by the regularity with which they are reactivated. He distinguishes these publics from the

crowds or gatherings of earlier times who attended to major league sports on an infrequent basis. His shows that the changes to the North American leagues are characterized by the constitution or creation of publics.

15. Coffey, *Canterbury XIII*.
16. Only three All Black teams toured Britain between the establishment of the NZRU and World War II. The first two, which toured Britain in 1905–6 and 1924–5, were later affectionately branded as 'The Originals' and 'The Invincibles'. In 1935 a third All Black team toured the northern hemisphere.
17. Dunning and Sheard, *Barbarians, Gentlemen and Players*; Collins, *Rugby's Great Split*.
18. Leifer, *Making the Majors*, 59.
19. Whitson, 'Circuits of Promotion', 58.
20. Fougere, 'Sport, Culture and Identity'.
21. O'Brien and Slack, 'Analysis of Change'; Malin, *Mud, Blood and Money*.
22. Smith and Williams, *Fields of Praise*, 474; Howe, 'Professionalism, Commercialism and the Rugby Club', 167; Williams, 'How Amateur was My Valley', 253; Williams, 'Rugby Union', 317; Collins, *Rugby's Great Split*, 165.
23. Ryan, *Forerunners of the All Blacks*.
24. Gallagher and Stead, *The Complete Rugby Footballer*, 37.
25. Ibid., 38–9.
26. Malin, *Mud, Blood and Money*; Malcolm, Sheard, and White, 'Changing Structure and Culture'.
27. Smith and Williams, *Fields of Praise*, 171.
28. Dunning and Sheard, *Barbarians, Gentlemen and Players*, 245; Williams, 'Rugby Union', 320–1.
29. Gallagher and Stead, *The Complete Rugby Footballer*, 40–1.
30. Ibid., 42, 47.
31. Vincent, 'Practical Imperialism'.
32. Gallagher and Stead, *The Complete Rugby Footballer*, 36.
33. Richardson, 'The Invention of a National Game'.
34. Swan, *History of New Zealand Rugby Football 1870–1945*; Swan, *History of New Zealand Rugby Football Volume 2*.
35. Gallagher and Stead, *The Complete Rugby Footballer*, 51.
36. Palenski et al., *The Encyclopaedia of New Zealand Rugby*, 230–6.
37. Dunning and Sheard, *Barbarians, Gentlemen and Players*, 263–4; Williams, 'Rugby Unions'.
38. Garland, *Fields of Glory*, 2.
39. Day, 'Sport, the Media and New Zealand'.
40. Becht, *A New Breed Rising*.
41. FitzSimons, *The Rugby Wars*; Hutchins, 'Rugby Wars'; Rowe, 'Rugby League in Australia'; Rowe, Lawrence, Miller and McKay, 'Global Sport?'.
42. Obel, 'Local and Global Publics'.
43. Markovits and Hellerman, *Offside. Soccer and American Exceptionalism*, 29.
44. McGovern, 'Globalization or Internationalization?'
45. NZRFU, *Handbook*, 89.
46. Misa, 'The Monday-to-Friday John Kirwan'; Howitt and Haworth, *Rugby Nomads*, 286, 288.
47. Jones, 'Full-time League'.
48. Dabscheck, 'Trying Times'.
49. Obel, 'Local and Global Publics'.
50. Rugby Union Players' Association.
51. Pengilley, 'Super League'.
52. Houlihan, *Sport, Policy and Politics*; Cameron, *Trail Blazers*; Whitson and Macintosh, 'Rational Planning'.
53. Boston Consulting Report, *Taking Rugby Union*. The NZRU commissioned the report from the Boston Consulting Group in 1993 the significance of which was that the union had gone to an independent firm to gain advice on how to protect the national position of the sport. Many of the recommendations in the report, not surprisingly given the centralized structure of New Zealand rugby union, were modelled on North American professional leagues rather than the community-based club model of European professional sports such as association football.

54. Robson, 'Crunching the Numbers'.
55. Obel and Austrin, 'End of Our National Game'.
56. Morgan, 'Optimizing the Structure'.
57. Cleary and Griffiths, *Rothmans Rugby Union Yearbook*.
58. Trelford, 'Brisbane Debacle'.
59. Baldock, 'Rugby Union'.
60. Cain, 'Peace Deal puts England'.

References

Baldock, A. 'Rugby Union: English Rugby's Club Versus Country Crisis Deepens', *Daily Post* October 28, 2005.

Becht, R. *A New Breed Rising: The Warriors Winfield Cup Challenge*. Auckland: HarperCollins, 1994.

Boston Consulting Group. *Taking Rugby Union into the 21st century: Strategic Choices Facing the New Zealand Rugby Football Union*. Auckland: The Boston Consulting Group – Incorporating Pappas Carter Evans & Koop, 1994.

Cain, N. 'Peace Deal Puts England on Level Footing with Rivals; Rugby Union: Guinness Premiership', *The Sunday Times*, Sepember 30, 2007.

Cameron, J. *Trail Blazers: Women Who Manage New Zealand Sport*. Christchurch: Sports Inclined, 1996.

Carman, A.H. *Ranfurly Shield Rugby: The Complete Book of Match Reports, Comments, Teams, Photographs and Records*. Wellington: Reed, 1960.

Cleary, M., and J. Griffiths. *Rothmans Rugby Union Yearbook 1996–97*. London: Headline Book Publishing, 1997.

Coffey, J. *Canterbury XIII: A Rugby League History*. Christchurch: Canterbury Rugby Football League, 1987.

Collins, T. *Rugby's Great Split: Class, Culture and the Origins of Rugby League Football*. London: Frank Cass, 1998.

Dabscheck, B. 'Trying Times: Collective Bargaining in Australian Rugby Union', *Sporting Traditions* 15 (1998): 25–49.

Day, P. 'Sport, the Media in New Zealand'. In *Sport, Society and Culture in New Zealand*, ed. B. Patterson. Victoria University, Stout Research Centre: Dunmore Press, 1999.

Dunning, E., and K. Sheard. *Barbarians, Gentlemen and Players: A Sociological Study of the Development of Rugby Football*. Wellington: Price Milburn, 1979.

FitzSimons, P. *The Rugby War*. Sydney: HarperSports, 1996.

Fougere, G. 'Barbed Wire and Riot Squads – What is Being Defended? The Springbok Tour of 1981', *New Zealand Journal of Cultural Studies Working Group Journal* 2 (1981): 11–14.

Fougere, G. 'Sport, Culture and Identity: The Case of Rugby Football'. In *Culture and Identity in New Zealand*, ed. D. Novitz and B. Willmott, Wellington: GP Books, 1989.

Gallaher, D., and W.J. Stead. *The Complete Rugby Footballer on the New Zealand System* (facsimile), Christchurch: Kiwi Publishers, 1906/1998.

Garland, S.J. *Fields of Glory: 21 NPC Years, 1976–1996*. Auckland: HarperCollins, 1997.

Houlihan, B. *Sport, Policy and Politics: A Comparative Analysis*. London: Routledge, 1997.

Howe, P.D. 'Professionalism, Commercialism and the Rugby Club: The Case of Pontypridd RFC'. In *Making the Rugby World. Race, Gender, Commerce*, ed. T.J.L. Chandler and J. Nauright. London: Frank Cass, 1999.

Howitt, B., and D. Haworth. *Rugby Nomads*. Auckland: HarperSports, 2002.

Hutchins, B. 'Rugby Wars: The Changing Face of Football', *Sporting Traditions* 13 (1996): 151–62.

Jones, S. 'Full-time League Role Not for Some', *Sunday Star-Times*, May 7, 1995 (London edition).

Leifer, E.M. *Making the Majors: The Transformation of Team Sports in America*. Cambridge, MA: Harvard University Press, 1995.

Malcolm, D., K. Sheard, and A. White. 'The Changing Structure and Culture of English Rugby Union', *Culture, Sport and Society* 3 (2000): 63–87.

Malin, I. *Mud, Blood and Money: English Rugby Goes Professional*. London: Mainstream Publishing, 1997.

Markovits, S., and S.L. Hellerman. *Offside. Soccer and American Exceptionalism.* Princeton, NJ: Princeton University Press, 2001.

McGovern, P. 'Globalization or Internationalization? Foreign Footballers in the English League, 1945–95', *Sociology* 36 (2002): 23–42.

Misa, T. 'The Monday-to-Friday John Kirwan', *North & South,* November, 1987.

Morgan, M. 'Optimizing the Structure of Elite Competitions in Professional Sport – Lessons from Rugby Union', *Managing Leisure* 7 (2002): 41–60.

Nauright, J. 'Sport, Manhood and Empire: British Response to the New Zealand Rugby Tour of 1905', *The International Journal of the History of Sport* 8 (1991): 239–55.

Nauright, J. 'Race, Rugby and Politics: New Zealand and South Africa 1921–1992', *Journal of Physical Education New Zealand* 26 (1993): 19–22.

NZRFU. *Handbook.* Wellington: New Zealand Rugby Football Union, 1994.

O'Brien, D., and T. Slack. 'An Analysis of Change in an Organizational Field: The Professionalization of English Rugby Union', *Journal of Sport Management* 17 (2003): 417–48.

Obel, C. 'Local and Global Publics: Shifting Popularity in Rugby Union and Rugby League'. In *Time Out? Leisure, Recreation and Tourism in New Zealand and Australia,* ed. H. Perkins and G. Cushman. Auckland: Longman, 1998.

Obel, C., and T. Austrin. 'The End of Our National Game: Rugby, Romance and Mobilities'. In *Tackling Rugby Myths: Rugby and New Zealand Society 1854–2004,* ed. G. Ryan, 173–93. Dunedin: Otago University Press, 2005.

Palenski, R., R.H. Chester, and N.A.C. McMillan. *The Encyclopaedia of New Zealand Rugby* (3rd ed.). Auckland: Hodder Moa Beckett, 1998.

Pengilley, W. 'Super League', *New Zealand Law Journal* (1998): 32–6.

Perry, N. 'Cinderella and the Silver Mercedes: Popular Culture and the Construction of National Identity'. In *Culture and Identity in New Zealand,* ed. D. Novitz and B. Willmott. Auckland: Bookprint Consultants, 1989.

Phillips, J. *A Man's Country? The Image of the Pakeha Male – A History.* Auckland: Penguin Books, 1987.

Richards, T. *Dancing on our Bones: New Zealand, South Africa, Rugby and Racism.* Wellington: Bridget Williams Books, 1999.

Richardson, L. 'Rugby, Race and Empire: The 1905 All Black Tour', *Historical News* 47 (1983): 1–5.

Richardson, L. 'The Invention of a National Game: The Struggle for Control', *History Now* 1 (1995): 1–8.

Robson, T. 'Crunching the Numbers', *Dominion Post,* November 4, 2005.

Rowe, D. 'Rugby League in Australia: The Super League Saga', *Journal of Sport and Social Issues* 21 (1997): 221–6.

Rowe, D., G. Lawrence, T. Miller, and J. McKay. 'Global Sport? Core Concern and Peripheral Vision', *Media, Culture and Society* 16 (1994): 661–75.

Rugby Union Players' Association v Commerce Commission (No 2). *New Zealand Law Review* 3 (1997): 301–29.

Ryan, G.J. *Forerunners of the All Blacks: The 1888–89 New Zealand Native Football Team in Britain, Australia and New Zealand.* Christchurch: Canterbury University Press, 1993.

Sinclair, K. *A Destiny Apart: New Zealand's Search for National Identity.* Wellington: Unwin Paperbacks and Port Nicholson Press, 1986.

Smith, D., and G. Williams. *Fields of Praise: The Official History of the Welsh Rugby Union, 1881–1981.* Cardiff: University of Wales Press on behalf of the Welsh Rugby Union, 1980.

Swan, A.C. *History of New Zealand Rugby Football 1870–1945.* Wellington: Reed, 1948.

Swan, A.C. *History of New Zealand Rugby Football Volume 2: 1946–1957.* Wellington: New Zealand Rugby Football Union, 1958.

Thompson, R. *Retreat from Apartheid: New Zealand's Sporting Contact with South Africa.* Wellington: Oxford University Press, 1975.

Thompson, S. 'Challenging the Hegemony: New Zealand Women's Opposition to Rugby and the Reproduction of a Capitalist Patriarchy', *International Review for the Sociology of Sport* 23 (1988): 205–11.

Torres, C., and P. Hager. 'Competitive Sport, Evaluation Systems, and Just Results: The Case of Rugby Union's Bonus-Point System', *Journal of the Philosophy of Sport* 32 (2005): 208–22.

Trelford, D. 'Brisbane Debacle due to Uncivil War', *Electronic Telegraph,* June 9, 1998.

Vamplew, W. *Pay Up and Play Up the Game: Professional Sport in Britain 1875–1914.* Cambridge: Cambridge University Press, 1988.

Vincent, G.T. 'Practical Imperialism: The Anglo-Welsh Rugby Tour of New Zealand', *The International Journal of the History of Sport* 15 (1998): 123–40.

Whitson, D. 'Circuits of Promotion: Media, Marketing and the Globalization of Sport'. In *Mediasport,* ed. L. A. Wenner. London: Routledge, 1998.

Whitson, D., and D. Macintosh. 'Rational Planning vs. Regional Interests: Professionalization of Canadian Sport'. *Canadian Public Policy* 15 (1989): 436–49.

Williams, G. 'How Amateur was My Valley: Professional Sport and National Identity in Wales 1890–1914'. *British Journal of Sport History* 2 (1985): 248–69.

Williams, G. 'Rugby Union'. In *Sport in Britain. A Social History,* ed. T. Mason. Cambridge: Cambridge University Press, 1989.

Zavos, S. *Ka mate! Ka mate!: New Zealand's Conquest of British Rugby.* Auckland: Viking, 1998.

The impact of televised football on stadium attendances in English and Spanish league football

Babatunde Buraimo[a], Juan Luis Paramio[b] and Carlos Campos[c]

[a]School of Sports, Tourism and the Outdoors, University of Central Lancashire, Preston, UK;
[b]Departamento de Educacion Física, Universidad Autonoma, Madrid, Cantoblanco, Spain;
[c]Universidad de Extremadura, Caceres, Spain

Since the early 1990s, sports broadcasting has emerged to become an important part of the sports industry. This is particularly important in the case of European football because revenues generated from the sport broadcast market tend to dominate those generated from gate attendance, which has traditionally been the main source of income for football clubs and leagues. In this article, we examine the broadcast regimes of the English Premier League and the Spanish Primera Liga (Liga de Primera Division) and examine the impacts that televising games from these leagues have had on their respective match-day attendances. We find that, although stadium attendances in both leagues respond to a series of factors in a similar manner, the effects of broadcasting on match-day attendance vary across the two leagues. We examine the economics issues and policy implications of these findings.

Introduction

European football has experienced dramatic changes since the early 1990s. Many of these changes have been brought about by developments within the broadcast market.[1] The development of direct-to-home satellite broadcasting created much needed competition with the dominant incumbent terrestrial broadcasters. This meant that leagues and clubs could generate greater rights fees from the sale of their broadcast rights. In England, the emergence of the British Sky Broadcasting (BSkyB) coincided with the breakaway of the top division in the English Football League. The loss of the Football League's top division saw the creation of the Football Association Premier League (FAPL), with competition commencing in 1992. From a sporting perspective, the breakaway had no discernable effect; promotion of the best and relegation of the worst-performing teams between the divisions were still features of league football. The real change was from an economic perspective. The breakaway of the top division was motivated by the top clubs, who wanted to put an end to the cross-subsidization of broadcast revenue that occurred across all divisions. Furthermore, these teams felt that league had not maximized potential earnings from the broadcast market.[2] BSkyB acquired the exclusive rights to broadcast 60 games per season on its subscription channels for five years at a cost of £304m.[3]

Spanish football's broadcasting experience constitutes an interesting, but partly divergent case with England's. At around the same time in Spain, the Liga Nacional de Fútbol Profesional (LNFP), who administered the broadcasting rights of all Primera and Segunda Division matches, invited bids for the rights to televised football for the first time. A mixture of existing public (TVE and regional TV channels) and new private (Tele 5, Antena 3 and Canal+) broadcasters,[4] as well as non-broadcasting companies (UNIVISION and DORNA) bid for these rights. Initially, DORNA,[5] an international management and marketing company founded one year before, obtained the exclusive rights to Spanish football for an eight-year period from 1990 to 1998 for a fee of 19 billion pesetas (around €114m). However, DORNA was facing financial problems and as a result, was forced to sell the rights to the Federation of Regional and Radio Organizations (FORTA), a network of regional public TV channels. Canal+ asked FORTA to extend the agreement allowing them to be part of the deal.[6] Unlike the FAPL's broadcasting rights, which were collectively sold to BSkyB for transmission on its subscription channels and later on its pay-per-view channel, the sale of broadcast rights by the LNFP since the early 1990s has experienced both collective and individual sales. As a unique example in Europe, the transmission of these matches has occurred not only on subscription and pay-per-view channels, but also on terrestrial free-to-air television. This article re-examines the impact of televised football on stadium attendance. In doing so, we provide a novel insight by examining the two major football leagues, the English Premier League and the Spanish Primera Liga, and the impact of transmission on different platforms.

Broadcasting in the Premier League and the Spanish Primera Liga

The relationship between league football and television is not new. As far back as the 1960s, the Football League reached an agreement with ITV, a network of independent regional commercial broadcasters, to televise 26 live matches. The league and the broadcaster, however, could not agree and the agreement was annulled.[7] It was not until 1983 that live transmission of league football in England began. The transmission of live matches was dominated by the incumbent broadcasters the British Broadcasting Corporation (BBC) and ITV. In negotiations over rights fees, the two broadcasters effectively operated a bilateral monopoly which limited the amount of broadcast revenue that the Football League could generate. The absence of competition within the broadcast market meant that economic power resided with the broadcast cartel. The agreement between the Football League and broadcasters was for two seasons at a cost of £5.2m. Clearly, the cartel had succeeded in suppressing the true market value for league football by acting as allies rather than competitors. Another contributor to this relationship was the limited broadcast spectrum. This meant that league football not only had to compete with other sports for (live) transmission, but also with other types of programming.[8] The Football League was of the knowledge that the rights fee was being suppressed and demanded a higher fee for renewal of the contract. The league and the broadcaster could not reach an agreement for the start of the 1985/1986 season and no football was televised during the first half of that season. Eventually, the league reached an agreement for the remainder of that season and six matches were televised. The cartel continued to exert its power for much of the 1980s. Surprisingly, the practices of BBC and ITV did not attract the attention of the UK competition authorities and the anticompetitive practices were never challenged.

It was during the latter part of this decade that advances in broadcast technology saw the emergence of DTH broadcasters. In the UK, the licences for DTH transmission were acquired by Sky Television and British Satellite Broadcasting (BSB). Sky Television was the dominant of the two, but it faced considerable competition from BSB in the pay television sector and even greater competition from the incumbent terrestrial broadcasters who provided television viewers with content for free.[9] The number of major broadcasters in the market was to reduce with the merger of Sky Television and BSB in 1990 to form British Sky Broadcasting (BSkyB). To offer distinctive programming that would allow BSkyB to justify its charge, significant investment occurred in the sports rights market and the acquisition of league football rights were to be the foundations of its new strategy. In 1992, BSkyB and the FAPL started a sport–broadcaster alliance that was to change the sports broadcast landscape.[10] Between 1992 and the 2006/2007 season, BSkyB acquired the exclusive rights to transmit FAPL football in the UK. This alliance has generated substantial levels of revenues for the league. Since the 2000/2001 season the FAPL's revenue from broadcasting has dominated those from match-day attendances or other commercial activities.[11] Figure 1 shows the breakdown of FAPL revenue from different sources from 1997/1998 to 2007/2008.

Many of the developments in broadcast technology that have occurred in Spain[12] mirror those in England and similarly, revenue from the broadcast sector dominated revenue from other sources (with the exception of 2005/2006) as shown in Figure 2. The policy initiatives implemented in the league, however, have been rather different. Until the 1995/1996 season, the statutes of LFP indicated that individual selling of broadcasting rights was not allowed. This requirement was modified in 1997 after

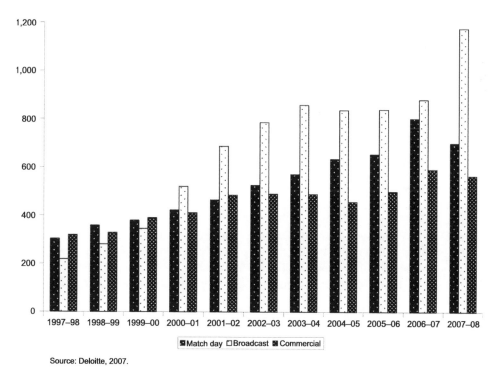

Source: Deloitte, 2007.

Figure 1.   English Premier League revenue by source and season (€m).

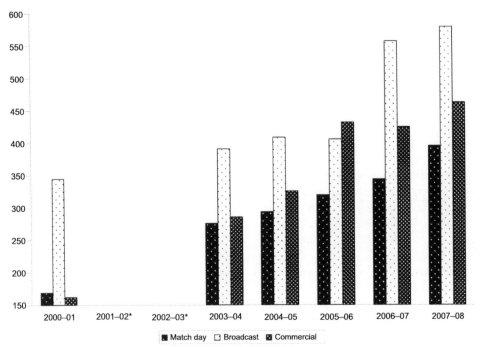

Figure 2.   Spanish Primera Liga revenue by source and season (€m).

pressure from the big clubs who wanted to put an end to the previous collective selling of rights. The bigger clubs demanded greater autonomy to exploit their market power in order to obtain more revenues.[13]

The league had to see out a long eight-season contract with the satellite broadcaster, Canal+, and the free-to-air broadcaster FORTA. Before the then-current contract between Canal+, FORTA and LNFP expired in 1998, the first TV football war between two Spanish big media communication groups, Grupo Prisa (owner of Canal+) and Grupo Z (owner of Antena 3) started in the summer of 1995. This was over the broadcasting rights of Primera and Segunda Division football clubs. Antena 3 wanted to gain entry into the football market and took a decisive and also risky approach offering five-year contracts to all Primera and Segunda Division clubs on an individual basis.[14] Such was the intensity of competition between Grupo Z and Grupo Prisa, with the former offering 155 billion pesetas for five years, while Canal+ was offering 250 billion pesetas for seven years that clearly increased the price for TV rights. This war meant more than football, and both broadcasters aspired to obtain the monopoly of the incoming Spanish digital TV market.

In August 1996, all parties involved in the war (football clubs, the Spanish Football Federation, FORTA, Canal+ and Antena 3) came to an agreement. As such, in December 1996, Canal+ launched a new digital channel, Canal Satelite Digital. Antena 3 also launched Via Digital to broadcast football matches of teams that they had the exclusive rights for. Telefonica bought the stakes of Antena 3 a year later.

The television rights war came to an end after the so-called 'Agreement of Christmas Eve' and as a clear example of horizontal integration between companies involved in football broadcasting, both digital platforms decided to join forces and formed a new TV platform, Digital Plus (a merge between Canal+ and Via Digital). This platform is part of a new company, Audiovisual Sport owned by Sogecable which has exercised the monopoly of rights exploitation of football matches until recently. One of effects of the competition for football rights has been the strong price increase from 19 billion pesetas in 1989 for an eight-year contract to an astonishing 50 billion pesetas per season for over a seven-year period. As a reaction, the Spanish government decided to launch a new TV Law (Ley 21/1997, Reguladora de las Emisiones y Retransmisiones de Competiciones y Acontecimientos Deportivos) to regulate football broadcasting. The transmission of matches on free-to-air is a require-ment by law as these are listed events and therefore the broadcast rights cannot be exclusively sold to a pay television operator. For this reason, a match per weekend was shown on free-to-air television by Mediapro through the Sexta channel and the right for others belonged to Audiovisual Sport. In July 2006, a new war over TV rights started between Audiovisual Sport and Mediapro.[15] Although Audiovisual Sport reached an agreement with Mediapro, a new media company, to provide it with the commercial rights for live free-to-air matches, highlights of league matches, and the international rights of football matches for €150m, this agreement was subject to several conditions. The Spanish competition authorities found evidence of abuse of the dominant position and the agreement was only allowed subject to a series of conditions, mainly providing access to third parties. At the time of writing, this conflict in Spain is ongoing and is affecting broadcasters, football clubs and undoubt-edly the viewing public.

In addition to individual selling in Spain, another difference between the football broadcast regimes of Spain and England is the volume of matches that were televised. During the first five seasons of the FAPL, only 60 matches were permitted to be screened. This was increased to 66 matches at the start of the 2001/2002 season and then to 88 matches in 2004/2005. At the start of the 2004/2005 season, an additional 50 matches were televised on pay-per-view. The gradual increase in the number of matches has been to keep the competition authorities at bay and prevent any investi-gation into what might be viewed as anticompetitive practices aimed at minimizing output and extracting as much consumer surplus as possible. By contrast, the abandon-ment of collective selling in favour of individual selling in Spain has seen the screen-ing of all matches. The majority of these are on a pay-per-view basis with a modest, but significant number on both free-to-air and subscription television. Currently, and per season, 38 matches are shown on a free-to-air basis, another 38 on a subscription basis and the remaining 308 on a pay-per-view basis. Therefore, Spanish football fans are able to view any of the 380 matches per season on television subject to meeting the cost.

Individual selling, as well as the volume of televised matches, mean that the total revenues generated by the Liga teams from the Spanish broadcast sector are modest in comparison with those generated by FAPL teams from the English broad-cast market. In all likelihood, it also means that the distribution of television reve-nue among the clubs in the Primera Division is likely to reflect the television audience ratings for those matches and therefore be skewed in favour of the popular big teams. In fact, during the 2005/2006 season, Barcelona's and Real Madrid's share of the total broadcasting income was 46%. Although this value includes broadcasting revenue from other sources such as other domestic and European competitions, the dominance with respect to this source is substantive. This is in contrast to England where 50% of FAPL broadcast revenue is shared equally, 25% is shared on merit based on end-of-season rankings and the remaining 25% distributed based on the frequency by which a team's matches were televised. Under the English system even the weakest team will extract a significant share of the total broadcast revenue.[16]

Televised football and stadium attendances

The principle focus in this article is to illuminate how transmission of live football on television impacts stadium attendance. The analysis offers new insight by, first, providing a comparative perspective of English and Spanish football. Second, the analysis is able to offer insights into the impact of transmission on different platforms, namely pay television, a subscription basis, and free-to-air. Furthermore, the analysis provides a view on how stadium attendees respond to different broadcasting regimes across the two leagues.

Previous studies have sought to provide an analytical insight into the impact of televising games on stadium attendance. One of the very first studies to investigate the impact of television on stadium attendances focused on the 1993/1994 FAPL season.[17] During this particular season, 60 matches were televised on BSkyB's subscription sports channels on Sunday afternoon and Monday evening. The analysis concluded that matches televised on Sunday had no significant impact on stadium attendance; however, those matches which were televised on Monday reduced attendances by 15%. The results of the analysis need to be interpreted with care for the following reason. During the 1993/1994 season (and many more seasons since), attendances at a significant number of matches would have been constrained by the capacities of the clubs' stadia. These constrained matches are not accounted for in their modelling of attendance. The reduction in attendances noted on Monday could equally (or at the very least partly) be apportioned to the fact that the match was scheduled on a weekday, when leisure time is relatively scarce compared with the weekend. Using the same season, a study by Kuypers notes the capacity constraints problem and uses an alternative modelling approach.[18] He finds no significant impact of live satellite broadcasting on attendance. The problem with the two aforementioned studies is that the period of analysis is a single season. Using a cross-sectional model in this manner can often result in biased estimates, particularly if the cross-section is peculiar and significantly different from other cross-sections. A means of overcoming this potential problem is to pool data across numerous cross-sections (or seasons).

A study of the inefficiency of cartels[19] in English soccer examined the effects of satellite broadcasting in different seasons and on different days of the week. It showed that, on the whole, satellite broadcasting had no systematic effect on attendance in the FAPL and further concluded that if there were any negative effects, teams were more than compensated by the facility fees they received from the broadcaster. A study by Allan using the data for a single club (Aston Villa) across six seasons found that live television coverage impacted negatively on attendance and reports a 7.75% decline. The extent to which this can be used to generalize for the rest of the league is open to questions because certain features of the subject club may be peculiar to it and therefore not be representative of other clubs within the league. A study[20] of attendance demand in Spanish football found that televised games, on both public and private (subscription) television, had a negative effect on attendances but the study does not differentiate between matches played at the weekend and during the week. This is important because the availability of leisure time will impact differently at the weekend compared with the week.

The conclusion that can be drawn from examination of these studies is that there is no firm consensus on the effects of broadcasting in football. This lack of consensus is not limited to football. Studies on the impact of broadcasting in sports have also failed to reach consensus. For example, an empirical analysis of the impact of television on National Collegiate Athletic Association (NCAA) American football found that televising games had the effect of improving attendances at games. Contrastingly, another empirical study of the same sport using the same data period found that televising games had a negative impact.[21] For a survey of studies on the demand for sports and the effects of television, see Borland and Macdonald's review.[22]

Variables and model specification

To model the effects of television on stadia attendance, data across four seasons in both the English Premier League and the Spanish Primera Liga are used. By pooling data from four different seasons, any peculiar effects that distinguish one season from another can be controlled. Also by using both the English and Spanish leagues, the responses of the two different audiences can be compared and the effects of different platforms can be analysed; in the case of English football, subscription television and in the case of Spanish football, subscription and free-to-air television.

A series of control variables are established. The first of these is intended to capture the habit persistence of fans. This represents those core fans likely to attend, all things being equal. Habit persistence for the home and away teams is taken as the (logarithm of the) mean home and away teams' attendances from the previous season. Across the two leagues, the impact of habit persistence is expected to be significant and positive with that of the home team having the greater effect.[23] Another control variable is the performance of the teams prior to the match. *A priori*, the size of the crowd is likely to be directly proportional to the performances of the two teams involved in the match. To capture the current performances of the two teams involved in the match, the points per game of the home and away teams prior to the match are used. By construction, the maximum value of points per game is 3 and the minimum value is 0 reflecting the zero points awarded for a loss and three points awarded for a win. In the event of a draw, each team is awarded a single point. As this measure cannot be computed for the first round of matches, these are omitted from the analysis.

Another important sporting variable is whether the match is of historical signifi- cance involving local rivals. There are many matches in English and Spanish football that motivate greater attendances because of the historical rivalry between teams. *Derby* is a dummy variable which takes the value 1 if the match is a derby and 0 otherwise. A further series of dummy variables are also used to capture the glamour of certain away teams. All other factors being equal, attendance is likely to be higher than normal if the visiting team is any one of the English or Spanish *super* teams. The nominated *super* teams are Arsenal, Liverpool and Manchester United in England and Barcelona, Real Madrid and Deportivo La Coruña in Spain. A dummy variable for each of aforementioned teams is equal to 1 if that team is the away team and 0 otherwise.

To distinguish between the effects of scheduling and broadcasting, a dummy variable to capture matches scheduled from Monday to Friday inclusively and not broadcast is included in the analysis. *Mid-week no TV* is equal to 1 if the match takes place on a weekday and is not televised and 0 otherwise. The final set of control variables are for the various months and different seasons. August along with September, and 2003/2004 are the reference months and seasons, respectively.

The focus variables capture the effects of broadcasting. Because both broadcast on a pay television platform – BSkyB in England and Canal + in Spain – Subscription weekend and Subscription midweek are dummy variables to capture matches shown on pay television channels at the weekend and during the week respectively. In addition, for Spain, where matches are also shown on free-to-air television, *free-to-air weekend* and *free-to-air weekday* capture matches televised on terrestrial channels at the weekend and during the week, respectively.

The empirical modelling of attendance needs to reflect structural issues within each of the leagues. For example, in the fours seasons from 2003/2004 to 2006/2007 of the FAPL, 61% of attendances at matches are at or near the capacities of the various stadia used in the league.[24] Another important consideration in the empirical estimations is team heterogeneity and omitted variables. To control for these factors, attendances are modelled using random effects. This allows the models to control for omitted factors such as ticket prices and team budgets that might cause coefficients to be biased. Some attendances in the Primera Liga suffer from being constrained, but not to the same degree as its English counterpart. In the same four seasons, fewer than 10% of those matches can be viewed as being constrained by the stadia's capacities. For this reason, an alternative model is used to model attendance in the Primera Liga, a Prais–Winsten regression with home team fixed effects. This overcomes the omitted variable bias and corrects of any autocorrelation between rounds of home matches.[25]

Empirical results

The results of the models for the English Premier League and Spanish Primera Liga are shown in Table 1. The coefficients and corresponding t statistics of the control variables used in the model are as expected. With respect to habit persistence, the (logarithm of the) previous season's mean attendances intended to capture persistence by supporters is significant in explaining match-day attendance for both leagues. This level of persistence can be viewed as the base level of core support given the identities of the two teams competing. Habit persistence by the home team more readily transformed into match-day attendance in the Spanish Primera League compared with the English Premier League. The reverse, however, is true for the away team. This may be due the relatively shorter distances that away fans have to travel in the English league compared with in Spain. As expected, the performances of the teams prior to the match influences match-day attendance; the exception being the away team's performance in the English Premier League. Attendances at matches in both leagues respond positively to better performances by the home team. In the Primera Liga, attendances also improve if the points per game of the away team are better. Derby matches have a positive influence on match-day attendance in both leagues. In the English league, a derby match, *ceteris paribus*, improves match-day attendances by an estimated 8.3% compared with non-derby matches. This rises to 12.4% in the Spanish league. It would seem that supporters in both leagues value

Table 1.   Random effect Tobit model for English Premier League and Prais–Winsten model for Spanish Primera Liga.

Dependent variable is Ln (attendance)	English Premier League		Spanish Primera Liga	
Explanatory variable	Coefficient	t statistic	Coefficient	t statistic
Ln(home teams mean attendance)	0.259	8.84	0.870	42.37
Ln(away teams mean attendance)	0.087	6.40	0.028	2.71
Home team's points per game	0.031	3.01	0.032	2.06
Away team's points per game	0.009	1.05	0.034	3.20
Derby	0.083	3.28	0.124	6.63
Mid-week no TV	−0.038	−3.28	−0.071	−3.97
Arsenal as away team	0.089	3.91		
Chelsea as away team	0.081	3.33		
Liverpool as away team	0.187	6.57		
Manchester United as away team	0.125	4.22		
Barcelona as away team			0.177	7.03
Deportiva La Coruña as away team			0.038	1.75
Real Madrid as away team			0.173	7.07
October	0.011	0.69	−0.043	−1.91
November	0.002	0.12	−0.035	−1.29
December	0.025	1.71	−0.085	−3.03
January	0.009	0.57	−0.041	−1.42
February	0.035	2.04	−0.065	−2.27
March	0.026	1.51	−0.043	−1.55
April	0.046	3.05	−0.034	−1.25
May	0.104	4.81	−0.007	−0.27
June			−0.187	−2.99
2004/2005	0.003	0.21	0.017	0.81
2005/2006	−0.033	−2.79	−0.025	−1.13
2006/2007	−0.053	−4.27	0.006	0.29
Constant	6.716	20.07	0.996	4.22
Subscription weekend	−0.029	−2.15	−0.082	−1.54
Subscription weekday	−0.083	−5.36	−0.020	−1.19
Free-to-air weekend			−0.038	−2.18
Free-to-air weekday			−0.186	−4.04
Home team fixed effects	Significant		Significant	
Number of observations	1480		1480	
Constrained observations	908			

the added impetus that is generated from matches involving teams with historical rivalry. As expected, matches which are scheduled for weekdays and not televised attract fewer audiences than those scheduled for the weekend. The reduction in match-day attendance is 3.8 and 7.1% in England and Spain, respectively. This provides some insight for league administrators when it comes to scheduling fixtures and the cost imposed on teams who have their matches (re)schedule outside Saturday or Sunday.

Given the status of some teams in both England and Spain as super teams, it is not surprising that if such teams are the visitors, the home teams is, on average, likely to generate attendances that are greater than normal. All the teams nominated as super teams generated significant coefficients at the 1% level with the exception of Deportiva La Coruña, which was significant at the 10% level. In the FAPL, mean attendance improved by 8.9% if the away team was Arsenal. If the away team was Chelsea, Liverpool or Manchester United, the corresponding improvements were 8.1, 18.7 and 12.5%, respectively. This shows that in the English Premier League, fans find Liverpool to be the most desirable team to host as visitors. In the Primera Liga, Barcelona and Real Madrid have similar effects, improving match-day attendances by 17.7 and 17.3% when compared with other visiting teams. This is not too surprising given that all these teams, with the exception of Chelsea, are members of G-14, an elite group of European football clubs.

The other control variables within the model are the month and season dummies. These generally capture the month and seasonal trend within the two leagues. Close inspection of the month dummies shows that in England, as the season draws to a close, match-day attendances rise, particularly for matches in April and May compared with attendances in August and September. This is also the case in Spain, although the end-of-season increase in attendances follows a severe decline in the previous months.

The last group of variables is the focus broadcasting variables. The coefficient of *Subscription weekend* is negative and significant at the 10% level in the FAPL. This suggests that if matches are televised on Saturday or Sunday on BSkyB's subscription channel, attendances are, on average, 2.9% lower compared with weekend matches that are not televised. *Subscription weekday* also attracts a negative coefficient but of a larger magnitude and is significant at the 1% level. The interpretation is that matches televised on weekdays attract 8.3% fewer audiences compared with those not televised taking place at the weekend. Consequently, televising FAPL matches on BSkyB's subscription channel is harmful to match-day attendances. Given the facility fees provided by BSkyB to clubs whose matches are televised, any loss in gate attendance revenue caused by television is more than likely to be compensated for.

In Spain, the broadcasting regime is different, given that matches are televised on free-to-air as well as subscription television. In contrast to the FAPL, televising Spanish matches on a subscription basis has no significant effect on match-day attendances compared with other matches that were televised on pay-per-view. By contrast, matches that are televised on free-to-air during the week and at the weekend caused a decline in attendance. If a match is to be televised during the week, its attendance is estimated to fall by 18.6% compared with a match on pay-per-view. If the match is at the weekend, attendance is estimated to fall by 3.8%.[26] The results of the analysis show that English and Spanish football attendances are both affected by television but in different ways. The differences are, in part, caused by the different broadcast regimes and also by the different sets preference expressed by the two sets of supporters.

Discussion and policy implications

There are a number of policy implications surrounding broadcasting and professional football, particularly in the context of the premier leagues in England and Spain. Of direct inference from the results of this study is the impact of televised live matches on stadium attendance. Leagues and teams need to be aware of the short- and long-term impacts that televised matches are likely to have on their attendances. Although revenue from match-day attendance is dominated by that achieved from television, it still remains a significant and important portion of total revenue (see Figures 1 and 2). The effect estimated in this article is the direct short-term impact of television, which on the whole is negative.[27] Consequently, the results can be used to assess the extent to which compensation in the form of a rights fee is adequate for leagues and individual clubs. Furthermore, improvements in economic efficiency and optimization can be achieved if league administrators and broadcasters select and schedule matches in a manner that minimizes the impact of television on match-day attendance and at the same time maximizes television audience ratings. This is an area for further research.

With regards to optimizing attendances at matches selected for television, there is also an important dimension that should be considered. That is the quality of the televised product. The quality of televised matches is dependent not only on the quality of the two teams involved in the contest, but also on the stadium's atmosphere, provided by the fans. Hence the quality of the televised product, all things being equal, can be enhanced by ensuring that the number of fans in the stadium is maximized.[28] The relationship between stadium and television is therefore a complex one[29] that league administrators should be aware of in the management of sport and broadcasting.

Another important policy implication is the organization and sale of television rights. In England, the sale of rights has been collective by the FAPL acting on behalf of its incumbent members. Acting as a cartel in this manner allows the league to maximize its revenue by restricting the number of televised matches, and exercising its monopoly in the sale of rights.[30] In fact, the collective sale of FAPL television rights has caught the attention of competition authorities in England and at the European level. The Spanish experience is different in this respect. Aspects of the league's broadcasting rights are sold collectively, whereas others are sold on an individual basis. This no doubt creates difficulties for broadcasters when scheduling matches. There is also the added complexity of how much teams should be compensated. This can distort levels of competitive balance reinforcing the dominance of a small number of big teams within the league as they generate more substantially more revenue from the individual sales of their broadcast rights compared with their smaller counterparts.

Concluding remarks

The analysis of this study has examined the impact of televised football on match-day attendance in the English FAPL and the Spanish Primera Liga. Given that many of the matches played in the Premier League are constrained by the various capacities of the stadia, special measures in modelling attendances are necessary and a Tobit model is used. Although some matches are constrained in Spain, the extent of the problem does not merit the use of a Tobit model and a Prais–Winsten regression model is used instead. One of the benefits of this model is that the correlation between different rounds of home matches can be taken into account. In England, the analysis shows that attendances in the FAPL are negatively affected by televised games on BSkyB's subscription service. Those matches televised at the weekend are estimated to reduce stadium attendance by 3% and those televised on weekdays by 8%, compared with non-televised matches at the weekend.

By comparison, all matches in the Primera Liga are televised and are across three different platforms: pay-per-view, subscription and free-to-air. Because the data period in the analysis does not comprise any matches that were not televised, it is not possible to comment as to whether matches televised on pay-per-view television have any adverse impact on attendance. The analysis shows that the effect of matches televised on subscription television is no different from those matches televised on a pay-per-view basis. The biggest impact results from those matches shown on free-to-air television. By statute, a match from each round must be televised on terrestrial television because such matches are listed events. When such matches are televised at the weekend, attendances fall by approximately 4%. For matches televised on free-to-air during the week, the estimated impact on stadium attendance is 19%. The analysis shows that stadium attendances in both countries are adversely affected when matches are selected for live broadcast. The decision as to whether matches should be broadcast and when this should take place ultimately depends on the size of the television audiences and the extent to which the teams are compensated for their losses.

Notes

1. See, for more details, of TV broadcasting rights and football, Solberg, 'Sports Broadcasting'; Solberg, 'TV Sports Broadcasting'.
2. Dobson and Goddard, *The Economics of Football.*
3. The headline figure of £304 was not realized as this included the rights for overseas broadcast, which was not taken up by BskyB (Baimbridge, Cameron, and Dawson, 'Satellite Television and the Demand for Football').
4. In 1989, the Spanish Government favoured, for the first time, the emergence of the commercial TV channels in Spain (Ley de la Televisión Privada). As part of this law, two terrestrial broadcasters Antena 3, Tele 5 and a DTH satellite, Canal+ entered in the Spanish TV market. As stated in the discussion, Canal+ used football and in particular, getting the broadcasting rights of Spanish football to improve its position in the Spanish TV sector (see Bonaut, 'Relación de Necesidad entre Deporte y Televisión').
5. As was found in http://www.dorna.com/ (Accessed October 22, 2007), Dorna states that 'this company is the exclusive holder of all commercial and TV rights of the MotoGP World Championship since 1992, and from 2001 also holds the rights of the SX World Championship. The company also participates in the management and marketing of other motorsports events: Spanish Road Racing Championship (CEV), British Superbike Championship (BSB) and Trials World Championships (Indoor and Ooutdoor)'.
6. This agreement has clearly been more beneficial to Canal+ which has extended the number of subscribers to over 1.4 million. See also Ascari and Gagnepain, 'Spansih Football'.
7. Forrest, Simmons, and Szymanski, 'Broadcasting, Attendance and the Inefficiency of Cartels'.
8. See Whannel, 'The Unholy Alliance'.
9. The BBC is a state broadcaster and generates its revenue from licence fee payable by all households with a television. ITV, by contrast, is commercial broadcaster which generates its revenue by selling advertising space during programming. Both broadcasters are able to offer programme to audience with no direct charge.
10. The exclusive acquisition of FAPL matches by BSkyB has through the years attracted the attention of competition authorities in both the UK and Europe. In 1999, the FAPL had to justify the collective selling of its television rights to BSkyB, which foreclosed the involvement of other would-be broadcasters and maintained BSkyB's monopoly in this market. The Restrictive Practices Court ruled in favour of the league, who argued that collective selling was necessary to maintain competitive balance within the league. Since this ruling, the European Competition Commission has taken steps to abolish the exclusive acquisition of FAPL by BSkyB. In 2007/2008, Setanta, Irish based pay television broadcaster, acquired a portion of FAPL for transmission in the UK.

11. See Buraimo, 'Stadium Attendance and Television Audience Demand in English League Football'; Buraimo, Simmons and Szymanski (2006) for a review of the finances of English football teams.

12. The introduction of TV in Spain in 1956 clearly affected the economies of football clubs. As an example, the first televised match was Barcelona versus Real Madrid on 15 February 1956 at Nou Camp. Barcelona got 150,000 pesata (less than €1000) for the television rights to this match (see Paramio, Buraimo and Campos, 'From the Modern to the Post-modern Stadia'). From this time until 1983 when the so called the Law of Third Channel opened the market to other broadcasters, the Spanish public service broadcaster, Television Española (TVE) exercised the monopoly over the football rights which in many cases influenced negatively the rights fees for football clubs.

13. See Ascari and Gagnepain, 'Spanish Football'; Barajas, *El Valor Económico del Fútbol*.

14. These negotiations with all clubs forced to LNFP to change their regulations to allow individual football teams to negotiate individually their contracts with broadcasters (Campos, *Estrategias de Saneamiento en el Deporte Profesional*).

15. See more details on the process and their effects on the economies of football clubs and the competitive balance of Spanish football in http: www.iusport.es (accessed October 22, 2007). This conflict is still under revision by the Spanish judicial system. Going back to 2003, most of the Spanish teams as part of what is known as G-30 (formed by all 22 clubs in the Second Division plus eight clubs like Mallorca, Celta Vigo, Racing Santander, Osasuna, Valladolid, Recreativo, Rayo Vallecano and Alaves), except the big teams, were forced to sign a new contract with Sogecable with less revenues. This situation has created a profound division between Spanish football clubs who are split between two groups named as G-30 and G-12 (which includes, among others, clubs like Real Madrid, Barcelona or Atletico de Madrid). This situation was modified after Mediapro bought the rights of most teams. For example, in June 2006, Mediapro obtained the rights to FC Barcelona for €105m per year for a seven-year contract (2008 to 2013) and later, in November, obtained got the rights to Real Madrid for 1100m for a seven-year period. Similarly, Mediapro has bought the rights to other Primera Division teams like Zaragoza, Racing Santander, Athletic Bilbao and Sevilla. However, the revenues for these deals are much lower than with those with Barcelona and Real Madrid.

16. During the 2005/2006 season, Watford, who were places 20 and accrued the smallest share, received 3.6% of the broadcast revenue available to the 20 teams. Manchester United accrued the largest proportion of 6.9%.

17. See Baimbridge, Cameron, and Dawson, 'Satellite Television and the Demand for Football'

18. Kuypers (*The Beautiful Game?*) uses a Tobit model which takes into account that the distribution of attendances is truncated and some values of attendance cannot be observed because of the constraining size of some stadia.

19. Forrest, Simmons and Szymanski, 'Broadcasting, Attendance and the Inefficiency of Cartels'.

20. See García and Rodríguez, 'The Determinants of Football Match Attendance Revisited'.

21. See Kaempfer and Pacey, 'Televising College Football'; Fizel and Bennett, 'The Impact of College Football Telecasts on College Football Attendance'.

22. Borland and Macdonald, 'Demand for Sport'.

23. See Forrest and Simmons, 'New Issues in Attendance Demand'.

24. Often in English league football, parts of the stadia are left empty for safety and security, separating the fans of the home and away teams. Therefore, attendances which are at or above 95% of the stadia's capacity are taken to be constrained.

25. See Greene, *Econometric Analysis*.

26. This is significant at the 5% level.

27. There is likely to be a long-term dimension to the impact of televised matches on stadium attendance, however, a long-run time series analysis of several seasons is necessary to assess such long-term effects.

28. See Buraimo, 'Stadium Attendance and Television Audience Demand in English League Football'.

29. Fans are needed in the stadium to provide atmosphere and enhance the quality of the product for television, however, televising games causes a reduction in attendances at the stadium.

30. See Forrest, Simmons and Szymanski, 'Broadcasting, Attendance and the Inefficiency of Cartels' for a discussion on the inefficiencies of cartel with specific reference to the FAPL.

References

Ascari, G., and Gagnepain P. 'Spanish football' *Journal of Sports Economics,* 7, no. 1 (2006): 76–89.

Baimbridge, M., Cameron, S., and Dawson, P. 'Satellite Television and the Demand for Football: A Whole New Ball Game?' *Scottish Journal of Political Economy,* 43, no. 3 (1996): 317–333.

Barajas, A. *El Valor Económico del Fútbol. Radiografía Financiera del Fútbol Profesional,* EUNSA: Pamplona Navarra, 2005.

Bonaut, J., 'Relación de Necesidad entre Deporte y Televisión: La Influencia del Deporte en la Evolución Histórica de la Televisión en España (1956–1989)' *Comunicazione Sociali,* 28, no. 1 (2006): 60–70.

Borland, J. and Macdonald, R. 'Demand for sport' *Oxford Review of Economic Policy,* 19, no. 4 (2003): 478–502.

Buraimo, B. 'Stadium attendance and television audience demand in English league football' *Managerial and Decision Economics,* 29, no. 6 (2009): 513–523.

Buraimo, B., Simmons, R., and Szymanski, S. 'English Football' *Journal of Sports Economics,* 7, no. 1 (2006): 29–46

Campos, C. *Estrategias de Saneamiento en el Deporte Profesional (Turnaround Strategies in Professional Sport),* Wanceleum: Sevilla, 2006.

Deloitte, *Annual review of football finance,* Manchester: Deloitte, 2007.

Dobson, S., and Goddard, J. *The economics of football,* Cambridge: Cambridge University Press, 2001.

Fizel, J., and Bennett, R. 'The impact of college football telecasts on college football attendance' *Social Science Quarterly,* 70, no. 4 (1989): 980–988.

Forrest, D., and Simmons, R. 'New issues in attendance demand: the case of the English football league' *Journal of Sports Economics,* 7, no. 3 (2006): 247–266.

Forrest, D. Simmons, R., and Szymanski, S. 'Broadcasting, attendance and the inefficiency of cartels' *Review of Industrial Organization,* 24, no. 3 (2004): 243–265.

García, J., and Rodríguez, P. 'The determinants of football match attendance revisited: empirical evidence from the Spanish football league' *Journal of Sports Economics,* 3, no. 1 (2002): 18–38.

Greene, W. *Econometric Analysis,* New Jersey: Prentice Hall, 2003.

Kaempfer, W., and Pacey, P. 'Televising college football: the complementarity of attendance and viewing' *Social Science Quarterly,* 67, no. 1 (1986): 176–185

Kuypers, T. *The beautiful game? An econometric study of why people watch English football,* (Discussion Paper in Economics No. 96-01). London: University College London, 1996.

Paramio, J.L., Buraimo, B., and Campos, C. 'From the modern to the postmodern stadia: The Development of Football Stadia in Europe', *Sport in Society* 11, no. 5 (2008): 517–534.

Solberg, H.A. 'Sports Broadcasting'. In *The Business of Sport Management,* edited by J. Beech and S. Chadwick. Harlow, Prentice Hall, 2004: 368–393

Solberg, H.A., and Helland, K. 'TV Sport Broadcasting: The role of Business Integration'. In Sports Business Conference, London, 2007, 17 April.

Whannel, G. 'The unholy alliance: notes on television and the remaking of British sport 1965–85' *Leisure Studies,* 5, no. 2 (1986): 129–145.

The model of governance at FC Barcelona: balancing member democracy, commercial strategy, corporate social responsibility and sporting performance

Sean Hamil[a], Geoff Walters[a] and Lee Watson[b]

[a]Department of Management, Birkbeck, University of London, London, UK; [b]Department of Iberian and Latin American Studies, Birkbeck, University of London, London, UK.

This article presents an in-depth case study of the governance of FC Barcelona up to the end of 2008. An historical account of how the membership-ownership model at FC Barcelona was threatened during the presidency of Josep Núñez between 1978 and 2000 is first presented. An analysis of the conditions over 2000–2003 which led to the election in 2003 of Joan Laporta as club president, on a radical platform for reform of the governance of the club, is then presented. A detailed analysis of the governance and management of FC Barcelona over the 2003–2008 period is then outlined, with the analysis focusing on four key strategic areas: the prioritisation of sporting success; the re-assertion of member democracy and improvements in transparency of club governance; the implementation of a commercial strategy designed to generate increased revenues; and the development of an innovative series of corporate social responsibility initiatives. The analysis concludes with a critical consideration of the reasons why the mutual ownership and governance structure of FC Barcelona does not appear to have hampered its ability to compete in financial and sporting terms and whether this model could be replicated in the English Premier League.

Between 2003 and 2008 a number of clubs in the English Premier League were the subject of takeovers by private investors, mainly from outside the UK; Chelsea by Russian oligarch Roman Abramovich (2003); Manchester United by the American Glazer family, owners of the Tampa Bay Buccaneers NFL football franchise (2005); Portsmouth by Russian émigré businessman Alexandre Gaydamak (2006 – since sold to a succession of other overseas investors before collapsing into financial administration); Aston Villa, by the American businessman Randy Lerner, owner of the Cleveland Browns NFL franchise (2006); Sunderland, by an Irish business consortium led by former Sunderland player Niall Quinn (2006 – since acquired by an American investor); West Ham United initially purchased as part of an Icelandic business consortium (2006) and now jointly owned by UK and Icelandic Investors; Liverpool, by American businessmen Tom Hicks (owner of the Texas Rangers Major League Baseball [MLB] franchise and the Dallas Stars National Hockey League [NHL] franchise) and George Gillett (owner of the Montreal Canadiens NHL franchise [2007]); Manchester City, taken over by Thaksin Shinawatra, the former prime minister of Thailand (2007) and later sold to investors from Abu Dhabi (2008); and Newcastle United, owned by English sporting goods retail entrepreneur Mike Ashley (owner of the Sports Direct retail chain, and a number of branded sports goods companies including the Lonsdale boxing brand [2007]). A popular justification for such takeovers of English football clubs by million-aire private owners is that, in order to be successful at the highest level, a club needs to be able to attract major private investment to allow it to compete effectively in the international football player labour market; a club therefore needs to be constituted as a limited company by shares to allow new equity investment.

It is somewhat ironic that the first and third largest clubs in Europe in the 2006/2007 season, Real Madrid and FC Barcelona (as measured by financial turnover[1]), are in fact not-for-profit sporting clubs owned by their members and are not private limited companies. This raises a critical question – how then can they afford to compete both financially and in terms of sporting performance when their mutually owned structure specifically precludes the raising of share capital to expand the finan-cial base of their organizations? This article addresses this question in relation to the recent history of FC Barcelona (sometimes known simply as Barça).

Based in the Catalonian region of Spain, as of 30 June 2008, FC Barcelona had 162,979 members, or *socios*, with 17% being foreigners.[2] The *socios* pay an annual fee that gives them the right to elect members to the board, headed by a president, who together then oversee the administration of the club. FC Barcelona also repre-sents a *polideportivo* – a multi-sports club – meaning that in addition to the football team, there are other professional teams in sports such as basketball, roller hockey, handball and futsal, as well as amateur teams in sports such as rugby, cycling, athlet-ics, volleyball and baseball.[3] The mutually owned FC Barcelona therefore effectively subsidises other nonfootball areas of sporting endeavour in the club. The club motto 'més que un club' – meaning 'more than a club' – reflects the fact that the role of FC Barcelona is not restricted to football, instead extending to all aspects of Catalan society. In effect, FC Barcelona is a cultural as well as sporting institution which enjoys a wider political significance in Catalan society; it is indeed more than just a football club, and certainly very different from a North American sports entertain-ment franchise.[4]

This article begins by briefly discussing the historical role of FC Barcelona as a symbol of Catalan nationalism, in particular during the years in which Spain was under the rule of the fascist dictator General Franco. It then considers how the membership model at FC Barcelona was threatened during the presidency of Josep Núñez who, between 1978 and 2000, 'systematically eroded the democracy enshrined in the club statutes'.[5] This led to the formation of L'Elefant Blau, an organization that campaigned for member democracy. The spokesman and key figure of L'Elefant Blau, Joan Laporta, was elected president of FC Barcelona in 2003 on a radical platform for change. At that point in time, FC Barcelona was in a precarious position, trailing Spanish rivals Real Madrid and other clubs in Europe in both sporting (having won no trophies for four years) and commercial performance (slipping to 13th largest club in Europe in terms of financial turnover[6]). This article considers the model of governance that Joan Laporta and his board of directors implemented at FC Barcelona over the 2003–2008 period, concentrating on four key strategic areas:

(1) The prioritization of sporting success, with the playing and football management team rebuilt and refinanced with positive results. FC Barcelona won successive Spanish La Liga titles in 2005 and 2006, in addition to Europe's premier club competition, the Champions League, in 2006 and again in 2009.

(2) The reassertion of member democracy and improvements in transparency of club governance, and the establishment of a campaign – 'The Big Challenge' (El Grand Repte) – to increase club membership as a vehicle to build the financial strength of the club.

(3) The implementation of a commercial strategy designed to generate increased revenues from off-field activities and improve financial performance. Between 2003 and 2008, financial turnover increased from €123.4m to €308.8m,[7] indicating that the strategy had enjoyed some success and had not been impeded by FC Barcelona's mutual ownership structure.

(4) In tandem with an aggressive commercial strategy, the implementation of an innovative series of corporate social responsibility initiatives as part of a carefully crafted strategy designed to demonstrate that it is indeed an institution that explicitly recognises a set of wider social and cultural obligations.

This article concludes with a critical consideration of the reasons why the untypical mutual ownership and governance structure of FC Barcelona did not appear to have hampered its ability to compete in financial and sporting terms over the 2003–2008 period. It also reflects on what, if any, have been the consequences of an attempt to remove Joan Laporta as president of Barcelona in July 2008, two years before the end of his scheduled tenure. Does this demonstrate that the mutually owned model of ownership is inherently political unstable? Or is this just a manifestation of the normal 'rough and tumble' of football politics played out in a more accountable arena than might be found in a privately owned football club?

The article concludes by posing the question; could the mutually owned model utilized by FC Barcelona work effectively at a major English Premiership club?

FC Barcelona: the most vibrant institutional expression of Catalan nationalism

FC Barcelona was founded in 1899 by a Swiss businessman, Hans Kamper. However, upon his arrival in Barcelona he adopted the Catalan name Joan Gamper – the name under which he has been acknowledged as the founder of FC Barcelona.[8] According to many texts which detail the club's history, his identification and devotion to a Catalan nationalism ensured that the club became a symbol for Catalan society. It should be noted that the majority of published works on FC Barcelona have a tendency to be written by fans for fans and thus are predisposed to be somewhat enthusiastic about the club and its heritage, adding to the mythologies of the football club's foundation. For example, few contemporary sources acknowledge the fact that Gamper actually left the club and ceased active participation in 1906.[9] However, as a result of an economic downturn that led to large-scale unemployment and economic hardship, the football club was struggling for funding and support by the end of the decade. Football throughout the city went into brief decline and many clubs, like rival FC Català, folded altogether. Many club histories report that at a club meeting in 1908, with membership at just 34 *socios* and on the verge of disintegration, Gamper intervened and returned to the club promising to save it from insolvency.[10]

Reinstated as club president from 1908 to 1925, Gamper resurrected the club and ensured that it became the most important sports' institution in the city. More importantly, he developed the club's cultural identity and laid the foundations upon which FC Barcelona's current identity and myths have been founded by exploiting the links between the football club and the Catalan nationalist movement. Through his aggressive search for funding, Gamper promoted the team as a 'Catalan' club in order to garner support from Barcelona's professional middle class who were increasingly mobilizing behind a nationalist ideology in the form of the Catalan nationalist and conservative Lliga Regionalista. Consequently, through cultivating a distinctly Catalanist identity, connections with the Lliga and the local government were developed and reinforced. With the Lliga in the ascendancy at the time, Gamper already had business connections with many of its key members who were also prominent professionals in the city.

However, it is undisputed that under Gamper, the club did eventually support initiatives designed to reinvigorate the cultural identity of Catalonia, e.g. campaigns for Catalan language schools, Catalan language courses for club members, and campaigns for independence from Spain.[11]

The status of FC Barcelona as one of the most prominent symbols of Catalan nationalism resulted in a six-month ban being placed on the football club in 1925 following the military coup led by General Rivera and the subsequent sustained campaign against Catalan nationalism.[12] FC Barcelona suffered further during the harsh environment of General Franco's fascist dictatorship when expressions of Catalan identity were suppressed as the regime moved swiftly to impose a broad spectrum of fascist symbols and rituals upon the sporting arena. The president of the Spanish football federation decreed that all clubs in Spain would be reconfigured in terms of 'obedience, submission and military discipline' in an attempt to mobilize and to forge the citizens of Spain in the national spirit and new values of the dictatorship.[13] For instance, in order to remove all traces of regional identity, the Catalan club was forced to change its name to the more Castilian sounding 'Barcelona Club de Fútbol' and to remove the Catalan flag from the club badge, while the use of the flag itself at the club's Nou Camp stadium was banned. The Franco regime was also responsible for appointing board members in a bid to counteract any future dissidence against the dictatorship regime.[14] The club only reverted back to its original name of FC Barcelona following Franco's death in 1975.

During the period in which General Franco was in power, FC Barcelona continued to strongly represent Catalan national identity and became a rallying point for regional identity and democratic values.[15] For instance, the stadium became one of the only places where it was safe for Catalans to congregate in large numbers and speak their own language,[16] and any win over Real Madrid was seen as a victory for democracy over the Franco regime, as Real came to represent the 'tyranny of a politically centralised and culturally uniform Spain'[17] for the Catalan people.

Following the death of Franco in 1975, political reforms in Spain restored rights and democracy to Catalonia. By the early 1990s, it was one of the most prosperous regions in Spain, its capital Barcelona being economically strong enough to stage the Olympic Games in 1992 and widely regarded as one of Europe's most dynamic cities in terms of cultural and artistic vitality.[18] Given that it is perhaps the region's most iconic institution, it was therefore ironic that the extension of democracy to Spain and Catalonia saw a parallel erosion of the democratic rights of the members, or *socios*, to influence the administration of FC Barcelona, notably under the presidency of Josep Núñez (1978–2000).[19]

The struggle for member democracy: the Josep Núñez years[20]

In 1978, Josep Lluís Núñez became the first president to be democratically elected by the entire membership of FC Barcelona since before the Spanish Civil War. Núñez was the president of his family business, Núñez y Navarro, the largest construction company in Catalonia. He brought his business pedigree to FC Barcelona, replacing what FC Barcelona biographer and *Financial Times* journalist Jimmy Burns described as a 'somewhat benevolent if patriarchal style of management with a sharper if more ruthless administration, with the emphasis on maximizing the club's economic potential'.[21] Of Basque origin and relatively humble beginnings, Núñez was not a member of the Catalan middle class that had traditionally been the driving force behind the club's nationalist associations. He was keen to emphasize his differences from the old ideals and management styles and from the outset he made it clear that he would strive to de-politicize the club. This 'de-politicization' of the club was linked to a process of de-Catalanization that satisfied those who wished to see any nationalist associations relegated to memory as, it was argued, this handicapped the club's ability to grow financially at a politically sensitive time when fears of separatism threatened to undermine Spain's transition to democracy. However, during Núñez's 22-year presidency, he also proceeded to undermine the membership model of ownership at FC Barcelona by reducing the rights of club members and eroding the democracy within the club statutes.[22,23] The dilution of a strong Catalan identity, alongside the erosion of the club's democratic principles would later form the bedrock of the staunchly nationalist Laporta's opposition to Núñez.

During this period, the mutual membership model of ownership that characterized all Spanish clubs was already under threat from another quarter – poor financial management and lack of cost control discipline. In the absence of a strong central regulatory body to exercise some restraint over financial risk-taking, a dramatic rise in costs, financial losses and debt took place at most Spanish clubs, all of which were transparently unsustainable.[24] The Spanish government was forced to intervene. This resulted in legislative changes which effectively brought an end to the membership model of ownership at the majority of Spanish clubs. In 1990, the Spanish government created Sport Law 10/1990 – *ley del deporte* – to regulate the legal structure of professional football.[25] The new regulations ensured that all club debts owed to public bodies (taxes, social security payments, etc.) were passed over to the Spanish Football League (LFP), which represents the clubs in the top two divisions; a series of levies on the revenue of the Spanish football betting pools – the *quiniela* (a popular form of gambling on football) – were then rebated to the LFP and to its ultimate governing body, the Spanish Superior Sport Council (CSD), to repay club debts. In total, *ley del deporte* aided the survival of football clubs by contributing €192m toward cancelling debts.[26,27]

The new regulation also required all professional clubs to convert into a new legal form, the *Sociedades Anónimas Deportiva* (SAD). A SAD was a joint-stock company with limited liability designed to increase financial accountability and ensure proper financial management. Initially, the share ownership in the new SAD structures was quite dispersed, but over time ownership has tended to become concentrated with the net result that by 2008, almost all clubs who converted to the SAD structure were controlled by high net-worth individuals, such as the Gil family at Atletico Madrid. It is also important to note in passing that the creation of the SAD structure has not resolved the chronic financial instability of Spanish football – Spanish clubs continue to make financial losses and run up huge debts,[28] which are then shed through the process of financial administration, as is also the case in the English Football League (the three divisions below the Premiership). In fact, it could be argued that the creation of SAD's has been a failed strategy in terms of improving the quality of financial management and government of Spanish football clubs.

However, not all clubs converted to a SAD. Those clubs that recorded a positive balance in their accounts during the 1985/1986 season were allowed to remain legally constituted as member clubs. Of the 42 professional clubs in Spain, only FC Barcelona, Real Madrid, Athletic Bilbao and Osasuna were able to retain their status as member-owned clubs.[29]

However, despite maintaining member-owned status, many of the *socios* at FC Barcelona were concerned about the lack of transparency regarding the administrative structures of the club. The assembly of delegates at FC Barcelona is a 3000-member body that operates as a parliament which has the power to censure the president and the board in the event they do not comply with the club's statutes. It also has the responsibility to appoint members of the economic committee to oversee the annual budget. Every two years, members of the assembly are picked at random. However, during the Núñez era, critics claimed there was a lack of transparency with regard to the process by which individuals were chosen for the assembly. The board also failed to reveal the list of assembly members (something that did not happen even in the Franco period) meaning that club members did not know who was representing their interests and who to approach to raise issues. Similarly, the list of actual members of the club was withheld on the grounds of privacy in order to avoid any unwanted commercial or political marketing. This made it virtually impossible for any competing candidate for the presidency of the club to then canvass members effectively in an election, thus providing a major advantage to the incumbent Señor Núñez. There was also an alleged lack of transparency regarding accounting procedures and the setting and monitoring of the annual budget, and the economic committee responsible for budgeting (chaired by Señor Núñez's son) was suffering from a clear lack of independence. The lack of transparent governance structures meant that although FC Barcelona was a members' owned club, President Núñez retained a high level of personal control over the management of the football club, with members unable to effectively exercise their democratic rights.[30,31] Indeed, one former club director opined that as Núñez's term of office became more prolonged, '…his junta [board] became largely decorative…'.[32]

In addition to the lack of transparency over club governance, there was also concern among many *socios* regarding the extent to which President Núñez wanted to introduce far-reaching commercial reforms to the football club which might erode its fundamental cultural identity. In public, Núñez rejected the idea that he wanted to float the football arm of the club on the Spanish stock exchange to raise additional capital; however, this option had been the subject of a feasibility study by the merchant banking group Rothschild.[33] In addition, as Burns[34] observed, Núñez was very impressed by a particular model of a football club:

> That Núñez and some of his advisors saw Manchester United as a commercial model during the late 1990s was apparent in countless consultancy papers and feasibility studies they examined behind the scenes, which drew comparisons with the English club's more developed merchandising and corporate hospitality, and its marketing overseas. It was estimated that the gap between Barça and Manchester United in terms of merchandising revenue was around 30%.

Of course, Manchester United was a stock exchange listed public limited company, an increasing trend in the ownership of English football in the late 1990s, and went on to win the Champions League in 1999. The proposed Barça 2000 project intensified concerns regarding the commercialization of the club with the project set to convert the area surrounding the Nou Camp stadium into a theme park with bars, restaurants and leisure facilities. The critics speculated that it would be difficult to achieve this ambition without resorting to external funding. In fact, an influential dissident group of *socios*, grouped under the L'Elefant Blau banner, saw the project as the first step in the process that would transform the FC Barcelona members' club to a company:

> The idea behind 'Barça 2000' was to build a kind of Disneyland park surrounding the stadium with all sorts of bars, cinemas, shops and other facilities tangential to our club's vocation, which is (as declared by the first article of the statutes) the promotion, practice, diffusion and exhibition of football and other sports. If the proposal for 'Barça 2000' had gone ahead it would have paved the way for the conversion of the club into a joint-stock company.[35]

Ultimately, the Barça 2000 project failed to materialize, largely due to the efforts of L'Elefant Blau, who organized a vote of censure against club President Núñez in 1997.

L'Elefant Blau

L'Elefant Blau was formed in 1997 as an opposition group to the presidency of Josep Núñez.[36] Their manifesto called for greater transparency in the club's accounting procedures and a limit on the presidential tenure to terms of four years.[37,38] It was the fear that under Josep Núñez, the identity and purpose of FC Barcelona was moving toward an American-style entertainment model, which drove Joan Laporta, a lawyer, and other like-minded individuals, to form L'Elefant Blau. Incidentally, Laporta was Johann Cruyff's lawyer; Cruyff, of course, was one of the world's greatest footballers and effectively a naturalized Catalan and iconic former player and manager of FC Barcelona who had famously fallen out with club President Núñez.[39,40] L'Elefant Blau was an attempt to re-assert FC Barcelona's identity as primarily a sporting and cultural institution, emphasizing that the main asset of the club was the *socios*:[41]

> ... this [the need to increase revenue] should not and cannot be used as an argument for cutting down the members' social and democratic rights. The club's main assets are its 100,000 members and its millions of fans. Similarly, the members are the club's only proprietors. No matter how much the club earns, the income of the whole club depends on its members, not on the television networks or on the sports equipment multinationals. That, at least, is our point of view....

The first course of action taken by L'Elefant Blau was to organize a vote of censure against President Núñez and the board. To organize a vote of censure, the statutes at FC Barcelona state that it is necessary to obtain signatures from 5% of the *socios*. However, the lack of transparency with regard to the membership base of FC Barcelona made it difficult to mobilize support. To ensure that L'Elefant Blau had sufficient signatures to put forward a vote of censure, members of the organization were positioned for a week on Las Ramblas, the main thoroughfare through the old historic section of Barcelona. In total, 6000 signatures were collected from *socios*, ensuring that a vote of censure went ahead in March 1997; of 40,000 voters, 15,000 voted in favour of the censure with 25,000 against.[42] Despite being unsuccessful, the high-level of support for the vote of censure made it clear to Núñez that he could not take the club's membership for granted.[43] The Barça 2000 project would subsequently be abandoned.

Furthermore, following the sustained attempt to depoliticise the club, Núñez had succeeded in driving a wedge between the football club and the nationalist politicians and affiliates who viewed Barça as an integral part of their cultural heritage. Jordi Badia – the communications director at FC Barcelona under Joan Laporta – referred to the atmosphere at the club and its relationship with the Catalan nation at that moment as a 'social fracture' and noted:

> Núñez opted for open confrontation with the media ... the resulting conflict with significant sectors of the Catalan press marked the beginning of a period of political isolation for Barça, which over time, left the club in an opposing position to practically every single institution in Catalunya.[44]

President Núñez resigned in 2000 after 22 years in the post and the shelving of the Barça 2000 project,[45] finally acknowledging his deep unpopularity among the club's supporters, which had manifested itself during the club's centenary (November 1998/ November 1999) with violent crowd protests against his continued tenure. The election to replace him was won by Joan Gaspart, his deputy during his 22-year reign; L'Elefant Blau had supported the challenger to Gaspart, Lluis Bassat. However, it was a narrow victory – on a 49% turnout, Gaspart garnered 55% of the vote against 43% for Bassat. Upon gaining the presidency, Gaspart acknowledged the need to reunite the club, inviting Bassat to work with the new board.[46]

However, Gaspart's tenure was not a success[47] and can best be summed up by the following assessment by management accountants Deloitte:[48]

> [Since winning La Liga in 1998/99] ... the club had struggled on and off the pitch. Four successive trophy-less seasons culminated in an annus horribilis in 2002/2003, when they finished in sixth position in La Liga, their lowest position since 1987/88 – and only qualified for the UEFA Cup on the final day of the season. The club's financial position was of equal, if not greater concern. Revenues of €123.4m (£85.9m) were less than half of Manchester United and left Barcelona in 13th position in the Football Money League. Player wages were €109.7m (£75.8m) or 88% of turnover, and the club's operating loss was €72m (£50m). A number of years of ongoing losses had left the club 186m (£128.6m) in debt. The club faced potentially serious financial difficulties.

Essentially, poor financial management had left the club in a position where if it had been a normal business it would have been technically insolvent.[49] There appeared to be no clear business strategy. This instability was also reflected in the football management department where there were three separate changes of team coach (Serra Ferrer, Carlos Rexach and Louis Van Gaal),[50] yet the club still remained trophy-less.

However, due to a lack of sporting success and poor financial management, Joan Gaspart resigned as president in February 2003 to be replaced in the short-term by caretaker president Enric Reyna Martinez.[51] In May 2003, President Martinez and his entire board resigned at an extraordinary general assembly of club *socios*, with an interim managing commission appointed to oversee the running of the club until the presidential elections in July.[52]

The July elections were notable for two reasons. First, there were six candidates standing for the presidency, including Joan Laporta and Lluis Bassat, the candidate that L'Elefant Blau had supported in the 2000 elections. Laporta's election campaign strongly promoted the traditional social role of the club and emphasized the importance of FC Barcelona as an expression of Catalan cultural identity and pride. His campaign slogan was '*Primer, el Barça* (Barça comes first)'.[53] Second, 54.7% of *socios* voted in the election – the highest ever turnout of club members. Laporta won by a clear margin, with 52.57% of the votes; Bassat was the nearest challenger receiving 31.8%.[54]

The corporate strategy of the Laporta era

Following his election as president in 2003, Joan Laporta was confronted with a major management challenge.[55] The club was very heavily indebted and making a loss at the operating level (incurring the largest net loss in its history in 2002/2003),[56] but the option of bringing in new capital in the form of equity investment was ruled out. In order to restore the club to sound financial health, and generate the resources necessary to re-build the football team and generate sporting success, it was necessary for the club's new management not only to control costs, but critically to drive new revenue. As management consultants Deloitte observed, in 2003 FC Barcelona's financial turnover was less than half that of Manchester United.[57] But all of this was to be achieved within an envelope of respecting, and indeed enhancing, the central role of FC Barcelona in Catalonian cultural and social life. However, critical to the vision of Laporta and his new management team was the view that the commercial potential of FC Barcelona remained under-exploited. The example of Manchester United continued to loom large, just as it had in the Núñez era, as Laporta later remarked in an interview:[58]

> The idea was to position Barça back at the top of the world of sport and media. Manchester United charges €2 million for each friendly. Barça charges only €300,000. We must succeed in achieving a situation where a young boy in Singapore or Tokyo wears a Barça shirt and not a Manchester United shirt.

The strategy was therefore unashamedly commercial in terms of its intentions to globalize what marketing professionals might describe as the Barça 'brand'. While the new board held fast to the principle that FC Barcelona was 'more than a club' they were not sentimental about the means required to build the strength of the club. Critically, they saw the application of modern management techniques in all areas as generic, and not exclusively linked to the private limited shareholder-owned company model. The discipline of shareholder governance was not necessary to incentivize the management. That would come from the desire of the management, as fans of the club, to seek the best for the club as a sporting and cultural institution.

Joan Laporta's first decision was to appoint successful professional managers to key executive positions in the club from outside the football industry in order to draw on their business and entrepreneurial experience; although all were supporters of FC Barcelona, all were high-achieving professionals in their respective fields. He also took the decision that the board of directors, though unpaid (in fact, club directors must also put a guarantee of €1.5m against any possible mismanagement during their term)[59], would become involved with the day-to-day management and operation of the club rather than simply setting the strategic direction for an executive management team to implement. This was deemed necessary as an exceptional measure given the scale of the change management challenge the organization faced. Again, all directors were high achieving individuals with considerable business experience. During the early stages of implementation of the management model, Joan Laporta explained the changes:

> The impact of the management team was one of renewal and even complete substitution, with the incorporation of new executives with expertise in each of the entity's fundamental areas. The management model we want to implement during this shock phase consists of directing the club with the entity's new executives and managers involved in management operations. One specific case is that of the economic vice-chairman, who is also acting as managing director. Each of the vice-chairmen directly intervene in

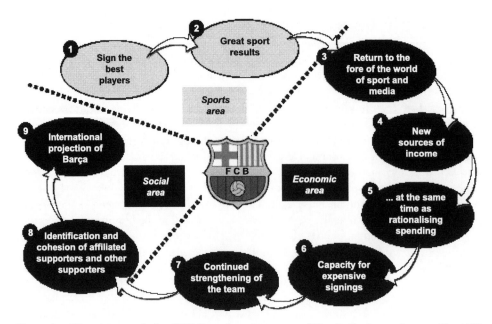

Figure 1. The virtuous circle of FC Barcelona (courtesy of Ferrán Soriano, vice president FC Barcelona, 2003–2008).[63]

> management and, as executive chairman, I coordinate the team as a whole. This is not an orthodox management model, but it has been necessary as a result of the extremely complicated situation in which we found the club.[60]

Implementing this system meant that immediately on arrival, Laporta conducted a purge of the existing executive team, with seven of nine leaving the organization.[61,62]

The new board of directors and executive management team were responsible for implementing strategic change in four key areas at FC Barcelona. First, restoring sporting competitiveness was prioritised. Second, the club sought to re-assert member democracy and improve the transparency of club governance, and to use this also as a vehicle to build the financial strength of the club. Third, a commercial strategy was implemented to generate revenue from off-field activities and improve financial performance. Fourth, steps were taken to ensure that the club balanced the need to build its commercial strength by addressing wider issues of corporate social responsibility. The detail of how these four strategic aspects is summarized in Figure 1.

Each of these four strategic aspects will now be interacted with and examined in turn.[64]

Sporting performance

As is the case at any football club, achieving sporting success is a (if not the) primary objective. Part of the reason for the continuing influence of Dutchman Johann Cruyff in the politics of FC Barcelona is that in his first season with FC Barcelona in the 1973/1974 season, the club won its first La Liga title since 1960. He subsequently went on to manage the so-called 'Dream Team' which won four La Liga titles from 1991 to 1994 and a European Cup in 1992 (and were European Cup runners up in 1994). Although they won La Liga again in 1998 and 1999, and the European Cup

Winners Cup in 1997, as they entered the new century there was a popular perception that the club was stagnating on the field of play.

Between 2000 and 2003 in particular, the presidency of Joan Gaspart was characterized by a high level of sporting instability with three coaches employed in three seasons (Serra Ferrer, Carlos Rexach and Louis Van Gaal), high spending on transfer fees, and a failure to win any trophies. At the beginning of Laporta's tenure, it was a measure of how far the stature of the club had fallen during the Gaspart era that they would be snubbed by David Beckham in favour of Real Madrid.[65] This followed the decision of Portuguese star Luis Figo to leave FC Barcelona in 2000 for Real Madrid, creating the impression that FC Barcelona was a club that the best players moved on from to fulfil their potential.

Under the presidency of Joan Laporta, the sporting performances of FC Barcelona improved significantly. Even before he was elected, the ultimately unsuccessful attempts by Laporta to secure the transfer of David Beckham from Manchester United demonstrated his understanding of the critical importance of building a strong team in order to compete successfully on the field of play as a prerequisite for driving all other revenues.[66] Having failed to sign Beckham, FC Barcelona went on to sign Ronaldinho from Paris St. Germain. In the view of management consultants Deloitte, this policy of immediate squad investment, 'Although carrying greater financial risk ... delivered better prospects for the club on the pitch'.[67] This of course was an essential prerequisite for driving commercial revenues from TV broadcast income to sponsorship to ticket sales to merchandising. As FC Barcelona's marketing vice president observed shortly after the Laporta presidential era began, '... the best promotion is a good performing team and a great show on the field'.[68] Furthermore, the attempt to sign David Beckham was paradigmatic of a strategy for the club to raise its profile on a global scale.

Kase et al.[69] analysed the sporting strategy of FC Barcelona between 2003 and 2006. They illustrated that the appointment of the Dutch coach Frank Rijkaard in 2003, and the decision of the club board to support him through an initial fallow period, resulted in a level of continuity and stability at the club. Rijkaard developed a playing squad that was evenly balanced between junior players from the youth academy and a number of top international players supplemented with a small number of world-class players such as Ronaldinho and Samuel Eto'o. FC Barcelona has now developed a strong youth development system,[70] and recently graduated the talented Argentinean Lionel Messi who came through the system and therefore under the category of 'home-grown' talent. In contrast to the 'galactico' policy implemented by Real Madrid (whereby a series of truly global superstar players were signed), the sporting strategy of FC Barcelona emphasized the importance of the team, rather than a collection of individuals.[71] The Laporta team identified that any strategy that was dependent upon the marketability of star players could easily be destabilized by rapid changes. For example, a star player might damage the brand image by having an extra-marital affair, suffer a long-term injury or worse still, transfer allegiance to a rival club. It became apparent that the strategy of defining the brand on the back of individual media stars carried unpredictability and, although it permitted market penetration, it was precarious in terms of market retention. This was to prove to be the case with the Real Madrid *Galactico* experiment. In contrast to Real Madrid, FC Barcelona director Marc Ingla told the leading Catalan language newspaper *Avui*:[72]

A survey has shown that in the emerging markets of China and Japan, there are at least 21 million people who say that they identify more strongly with FC Barcelona than any other club. The study also revealed that these fans identified more strongly with the identity of the club than with any one particular player. This is the key to the Barça brand and what makes it much stronger than if these fans followed one player – like David Beckham at Madrid. What happens to all of these supporters – female supporters – when that player leaves for another club? He takes his fans with him.

It appears that it became apparent to Ingla that, unlike Real Madrid, Barcelona's brand strength was embedded in the image of the football club itself rather than in the stars that it could recruit.

It is important to note that having appointed their manager, Laporta and his team were prepared to give him not only resources, but critically time, to make the team work on the field of play. This strategy proved highly successful, with FC Barcelona winning successive La Liga titles in 2005 and 2006, the Champions League in 2006, and the Spanish Supercup in 2005 and 2006.

Performance dipped in 2006/2007 and 2007/2008 with FC Barcelona finishing second and third respectively in the La Liga, and exiting the Champions League in the last 16 and semi-final; however, when measured against performance in the Gaspart era, it was still highly creditable and the club is now again acknowledged as amongst the most powerful in sporting terms in Europe. For the 2008/2009 season, after five seasons in charge, Frank Rijkaard was replaced by the reserve team manager, former player and – significantly – product of the youth system and a Catalan, Josep Guardiola, demonstrating that even in transition, there appeared to be an emphasis on maintaining stability, continuity and the club's identity. Critically, the member-owned structure of FC Barcelona had not proved an impediment to hiring and retaining high-quality players and management and to securing success on the field of play.

Member democracy

FC Barcelona had nearly 163,000 members (*socios*) at the end of June 2008.[73] Adult membership cost a fee of approximately €175 in 2008.[74] It entitled the *socios* to vote for the club president every four years at the presidential elections. *Socios* are also able to vote on a range of other issues. For instance, in 2003 members voted to allow shirt sponsorship for the first time in the club's history.

FC Barcelona is also governed by an assembly of delegates – a 3000-member body – made up of club members drawn at random by computer, members of the board of directors, former club presidents, members of the disciplinary committee, members of the economic commission, and up to 25 members chosen by the board of directors. It is only when one tries to imagine the implications of the application of such a system at a club in Britain that its extraordinary radicalism becomes apparent. For example, imagine if Malcolm Glazer and his board of directors had to stand for election every four years and account for their stewardship of Manchester United to an assembly of United supporters?

During the 22-year presidency of Josep Núñez, a lack of transparency over the governance of FC Barcelona and the inability of club *socios* to exercise their democratic rights were key concerns. Joan Laporta and his fellow directors sought to increase the level of transparency between the football club and the *socios* by improving communication channels. Every two months, a magazine is published in Spanish and Catalan and sent to all *socios* informing them of the latest developments at the club. Members with an email account also receive an electronic newsletter every month and news bulletins are sent via email. Barça TV, the club's designated subscription-based TV channel, is the official communication link between the football club and supporters, offering 10 hours of daily broadcasting to 40,000 subscribers.[75] There is also a degree of candour expressed in much of the commentary on club affairs in news coverage on the FC Barcelona website, which is extraordinary by the standards of English Premier League clubs.[76]

However, the new board were not only interested in promoting member democracy for its own sake or as a bulwark against any future dilution of FC Barcelona's wider social and cultural mission. They also explicitly sought to turn the fact that FC Barcelona was a democratic member-owned organization to the club's financial advantage by seeking to increase the number of *socios* through a huge membership recruitment drive called *El Gran Repte*, or 'The Great Challenge', designed to increase both the number of members and supporters' clubs. In a 2004 interview, Joan Laporta observed that for every 10,000 extra *socios* recruited, the club received 1m in additional revenue in membership fees.[77] Another board member, Marc Ingla, commented:

> FC Barcelona's competitive edge is the level of adhesion and identification of its affiliated supporters and other supporters with the club and the close link that is generated between the two.[78]

Of course, these were all committed supporters to whom various FC Barcelona goods and services could be sold. A designated supporters' office was established to drive forward the project. The success of the project can be gauged by fact that on 30 June 2008, FC Barcelona had 162,979 members, with 17% being foreigners,[79] up from approximately 105,000 in 2002.[80]

In an interview with the respected sports' journalist David Conn, in an article for the *Guardian* newspaper in the run-up to the 2006 Champions League Final with Arsenal, FC Barcelona's Finance Director Ferrán Soriano observed:[81]

> The need for the [FC Barcelona] Board to be accountable and stay popular with the fans means that season tickets are affordable compared with other major clubs, with the cheapest E101 (£69), enough to make the holder of a seat at Arsenal's new Emirates Stadium weep into his credit card statement. 'It is a challenge to remain member-owned and compete against the richest clubs,' Soriano said. 'For example, we run other sports, like handball and basketball – which make a loss – because our constitution states we must promote all sport in Barcelona. But we do compete, with pride in who we are, our history and values. Our supporters would feel alienated if we had a structure like Arsenal or Chelsea... The fans truly own this club... They control its destiny and can decide how it will be managed. This is totally different from Arsenal (two-thirds owned by ITV [the UK broadcasting company], businessmen Danny Fiszman and David Dein, and Lady Nina and Sir Charles Bracewell-Smith) or Chelsea, owned by one guy who could one day withdraw his investment.

Ferrán Soriano cited Roman Abramovich, but could he have not just as easily cited the Glazer family at Manchester United?

Further evidence of the distinctive relationship the club enjoys with its supporters can be seen in the mission statement of the Social Commission, the club department charged with the maintenance, promotion and development of the club's relationship with the FC Barcelona Official Supporters Clubs (*Penyes*). As outlined on its website:[82]

> Its objectives include transmitting and promoting the historic values and meaning of FC Barcelona, such as: civilian duty, social integration, democracy, Catalanism, universality

and others that reflect FC Barcelona's commitment to society. Another objective is to assist with and actively develop the global position and solidarity of being 'more than a club in the world' and the [the FC Barcelona's charitable] Foundation's projects such as UNICEF and Solidarity Schools.

Again, it is only when one attempts to translate this mission statement into the context of an English Premiership club that the sheer scale of the difference and radicalism becomes obvious. Although the new board of directors sought to derive financial strength from the members' owned model, the model brought with it very specific social obligations, and also to some extent constrained the board's room for manoeuvre in some key commercial areas. This meant that the club could not seek to invite external equity investment to raise funds as this would compromise the mutual ownership structure. They also had to seek the specific permission of the members through a ballot if they were to put a sponsor's logo on the team shirt. Similarly, the board was constrained in the extent it could increase ticket prices for fear of a backlash by members inviting a vote of censure by the governing assembly of the club. These were all challenges that the private owners of an English Premier League club do not have to manage.

Commercial strategy

The new board of FC Barcelona implemented a strategic plan which aimed to generate increased revenue from off-field activities, in particular by increasing the proportion of revenues generated internationally. The strategy proved very successful.

As illustrated in Figure 2, revenue rose between 2002/2003 and 2007/2008 from €123.4m to €308.8m, a growth rate of 250%. The club moved from being the 13th largest in Europe in terms of financial turnover to the third. Figure 2 also illustrates that over the same period the club made a consistent profit each year, in contrast to the 2000/2001 to 2001/2003 period where losses were made in two out of three years.

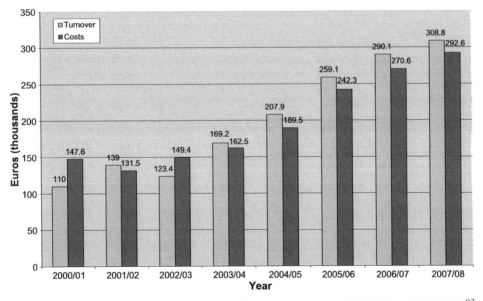

Figure 2.   FC Barcelona's cost management and revenue generation 2000/2001 to 2007/2008.[83]

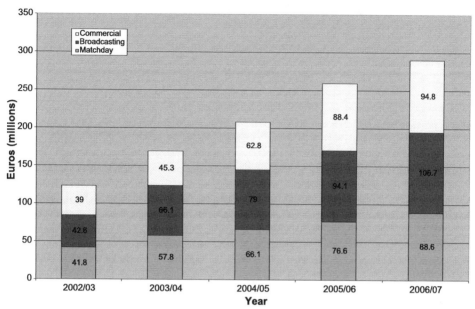

Figure 3.   FC Barcelona's revenue generation by category 2002/2003 to 2006/2007.[84]

As illustrated in Figure 3, it also managed to operate a balanced revenue model with income split evenly between match-day, commercial and broadcasting revenues.

There were a number of key factors underpinning the commercial strategy of FC Barcelona that were instrumental in improving financial performance. These included improved cost control, increasing broadcasting revenues, increasing club membership, and a marketing strategy focused on merchandising and the development and promotion of the club brand.

One of the first moves by the new regime was to stabilize and refinance the club's debt under the leadership of Finance Director Ferrán Soriano.[85,86] Debt was refinanced on less costly terms following an agreement with a syndicate of financial institutions led by its main bank La Caixa. This meant that, despite the heavy overall level of debt, the club was able to have some room for manoeuvre in terms of investing in the playing squad.

Cost control was a major problem in 2003; player wages increased from 66% of revenue in 2001 to 83% in 2003. To address this, a performance related pay scheme[87] was introduced and by 2004, player wages had been reduced to 52% of turnover, further reduced to 49% in 2005.[88] Deloitte reported that 18% of the club's 2005/2006 wage bill was related to the team's on-pitch success, whilst another 18% was related to player performance.[89,90] The decrease in player wages relative to revenue enabled FC Barcelona in 2005 to deliver a balanced budget for the first time in four years.[91] A similar performance-related pay system was introduced for management executives, and significant savings were made by virtue of the fact that the *de facto* executive board members were not paid. Essentially, the new board aimed to move to a break-even operating position in their first year of tenure. Interestingly, they also addressed the issue of free tickets. Allen and Recuero (2005) reported that:

> Another of the measures taken by the [new] board was to review the guest and invitation packages implemented by the previous directors. Up to the previous season [2002/2003].... The club gave away 4,800 tickets, 600 season tickets and 1,500 invitations. The directors used most of them, as they did almost 600 tickets to the chairman's box...[92]

Similarly, Laporta made a point early in his tenure of confronting the hooligan fringe of FC Barcelona's support, the so-called 'Mad Boys',[93,94] refusing to offer tickets and other favours in return for good behaviour and essentially banning them from the ground. This led to threats of physical violence against him with allegations that previous employees and directors of the club were at least in part fermenting this hostility against Laporta in particular.[95]

Critically, the new board adopted a forensic approach to cost control across the organization. They were equally aggressive in their approach to revenue generation. Figure 3 illustrates that between the 2002/2003 and 2006/2007 seasons, broadcasting revenue at FC Barcelona increased from €42.6m to €106.7m. Spanish football clubs are allowed to sell their broadcasting rights individually, with FC Barcelona able to charge a premium price for the rights to show their matches, many of which are sold on a pay-per-view basis. Barcelona also runs its own Barça TV channel, which is reported to be profitable. Initially, the large increase in broadcasting revenues came from a negotiated five-year broadcasting deal with Televisió de Catalunya in 2003, worth a reported €54m a year. In 2006, the Mediapro company took over the contract from Televisió de Catalunya, paying €210m for the remaining two years of the contract[96] while also signing up to a future agreement which will pay over €150m per annum from 2008/2009.[97] In addition, the club generated significant media revenues from its consistent participation in the latter stages of the UEFA Champions League. Essentially, from 2002/2003, FC Barcelona's management were able to dramatically increase the value of the rights to broadcast the team's matches in the marketplace, and the success of the team on the field of play saw it broadcast more frequently thus boosting revenue further.

Between 2002/2003 and 2006/2007, FC Barcelona increased match-day income from €41.8m to €88.6m.[98] This was driven by increased club memberships and gate revenue. In 2003, club membership stood at 106,000 *socios* and 'The Big Challenge' (*El Grand Repte*) campaign was launched with the objective of increasing club membership. As mentioned above, between 2003 and 2008, membership rose substantially to approximately 163,000. It is perhaps not unreasonable to speculate that the rise in membership might have been a key factor in the 12.7% increase in attendance figures between the 2002/2003 season and the 2005/2006 season.[99]

FC Barcelona had 85,000 season ticket-holders in 2005/2006. A scheme to facilitate the resale of up to 5000 tickets was implemented with the club receiving 50% of the proceeds. Deloitte reported that combined ticket and hotel packages target overseas supporters. 'Other stadium related revenues have increased from €4m in 2002/2003 to €21m in 2005/2006, by marketing the stadium and its facilities as a venue for conferences and conventions, while stadium tour revenue continues to grow. In 2004/2005, 36 new executive boxes were created and these have all been sold for the past two seasons. The club is investigating options to expand corporate facilities at the stadium, and the stadium capacity overall'.[100] Indeed, the Nou Camp stadium was already the most visited museum in Catalonia.[101] The average attendance at La Liga games in the Nou Camp in 2006/2007 was 74,100. In 2007, the club announced plans to redevelop the stadium adding 10,000 seats and taking capacity above 100,000.[102] The scale of their ambition was underlined by the fact that the contract to remodel the stadium went to the firm of award-winning architect Norman Foster.[103] The new stadium was not just to be a vehicle through which to drive increased revenues, but a statement of architectural and cultural, as well as sporting, pride and power. Again, it is hard to imagine any English Premiership club demonstrating the same dramatic sense of wider cultural significance of being 'more than just a football club'. However, it is also worth noting that as of December 2008, no start date for the project had been announced nor had the nature of the associated financing package.

Interestingly, FC Barcelona did not pursue a policy of maximizing ticket prices at levels the market would bear, as has been the case with English Premiership clubs. Although ticket prices, and the price of membership of the club, increased signifi-cantly in the 2003/2004 season as a short-term measure necessitated by the club's financial crisis, tickets were still very inexpensive when compared with tickets in the English Premier League.[104] Instead, there appeared a deliberate policy of pitching ticket prices at very affordable levels so as not to exploit the loyalty of the *socios*, or perhaps, as outlined above, to incite their dissatisfaction. It is worth noting that if such an aggressive ticket pricing strategy were to be adopted, then the club management would be open to censure by its members through the Members' Assembly. David Conn, in an article in the *Guardian* newspaper written just before the 2006 European Champions League final with Arsenal, observed that the cheapest adult season ticket in Barcelona's Camp Nou stadium was £69, while the equivalent at the Arsenal's Emirates stadium was £885. The most expensive adult season ticket at the Camp Nou was £579 whilst the equivalent at the Emirates was £1825.[105]

The club also pursued an aggressive commercial/sponsorship strategy, leading to a rise in revenues from €39m in 2002/2003 to €94.8m in 2006/2007.[106] In 2006/2007, the club notably extended their kit-manufacturing deal with Nike to June 2013, a deal worth a reputed €30m annually.[107] The relationship took the form of a 50:50 joint venture company which managed all of FC Barcelona's merchandising, in addi-tion to Nike being the kit manufacturer. FC Barcelona also secured commercial spon-sorship deals with major international partnerships such as Coca Cola (soft drinks), Estrella Damm (brewing) and La Caixa (banking).[108]

However, the strategy was also innovative. After first considering a conventional shirt-sponsorship deal in 2006, the club signed an agreement with UNICEF (the children's charity of the United Nations) from which the club received no payment (a more detailed analysis of this initiative is outlined below). Rather, the club promoted UNICEF on its shirt and supported the organization's projects. Deloitte reported that:[109]

> UNICEF and Barcelona believe they share a similar social outlook, and the five year partnership sees Barcelona promoting UNICEF on its shirts, while UNICEF receives 0.7% of Barça's operating revenue – €1.5 million per year – in support of a number of projects focusing on helping to protect children in areas of humanitarian crisis.

The marketing strategy at FC Barcelona also concentrated on the development and promotion of the club brand, particularly in countries outside Spain where the club had international recognition and a high level of brand equity in Asia, South and Central America, Europe and Africa.[110] With FC Barcelona the most well-supported overseas club in Japan and enjoying strong levels of popularity in China, Asia in particular became a target market for developing the club brand.[111] The club subsequently made a number of trips to play friendly matches in Asia, while signing deals to set up a dedicated Barcelona magazine and internet sites in Japan and China.[112]

Thus, over the 2002/2003 to 2006/2007 period, the financial performance of FC Barcelona was transformed. Through the application of tight cost management systems, combined with the shrewd and rigorous application of modern management techniques, revenues dramatically increased thus allowing greater expenditure on players but not at the expense of profitability. This was a rare achievement in the modern European football environment. Extraordinarily, in October 2008 the club was able to announce that it had completely eliminated the syndicated loan taken out on the election of Joan Laporta and his new board colleagues in 2003, having paid back €92.5m over the five-year period.[113] The fact that the club was member-owned, and that this put a break on potential revenue-generating measures that were the norm in the English Premiership – premium ticket pricing and corporate-branded shirt sponsorship – was not an impediment to achieving these objectives.

Corporate social responsibility

The way that FC Barcelona was now applying financial discipline to all its activities, and the way it was now marketing itself and its related merchandise on a global basis was widely acknowledged to be infinitely more sophisticated than during the Núñez era. It might therefore have appeared ironic that one of the motivations that drove the formation of L'Elefant Blau was the concern that FC Barcelona was becoming too commercialized and thereby losing touch with its social and cultural roots. However, the new board of directors implemented a parallel strategy to develop the club's corporate social responsibility activities in order to ensure that the club retained its traditional social and cultural raison d'être.

Critical to this was the expansion of the activities of the FC Barcelona Foundation, which had been founded in 1994. Under the new board, the charitable activities of the Foundation were globalized and developed far beyond what had been a previously narrow local focus. This expansion served to institutionalize community involvement at the club. Certainly, the club's corporate social responsibility programme must be among the most extensive of any sporting organization anywhere in the world with the club's website carrying extensive coverage of its activities in this area. The Foundation is the club's charitable arm, and board members are involved in charity events and fundraising events promoting social projects under the slogan 'Football is not everything'.[114] Through the Foundation, the club became the first sports organization to reach a partnership agreement with UNESCO – the United Nations Educational, Scientific and Cultural Organization – signing a five-year deal in 2006 to promote the role that sport can play in supporting the work of the organization in areas including education, social inclusion, literacy and citizenship.

FC Barcelona was quite explicit as to why it wished to globalize its CSR strategy:[115]

Today, football has become a global phenomenon, and support for Barcelona has spread spectacularly around the world. The number of club members from outside of Catalonia and Spain is increasing daily, and the club wants to respond to that show of passion for Barça. This has developed into a need and an obligation. And the best way for the club to do that has been to take a step further and become 'more than a club around the world' as well. This Barça that is so concerned for its people needs to be globalised. This caring and humanitarian Barça needs to be globalised. It is a strategic decision that is in keeping with the club's history and the way that football is continuing to develop on a worldwide basis. That is why the club has decided to contribute 0.7 per cent of its ordinary income to the FC Barcelona Foundation in order to set up international cooperation programmes for development, supports the UN Millennium Development Goals and has made a commitment to UNICEF's humanitarian aid programs through the donation of one and a half million euros for the next five years and now wears the UNICEF logo on its shirts. – an agreement that has made Barça unique.

The sponsorship deal between FC Barcelona and UNICEF, the United Nations children's charity, was a landmark development as an example of corporate social responsibility in practice. The FC Barcelona shirt is one of the most recognizable football shirts in the world and the value of the sponsorship rights would be sizeable. However, the club has historically resisted selling the shirt sponsorship rights as a strong sociopolitical statement to reinforce the traditional values of community and solidarity associated with the club. It was felt that to have a commercial sponsor on the shirt would somehow compromise the integrity of the club shirt and the spirit implied in the 'mes que un club/more than a club' slogan. Given that the four-year shirt sponsorship deal that Manchester United signed with American insurance company AIG in 2006 was worth nearly £56m, FC Barcelona's decision not to have a commercial shirt sponsor was not a vain gesture. It was thus a tangible expression that somehow FC Barcelona was different, not just another entertainment brand.[116]

However, some commentators underlined that being 'more than a club' could also pose dilemmas, as articulated by Chadwick and Arthur:[117]

> Sponsorship is … a major revenue stream for any club but it would appear that Barcelona is constrained by its past and by its brand image. By not carrying a corporate logo on its shirt, the club is once more making a strong socio-political statement, something that will reinforce the club's image in the minds of many people. This clearly has a value, no matter how intangible, and helps to reinforce the view that Barça is special – the club is about community, solidarity and care. But in an era of big name player signings and generous salaries, it also denies the club a very important source of revenue.

Though they went on to note:[118]

> Nevertheless, the move is clever brand management because it marks out Barça as being different to other clubs in not having a commercial shirt deal; it also reinforces the club's existing brand image as being 'mes que un club'. What the deal has done, therefore, is to help build equity in the Barça brand … particularly in terms of creating an affiliation between fans, the public and the club.

However, it was the case that not all club *socios* were happy with the UNICEF deal. At the previous year's Annual Assembly, they had been convinced by FC Barcelona Director Ferrán Soriano that the club needed to find a shirt sponsor *if* it was to be able to compete with Europe's biggest clubs. Soriano convinced the delegates that the club was losing out on a huge sum of money and so – reluctantly – the members agreed to allow shirt sponsorship for this reason. Many then felt aggrieved at the UNICEF deal over a year later because the financial reward was less tangible. While many acknowledged that it was positive for the club's image, this was not something that they had voted upon. Subsequently, the fact that Joan Laporta was perceived by some to have ushered in the deal through the back door formed one of the main motivating points in the motion of censure in the summer of 2008 by *socio* Oriol Giralt.[119]

Perhaps this was why the underlying message in Joan Laporta's address to the Barcelona member's assembly in September 2006, when he received criticism that *socios* had approved a break with the tradition of not carrying a sponsor on the club's shirt if it would generate revenue for the football club, was to stress that the UNICEF deal would indeed generate revenue through broader brand promotion in the future, and that the motivation was not purely philanthropic. Many members felt that the deal with UNICEF meant that the club was losing money rather than generating it and that, therefore, Laporta had been in contravention of the agreement. Defending the UNICEF deal, Laporta argued that it facilitated:

> The projection of FC Barcelona to a world level … This was the reason behind the deserved agreement with UNICEF; the agreement has increased the respect and prestige of the club enormously.[120]

Critically, the deal was therefore about globalizing the FC Barcelona brand and externally, the reaction to the deal was overwhelmingly positive. In summary, as Chadwick and Arthur noted:[121]

> As a model of corporate social responsibility it is exemplary, certainly in football, similarly in sport, possibly even in the business world as a whole.

In summary, FC Barcelona's UNICEF association has genuinely involved some sacrifices, notably the decision to forego income from shirt sponsorships. Arguably, the wider benefits that its corporate social responsibility (CSR) policy brought to building the unique FC Barcelona brand, 'more than a club', compensated for these sacrifices through their contribution to driving wider commercial revenues. Moreover, it is difficult to imagine many conventional privately owned football clubs (though interestingly, in the summer of 2008, Aston Villa in the English Premiership signed a small but similar deal with the Acorns Children's Hospice in the English Midlands region[122]) contemplating such a bold move when hard cash is directly available via a conventional shirt sponsorship deal. This is yet more evidence that FC Barcelona does not behave like a conventional football business.

The dream turns sour?

One of the first innovations introduced by the new board in 2002 was to limit the term of office of the president to two 4-year terms (assuming they were to be re-elected), a reaction to the 22-year reign of Josep Núñez, deemed to be unhealthy and undermining of the democratic structures of the club. However, the length of Joan Laporta's first term was challenged by a *socio* in the courts and as a result, the first eight days of Laporta's tenure in July 2003 were deemed to constitute the first year of his four-year term. Thus, shortly after having led the club to European Champions League glory, Joan Laporta was required to stand for re-election in September 2006, a year earlier than anticipated. However, he was the only club member that received the necessary 1804 signatures to stand for president, ensuring that he was reappointed for a second term. Given that FC Barcelona had just won the European Champions League, his popularity was at a high and the fact that he should be allowed to stand unchallenged was hardly a surprise. However, the episode clearly demonstrated the real power of the democratic principles enshrined in FC Barcelona's statutes.[123]

However, as in all football clubs, political tensions were never far from the surface. These first surfaced in 2005 when prominent board member Sandro Rosell (a successful former Nike executive) resigned along with four other directors[124] in protest at what they say was the allegedly domineering style of Joan Laporta. The remaining nine directors supported Laporta.

The wider political sensitivities involved in being president of FC Barcelona are perhaps best illustrated in an incident which occurred during a regional election campaign in Catalonia in 2005. The *Daily Telegraph*[125] reported that:

> The President of Barcelona Football Club has found himself at the centre of a bitter election campaign after seeming to align himself with one political party. Support for the Barça team is the one thing that unites Catalonia, a region torn between political allegiances that almost inevitably mean that no single party will gain an overall majority in the election on Wednesday. But the conservative Republican Party, CiU, delivered a last-minute coup on Saturday by apparently garnering support from the club's President when he was photographed having breakfast with the party's leader. Artur Mas, the CiU party's Presidential candidate, invited the press to witness his casual conversation with Joan Laporta, Barça's President, over croissants and orange juice in a street cafe in las Ramblas, in Barcelona. Images of the meeting were described as 'the campaign equivalent of a goal in the final minute of a match' in an editorial in yesterday's *La Vanguardia*, and caused immediate protests from other political parties. Josep Piqué, the Presidential candidate of the Right- wing nationalist Partido Popular, accused Mr Laporta of 'doing damage to Catalonia' by linking 'an entity that belonged to everyone with a political option'. Amid growing criticism, Mr Laporta organized a last-minute meeting yesterday with the leader of the current ruling party, the socialist PSC, in an attempt to avert accusations of favouritism. Recent opinion polls give the CiU party the lead with 35.5 per cent of the vote.

More pointedly, in October 2005, Laporta was forced to accept the resignation of his brother-in-law, Alejandro Echevarría, from the board of FC Barcelona when it was revealed Echevarría had once been a member of a foundation honouring former Spanish dictator Franco.[126]

Ultimately, FC Barcelona appears to illustrate that even at a club with such a substantial cultural, social and even political 'hinterland', the ultimate and critical arbiter of member opinion is the extent to which the team is enjoying success on the field of play. When FC Barcelona failed to emulate the successes of 2005/2006 in the following two seasons, the crowd at the Nou Camp began to turn against the board and Joan Laporta became the focus for their disenchantment. This culminated in a vote of no confidence in the board by members of the club in July 2008 in which nearly 40,000 members voted (approximately 33.2% of those eligible to vote) with 60.6% voting against the board.[127] (The Barça website actively encouraged members to vote,[128] and reported the comments of ex-presidents, including Josep Núñez, after they had cast their vote – not surprisingly, Núñez was unhappy with the Laporta regime).[129] As this fell short of the two thirds majority necessary to force a resignation of the board, Joan Laporta decided to remain on as president and complete the remaining two years of his term. However, four days later, eight members of the board, including prominent figures such Ferrán Soriano, Albert Vicens and Marc Ingla, resigned as they felt they no longer had a mandate to continue as directors.[130] At a general meeting of the members on 24 August, a majority of the nearly 1000 members present voted in support of Laporta continuing as president, which he interpreted as a mandate. Critically, he cited the need for 'stable governability' in his decision to see out the remaining two years of his presidency.[131] Joan Laporta was successfully able to complete his term of office which ended in June 2010.

Regardless of how one views Laporta's decision to remain in the presidency, what is clear is that the democratic structures of FC Barcelona allow the members (or supporters) a very real mechanism to influence, and indeed to force, the removal or resignation of Board members to an extent which simply would not be possible in a privately owned model of ownership.

FC Barcelona – 'more than a football club'?

In 2006/2007, FC Barcelona was the third largest football club in Europe, and still among the most successful in sporting terms. Its member-owned structure did not appear to have hampered its development on either account, despite all the political turbulence at the level of the Board and dissatisfaction among the *socios* culminating in the vote of no confidence. This defies the argument that to be truly competitive at the highest level in modern football, a club must be constituted as a limited company by shares capable of attracting major private investment from wealthy individuals.

FC Barcelona is a truly different club. It is a member-owned organization controlled by its members (supporters) and not a private company. These members elect the club president every four years. The club's members, or *socios,* enjoy the right to vote for the club president and board; the right to vote at the delegates assembly (the club members' parliament which has the power to censure the president and the board in the event they do not comply with the club's statutes); and the right to vote for charitable works proposed by the FC Barcelona Foundation, the club's charitable arm (FC Barcelona is committed to devoting 0.7% of its ordinary income to charitable and social projects). While this represents a far from utopian democracy, it is only when one tries to imagine the implications of the application of such a system at a club in Britain that its extraordinary radicalism becomes apparent.

The other notable aspect of the FC Barcelona member-owned model is that it actually works in practice, both as a form of participative democracy and effective corporate and business governance of the club, and also in terms of delivering the core objective of a successful football team on the field. In 2003, Joan Laporta defeated the previous club president incumbent, Josep Núñez, on a platform in which he explicitly set himself against Núñez's plan to float FC Barcelona on the Spanish Stock Exchange as a means for raising capital to strengthen the team. As he had previously argued while campaigning for L'Elefant Blau in 2000 (and was quoted earlier on page 481).[132]

> ...this [the need to increase revenue] should not and cannot be used as an argument for cutting down the members' social and democratic rights. The club's main assets are its 100,000 members and its millions of fans. Similarly, the members are the club's only proprietors. No matter how much the club earns, the income of the whole club depends on its members, not on the television networks or on the sports equipment multinationals. That, at least, is our point of view...

After winning the presidential election in 2003, Joan Laporta and his board successfully set about implementing a commercially successful alternative model to the private corporation model which had allowed the Glazer family to take control of Manchester United. This began with the appointment of successful professionals, who were also FC Barcelona fans, to key executive positions within the club – the fact that Barcelona is a members' club did not seem to deter serious applicants. The way that FC Barcelona sought to apply financial discipline to all its activities, and the way it sought to market itself and its related merchandise is now widely acknowledged to be infinitely more sophisticated than during the Núñez era. And, unlike under Núñez, the

Laporta regime has managed to market the club on a truly global scale while remaining faithful to the club's sociopolitical heritage, proving that the two are not mutually exclusive. As Ferrán Soriano explained, the economic benefits and the cultural benefits of the above are wholly compatible:

> Barça is relatively simple to explain to people from abroad: Catalunya is a country that, because of political circumstances, has been lacking, historically, in all of the most important symbols and institutions. Barça has become a very simple way for us to tell the outside world who we are. It would be much better if it was not like that, that Barça could just operate as any other football club and that Catalunya had always had a state and administrative structure that its culture and desire for self governance deserves – but that is not how things are. Consequently, FC Barcelona is one of the ways in which we, as Catalans, can project ourselves to the rest of the world, telling them that we are here and that we exist as a nation.[133]

Central to this strategy was the campaign to successfully increase the number of members in the club as a focus for driving revenue.[134] FC Barcelona demonstrated that supporters would buy increasing volumes of merchandise from their club, provided it was sold to them in an appropriate manner. Of course it helped that all the money raised went back into the club to support the team, as there were no dividends to be paid to investors.

Clearly the success of Laporta and his board's business model has been facilitated by the tremendous success that the football team currently enjoyed on the field. It is perhaps not unreasonable then to suggest that the two spheres of activity must feed off each other. The image of a well-run football club aggressively marketing itself around the world as the very embodiment of sporting excellence and cultural sophistication with all the associated romance of an institution that is truly owned by its members and that stands for something more than a commercial entertainment franchise must be an attractive package for any ambitious player. It certainly seemed to work for Ronaldinho and Henrik Larrson.

At the heart of what makes FC Barcelona work as a great sporting institution is the fact that, in the words of the club motto, it is 'More than a Club' – it is an expression of Catalan cultural identity and pride.[135] In 2000, Joan Laporta, then the leader of the fringe campaigning group of Barcelona members called the L'Elefant Blau[136] had this to say:

> Football and FC Barcelona are a way of life for many Catalans. It is that tribal spirit that is so important to football. Without it football means nothing.

It was feared that under Josep Núñez, the identity and purpose of FC Barcelona was moving toward an American-style entertainment model, as exemplified by the Glazer-owned Tampa Bay Buccaneers, which drove Laporta and his colleagues to form the L'Elefant Blau to reassert FC Barcelona's identity as primarily a sporting and cultural institution. Fortunately for them, the member-owned structure of FC Barcelona allowed this determined group to win the argument with the club's supporters in the democratic forum of an election. This option is not open to supporters of Premier League clubs in England, all of which are privately owned, unless they themselves can buy control of their club. During the progress of elections at FC Barcelona, and during Joan Laporta's subsequent stewardship of the club, there has been a certain amount of political name-calling by opponents, emotional resignations from the board, and agitation that one might more commonly associate with party political campaigning, but as

Sir Alex Ferguson might observe, 'that's football'. It is also the case that sometimes the much vaunted corporate social responsibility programme of the club does not operate as planned as some of the players sometimes find these obligations irksome. The UK newspaper *The Times* reported in June 2007, under the headline 'Mandela Snubbed', that several players, including Ronaldinho, opted to skip a reception with Nelson Mandela on the club's tour of South Africa; in fact, only five actually attended the reception.[137] However, these problems ultimately do not seem to have affected the overall quality of management of the club. Critically, the example of FC Barcelona demonstrates that a mutually owned model can work successfully in the modern globalised football industry.

Conclusion – could the FC Barcelona model be replicated at an English Premiership Club?

Since the election of Joan Laporta in 2003 as president of FC Barcelona, the board of Directors and management at the football club have embraced a new era of commercialism, accepted the need to operate in the global market, and expanded commercial activities by appealing to new markets such as Asia in order to achieve success on the field and commercial success off it. This may seem ironic, given that one of the reasons Joan Laporta and L'Elefant Blau campaigned against former President Josep Núñez was because it was felt that the club was becoming too commercially oriented and they were worried about the club becoming a privately owned company rather than a members' club. However, where the business model at FC Barcelona differed from that during the Núñez era is that the commercially driven model was based on strong cultural and social principles. The commercial strategy was finely balanced with maintaining the traditions of the FC Barcelona, such as member democracy and corporate social responsibility, while at the same time achieving sporting success.

The model of governance at FC Barcelona appears to indicate that the relationship between member democracy, commercial strategy, corporate social responsibility and sporting success is symbiotic; the success of each strategic aspect is in part dependent on the success of the other strategic aspects and therefore, it is not unreasonable to suggest that the spheres of strategic activity feed off each other and work together to help propel the football club forward. For example, the success of the commercial strategy has been facilitated by the tremendous success that the team is currently enjoying on the field, while the importance of maintaining the democratic structures of governance and protecting the status of the club as a not-for-profit sports organization also helps to drive commercial revenue. FC Barcelona therefore epitomizes a well-run football club aggressively marketing itself around the world as the very embodiment of sporting excellence and cultural sophistication with all the associated romance of an institution that is truly owned by its members and that stands for something more than a commercial entertainment franchise.

A telling element in the FC Barcelona rules is that you do not have to be Catalan, or even Spanish, to stand for election as club president; at Real Madrid, for example, you must be Spanish. As one of many biographers of the club, Phil Ball, remarked:[138]

> ...the Catalans pride themselves on their lack of parochialism, on their cosmopolitan air, on their time-honoured practice of looking outward, of absorbing influences and of transforming them into their own eclectic dynamic. The motto for the club's centenary

was *El centenari de tots* (everybody's centenary) ... it [the motto] embodied a subtle message of inclusiveness while simultaneously managing to invite outsiders to take an admiring look. Time and time again footballers have arrived from foreign shores and rapidly become 'Catalanised' – which it not to say that they have learned the language, but rather they that they have absorbed the peculiar *taranna* (way of being) of the region which they have almost invariably found attractive. Even the notoriously ill-adapting British have not been immune ... Gary Lineker, Steve Archibald, and Terry Venables, who got off on the right foot at the Camp Nou by addressing the crowd in halting Catalan at his first training session.

The Dutchman Johann Cruyff is perhaps the most influential of all the 'Catalanized'.

This raises the question posed at the beginning of this article; if the very, very, Catalan FC Barcelona is so open to absorbing outside influences, could its mutually owned model equally be absorbed into a major English Premiership club? Or is its success specific to the Catalan situation?

Burns again, when assessing the reason for Josep Núñez's ultimate failure to re-model the club as a modern corporation, hits on why few, if any, private owners are likely to transform the clubs they own toward the FC Barcelona model:

> Núñez was in many ways typical of the new breed of businessman taking charge of football in the 1990s. In style and management he echoed the political ambition of AC Milan's Silvio Berlusconi, the abrasiveness of Tottenham Hotspur's Alan Sugar, and the pragmatism of Fergus McCann ... [controlling shareholder at] Celtic Football Club.... And yet in one key respect Núñez was handicapped: he did not have, nor was he allowed to have, the power that came with being a majority of shareholder in a club. Much as he tried to control Barça as his own fiefdom, he continued to be faced with a widely felt and deeply entrenched tradition of nationalism and fan power.[139]

FC Barcelona may be a highly dynamic business organization applying all the modern business management techniques, but it is still a mutually owned organization where senior management truly are accountable to the club's members, as Joan Laporta was discovering through the various votes by members in the summer of 2008. The answer to this question may be that while no large Premiership club may voluntarily convert to such a mutual model, a bankruptcy at a major club as the world entered an era of global economic recession in the summer of 2008 may well create an opportunity for a well-organized group of supporters at clubs like Liverpool and Manchester United, where there is a strong fan culture and sense of tradition and moral ownership. What the FC Barcelona example demonstrates is that there is nothing inherent in the mutually owned model that disallows the development of teams capable of winning the UEFA Champions League (as both FC Barcelona and Real Madrid have demonstrated in recent years) or of building a sustainable financial strategy independent of the need for equity/shareholder investment. At the end of 2007/2008, FC Barcelona reported its sixth straight year of revenue growth and pre-tax profits[140,141] and announced in October 2008 that the club had paid back all of the syndicated loan taken out in 2003.[142] What is required is the ability of English football supporters to organize themselves into a democratically accountable and disciplined body capable of taking over a large club, and the opportunity to engage in such a take-over. Only time will tell whether the current economic downturn will create the conditions where this might take place. In the meantime, the example of FC Barcelona continues as a working model of a functioning mutual football 'club' alternative to the privately owned football 'corporation'.

Notes

1. Deloitte. *Football Money League*, 2, 2008.
2. FCBarcelona.cat. 'Barça Reaches 163,000 Members'.
3. FCBarcelona.cat. 'FCB Other Sports'.
4. For a useful summary of the social, cultural and sporting history of FC Barcelona see: Ball, 'Sunshine & Shadow'.
5. Brown, and Walsh. 'Football Supporters' Relations with Their Clubs', 94.
6. Deloitte. *Football Money League*, 29, 2007.
7. FC Barcelona. *Annual Report & Accounts 2007/2008 Season*, 149.
8. Burns. *Barça*, 76.
9. Many contemporary club histories gloss over this fact and either ignore it altogether, as is the case with Sobreques (1998), and Barnils (1999), who offer no explanation as to why this happened, merely stating that he left the club.
10. See earlier work by author; Watson 'FC Barcelona: Identity and Nationalism' – Gamper's marriage to Emma Pilourd, a Catholic Swiss woman, enabled his acceptance by the Catholic population in the city, a fact to which the newspaper *Las Deportes* attested to at that time.
11. Caraben, Godall, Laporta, and Moix. 'The Struggle for Democracy at Barcelona FC', 203.
12. Burns. *Barça*, 97.
13. Bahamonde. *El Real Madrid en la historia de España*, 187.
14. Burns. *Barça*, 128.
15. Caraben, Godall, Laporta, and Moix. 'The Struggle for Democracy at Barcelona FC', 203.
16. Brown, and Walsh. 'Football Supporters' Relations with Their Clubs', 94.
17. Caraben, Godall, Laporta, and Moix. 'The Struggle for Democracy at Barcelona FC', 203.
18. Ball. 'Sunshine & Shadow', 82.
19. Brown, and Walsh. 'Football Supporters' Relations with Their Clubs', 94.
20. For a more detailed review of the Núñez era see: Burns. *Barça*, 346–57.
21. Burns. *Barça*, 347.
22. Brown, and Walsh. 'Football Supporters' Relations with Their Clubs', 93–5.
23. Caraben, Godall, Laporta, and Moix. 'The Struggle for Democracy at Barcelona FC', 204–6.
24. Ascari, and Gagnepain. 'Spanish Football', 76–89.
25. Ibid.
26. Ibid., 77–9.
27. Castillo. 'The Concept of Loyalty and the Challenge of Internationalisation in Post-modern Spanish Football', 24–5.
28. Ascari, and Gagnepain. 'Spanish Football', 86.
29. Ibid., 76–89.
30. Caraben, Godall, Laporta, and Moix. 'The Struggle for Democracy at Barcelona FC', 206.
31. Brown, and Walsh. 'Football Supporters' Relations with Their Clubs', 94–5.
32. Burns. *Barça*, 353.
33. Ibid., 355.
34. Ibid., 355.
35. Caraben, Godall, Laporta, and Moix. 'The Struggle for Democracy at Barcelona FC', 206.
36. Ibid., 202–8.
37. Burns. *Barça*, 356.
38. Caraben, Godall, Laporta, and Moix. 'The Struggle for Democracy at Barcelona FC', 207.
39. Ball. 'Sunshine & Shadow', 105.
40. Burns. *Barça*, 356.
41. L'Elefant Blau. 'The Struggle for Democracy at FC Barcelona and the Case for a European Independent Regulator of Professional Football', 137.
42. Caraben, Godall, Laporta, and Moix. 'The Struggle for Democracy at Barcelona FC', 206.
43. Burns. *Barça*, 354.
44. Badia. *Cronica de Núñisme*, 93
45. Brown, and Walsh. 'Football Supporters' Relations with Their Clubs', 95.
46. Ibid.
47. Ball. 'Sunshine & Shadow', 109.
48. Deloitte. *Football Money League*, 29, 2007.
49. Kase, Gomez, Urrutia, Opazo and Marti. *Real Madrid – Barcelona*, 4.
50. Ibid., 9.
51. FC Barcelona.cat. 'FC Barcelona History: Presidents – Enric Reyna i Martinez (2003)'.

52. FCBarcelona.cat. 'FC Barcelona History: Presidents – Interim Administrative Committee'.
53. Allen, and Recuero. *FC Barcelona*, 6.
54. FC Barcelona.cat. 'FC Barcelona History: Presidents – Joan Laporta Estruch (2003)'.
55. An interesting account of Laporta's first 18 months as president is provided by Webster, 'Viva Barça!'.
56. Allen, and Recuero. *FC Barcelona*, 10.
57. Deloitte. *Football Money League*, 29, 2007.
58. Allen, and Recuero. *FC Barcelona*, 7.
59. Webster. 'Viva Barça!'.
60. Allen, and Recuero. *FC Barcelona*, 11.
61. Davilla, Foster, and Llopis. *Futbol Club Barcelona*, 3.
62. Allen, and Recuero. *FC Barcelona*, 11.
63. Ibid., FC Barcelona, 7.
64. For an overview of FC Barcelona's business strategy in Ferrán Soriano's own words see: Soriano, 'Governance in a Big Soccer Club'.
65. Ball. 'Sunshine & Shadow', 109–10.
66. For an account of how Manchester United implemented a similar strategy over the 1992–2007 period see Hamil. 'Manchester United', 114–34.
67. Deloitte. *Football Money League*, 30, 2007.
68. Richelieu, and Pons. 'Toronto Maple Leafs vs Football Club Barcelona', 241.
69. Kase, Gomez, Urrutia, Opazo, and Marti. *Real Madrid – Barcelona*, 9–10.
70. Davilla, Foster, and Llopis. *Futbol Club Barcelona*, 5–6.
71. Chadwick, and Arthur. 'Més que un club (More Than a Club)', 4.
72. Martin, 'La Gira Asiatica', 34.
73. FCBarcelona.cat. 'Barça Reaches 163,000 Members'.
74. FC Barcelona.cat. 'FCB Members: Adult Member'.
75. Richelieu, and Pons. 'Toronto Maple Leafs vs Football Club Barcelona', 249.
76. See the FC Barcelona website: http://www.fcbarcelona.com/web/english/noticies/club/temporada08-09/11/n081113106033.html
77. Allen, and Recuero.' FC Barcelona', 18.
78. Ibid., 19.
79. FCBarcelona.cat. 'Barça Reaches 163,000 Members'.
80. Allen, and Recuero. 'FC Barcelona', 34.
81. Conn. 'Barcelona's Model of Integrity Shows Right is Might'.
82. FCBarcelona.cat. 'FC Barcelona Penyes: the Social Commission'.
83. Deloitte. *Football Money League*, 8, 2008; Deloitte. *Football Money League*, 5, 29–71, 2007; FC Barcelona. *Annual Report & Accounts 2007/2008 Season*, 149.
84. Deloitte. *Football Money League*, 8, 2008; Deloitte. *Football Money League*, 5, 29–71, 2007.
85. Davilla, Foster, and Llopis. *Futbol Club Barcelona*, 3–4.
86. Allen, and Recuero. *FC Barcelona*, 13.
87. Ibid., 14–15.
88. Kase, Gomez, Urrutia, Opazo, and Marti. *Real Madrid – Barcelona*, 7.
89. Deloitte. *Football Money League*, 30, 2007.
90. Davilla, Foster, and Llopis. *Futbol Club Barcelona*, 5.
91. Deloitte. *Football Money League*, 30, 2007.
92. Allen, and Recuero. *FC Barcelona*, 14.
93. Ibid., 20.
94. Webster. 'Viva Barça!'.
95. Davilla, Foster, and Llopis. *Futbol Club Barcelona*, 6.
96. Deloitte. *Football Money League*, 31, 2007.
97. Deloitte. *Football Money League*, 8, 2008.
98. Deloitte. *Football Money League*, 8, 2008; Deloitte. *Football Money League*, 30, 2007.
99. Ibid.
100. Deloitte. *Football Money League*, 30, 2007.
101. Gil-Lafuente. 'Marketing Management in a Socially Complex Club', 186–208.
102. Deloitte. *Football Money League*, 8, 2008.
103. FCBarcelona.cat. 'Norman Foster Admired by Peers.'
104. Allen, and Recuero. *FC Barcelona*, 16.
105. Conn. 'Barcelona's Model of Integrity Shows Right is Might'.

106. Deloitte. *Football Money League*, 8, 2008; Deloitte. *Football Money League*, 30, 2007.
107. Deloitte. *Football Money League*, 8, 2008.
108. Deloitte. *Football Money League*, 8, 2008; Deloitte. *Football Money League*, 31, 2007.
109. Ibid.
110. Richelieu, and Pons. 'Toronto Maple Leafs vs Football Club Barcelona', 242.
111. Chadwick, and Arthur. 'Més que un club (More Than a Club)', 5.
112. For a more detailed summary of FC Barcelona's international marketing strategy over the 2003–2006 period see Davilla, Foster, and Llopis. *Futbol Club Barcelona*, 10–14.
113. FCBarcelona.cat. 'Boix'.
114. FCBarcelona.cat. 'FC Barcelona – The Foundation'.
115. FCBarcelona.cat. 'More Than a Club'.
116. Chadwick, and Arthur. 'Més que un club (More Than a Club)', 5–6.
117. Ibid.
118. Ibid., 6.
119. *La Vanguardia*. 'La moción de censura contra Laporta ya está en marcha'.
120. FCBarelona.cat. 'UNICEF shows a solid commitment from Barça'.
121. Chadwick, and Arthur. 'Més que un club (More Than a Club)', FC Barcelona 9.
122. *The TimesOnline*. 'Aston Villa Forgoes £2 Million Sponsorship to Support Charity'.
123. Hawkey. 'Heart of Barça'.
124. Davilla, Foster, and Llopis. *Futbol Club Barcelona*, 4.
125. Govan. 'Barcelona Boss Scores Own Goal'.
126. CNN.com. 'Laporta to Resign for New Election'.
127. FCBarcelona.cat. 'The Vote of Censure is Unsuccessful'.
128. FCBarcelona.cat. 'The Importance of Participation'.
129. FCBarcelona.cat. 'The Ex-Presidents Also Take Part'.
130. FCBarcelona.cat. 'Eight Directors Resign'.
131. FCBarcelona.cat. 'Laporta to Continue as President.'
132. L'Elefant Blau. 'The Struggle for Democracy at FC Barcelona and the Case for a European Independent Regulator of Professional Football', 137.
133. Murillo, and Murillo. *El Nou Barça*, 199–200.
134. Presentation by FC Barcelona Finance Director Ferrán Soriano at Birkbeck College, University of London, on 22nd February 2006.
135. Caraben, Godall, Laporta, and Moix. 'The Struggle for Democracy at Barcelona FC', 209.
136. L'Elefant Blau. 'The Struggle for Democracy at FC Barcelona and the Case for a European Independent Regulator of Professional Football', 138.
137. The Times. 'Mandela Snubbed'.
138. Ball. 'Sunshine & Shadow', 84.
139. Burns. *Barça*, 355–6.
140. FCBarcelona.cat. 'FC Barcelona Financial Balance'.
141. FCBarcelona.cat. 'Historic Budget Approved.'
142. FCBarcelona.cat. 'Boix'.

References

Allen, D., and Recuero, R.E. *FC Barcelona: Changing the Rules of the Game. Case Study by the Instituto de Empresa Business School*. University of Cranfield: European Case Clearing House, 2005.

Ascari, G., and P. Gagnepain. 'Spanish Football', *Journal of Sports Economics* 7, no. 1 (2006): 76–89.

Badia, J. *Cronica de Núñisme*. Barcelona: Portic, 2003.

Bahamonde, A. *El Real Madrid en la historia de España*. Madrid: Santillan ediciones, 2002.

Ball, P. 'Sunshine & Shadow: The Ambiguous Truth About Barcelona'. In *Morbo: The Story of Spanish Football*, Chapter 4. London: WSC Books, 2003.

Barnils, R. *Història Crítica del futbol Club Barcelona 1899–1999*. Barcelona: Empuries, 1999.

Brown, A., and A. Walsh. 'Football Supporters' Relations with Their Clubs: A European Perspective', *Soccer & Society* 1, no. 3 (2000): 88–101.

Burns, J. *Barça: A People's Passion*. London: Bloomsbury, 1999.

Caraben, A., A. Godall, J. Laporta, and J. Moix. 'The Struggle for Democracy at Barcelona FC'. In *A Game of Two Halves? The Business of Football*, ed. S. Hamil, J. Michie, and C. Oughton. Edinburgh: Mainstream, 1999.

Castillo, J.C. 'The Concept of Loyalty and the Challenge of Internationalisation in Post-modern Spanish Football', *International Journal of Iberian Studies* 20, no. 1 (2007): 23–40.

Chadwick, S., and Arthur, D. 'Més que un club (More Than a Club): The Commercial Development of FC Barcelona'. In *International Cases in the Business of Sport,* ed. S. Chadwick, and D. Arthur. Oxford: Elsevier, 2008.

CNN.com. 'Laporta to Resign for New Election', CNN.com, July 21, 2006. http://edition.cnn.com/2006/SPORT/football/07/21/spain.Barcelona/index.html. Accessed July 10, 2009.

Conn, D. 'Barcelona's Model of Integrity Shows Right is Might', *Guardian,* May 17, 2006. http://www.guardian.co.uk/football/2006/may/17/championsleague.europeanfootball. Accessed March 10, 2009.

Davilla, A., G. Foster, and J. Llopis. 'Futbol Club Barcelona: Globalisation Opportunities', Stanford Graduate School of Business Case-Study Series. Case SPM-33, January 2, 2007.

Deloitte. *Football Money League.* Manchester: Deloitte Sport Business Group, 2007.

Deloitte. *Football Money League.* Manchester: Deloitte Sport Business Group, 2008.

FC Barcelona. *Annual Report & Accounts 2007/2008 Season.* FC Barcelona, 2008.

FC Barcelona.cat. 'FCB Members: Adult Member'. http://www.fcbarcelona.com/web/english/socis/fes-te_soci/nova/info_senior.html. Accessed September 9, 2008.

FCBarcelona.cat. 'FC Barcelona Financial Balance'. http://www.fcbarcelona.com/web/english/club/club_avui/informacio_corporativa/situacio_economica/situacio_economica.html. Accessed September 9, 2008.

FCBarcelona.cat. 'FC Barcelona – The Foundation'. http://www.fcbarcelona.cat/web/Fundacio/english/. Accessed August 6, 2008.

FCBarcelona.cat. 'FC Barcelona History: Presidents'. http://www.fcbarcelona.com/web/english/club/historia/presidents.html

FC Barcelona.cat. 'FC Barcelona History: Presidents – Enric Reyna i Martinez (2003)'. http://www.fcbarcelona.com/web/english/club/historia/Presidents/enricreyna.html. Accessed September 9, 2008.

FCBarcelona.cat. 'FC Barcelona History: Presidents – Interim Administrative Committee'. http://www.fcbarcelona.com/web/english/club/historia/Presidents/comissiogestoratrayter.html. Accessed August 4, 2008.

FC Barcelona.cat. 'FC Barcelona History: Presidents – Joan Laporta Estruch (2003)'. http://www.fcbarcelona.com/web/english/club/historia/Presidents/joanlaporta.html. Accessed August 4, 2008

FCBarcelona.cat. 'More Than a Club'. http://www.fcbarcelona.com/web/english/club/club_avui/mes_que_un_club/mesqueunclub.html. Accessed August 6, 2008.

FCBarcelona.cat. 'FC Barcelona – Penyes: The Social Commission'. http://www.fcbarcelona.com/web/english/penyes/organs_penyes/comissio_social.html. Accessed August 26, 2008.

FCBarcelona.cat. 'FCB Other Sports.' http://www.fcbarcelona.com/web/english/altres_esports/altres_esports.html. Accessed September 9, 2008.

FCBarelona.cat. 'UNICEF Shows a Solid Commitment from Barça', September 23, 2006. http://www.fcbarcelona.com/web/english/historic_noticies/club/06/Setembre/n06092310.html. Accessed November 26, 2008.

FCBarcelona.cat. 'Norman Foster Admired by Peers', March 6, 2008. http://www.fcbarcelona.com/web/english/noticies/club/temporada07-08/03/n080306103519.html. Accessed August 26, 2008.

FCBarcelona.cat. 'The Importance of Participation', July 5, 2008. http://www.fcbarcelona.com/web/english/noticies/club/temporada08-09/07/n080705104829.html. Accessed September 9, 2008.

FCBarcelona.cat. 'The Ex-Presidents Also Take Part', July 6, 2008. http://www.fcbarcelona.com/web/english/noticies/club/temporada08-09/07/n080706104846.html. Accessed September 9, 2008.

FCBarcelona.cat. 'The Vote of Censure is Unsuccessful', July 6, 2008. http://www.fcbarcelona.com/web/english/noticies/club/temporada08-09/07/n080706104849.html. Accessed September 9, 2008.

FCBarcelona.cat. 'Eight Directors Resign', July 10, 2008. http://www.fcbarcelona.com/web/english/noticies/club/temporada08-09/07/n080710102448.html. Accessed September 9, 2008.

FCBarcelona.cat. 'Barça Reaches 163,000 Members', July 27, 2008. http://www.fcbarcelona. com/web/english/noticies/club/temporada08-09/07/n080727102587.html. Accessed September 9, 2008.

FCBarcelona.cat. 'Historic Budget Approved', August 24, 2008. http://www.fcbarcelona.com/ web/english/noticies/club/temporada08-09/08/n080824102957.html. Accessed September 9, 2008.

FCBarcelona.cat. 'Laporta to Continue as President', August 24, 2008. http://www.fcbarce-lona.com/web/english/noticies/club/temporada08-09/08/n080824102958.html. Accessed September 9, 2008.

FCBarcelona.cat. 'Boix: We'll Settle the Syndicated Loan on 31 October', October 13, 2008. http://www.fcbarcelona.com/web/english/noticies/club/temporada08-09/10/n081013103 185.html http://www.fcbarcelona.com/web/english/club/club_avui/informacio_corporativa /situacio_economica/situacio_economica.html. Accessed May 16, 2010.

Gil-Lafuente, J. 'Marketing Management in a Socially Complex Club: Barcelona FC'. In *Marketing & Football: An International Perspective,* ed. M. Desbordes, 186–208. London: Butterworth-Heinemann/Elsevier, 2007.

Govan, F. 'Barcelona boss scores own goal', *Daily Telegraph,* October 30, 2006.

Hamil, S. 'Manchester United: The Commercial Development of a Global Football Brand'. In *International Cases in the Business of Sport,* ed. S. Chadwick, and D. Arthur, 114–34. London: Butterworth-Heinemann/Elsevier, 2008.

Hawkey, I. 'Heart of Barça', *The Sunday Times,* July 23, 2006. http://www.timesonline.co.uk/ tol/sport/football/article691339.ece. Accessed March 10, 2009.

Kase, K., S. Gomez, I. Urrutia, M. Opazo, and C. Marti. *Real Madrid – Barcelona: Business Strategy V Sports Strategy: 2000–2006,* IESE Business School Occasional Paper Series, No 6/12, University of Navarra, 2006.

La Vanguardia. 'La Moción de Censura Contra Laporta ya Está en Marcha', *La Vanguardia,* September 5, 2008. http://www.lavanguardia.es/lv24h/20080509/53462264978.html. Accessed November 26, 2008.

L'Elefant Blau. 'The Struggle for Democracy at FC Barcelona and the Case for a European Independent Regulator of Professional Football'. In *Football in the Digital Age: Whose Game is it Anyway?,* ed. S. Hamil, J. Michie, C. Oughton, and S. Warby, 138. Edinburgh: Mainstream, 2000.

Martin, I.L. 'La Gira Asiatica', *Avui,* July 26, 2006, 34.

Murillo, E., and Murillo, C. *El Nou Barça,* 199–200. Barcelona: Edicions 62, 2005.

Richelieu, A., and Pons, F. 'Toronto Maple Leafs vs Football Club Barcelona: How Two Legendary Sports Teams Built Their Brand Equity', *International Journal of Sports Marketing and Sponsorship* 7, no. 3 (2006): 231–50.

Sobreques, S. *FC Barcelona. Cent Anys D'historia.* Barcelona: Edi-Liber editorial, 1998.

Soriano, F. 'Governance in a Big Soccer Club'. In *Governance and Competition in Professional Sports Leagues,* ed. P. Rodìguez, S. Késenne, and P. García. Oviedo: Universidad de Oviedo, 2007.

Soriano, F. Presentation by FC Barcelona Finance Director Ferrán Soriano at Birkbeck College, University of London, February 22, 2006.

The Times. 'Mandela Snubbed', *The Times,* June 22, 2007.

TimesOnline. 'Aston Villa Forgoes £2 Million Sponsorship to Support Charity', *TimesOnline,* June 30, 2008. http://www.timesonline.co.uk/tol/life_and_style/court_and_social/ article4236874.ece. Accessed November 26, 2008.

Watson, L. 'FC Barcelona: Identity and Nationalism', unpublished PhD Thesis, 2003.

Webster, J. 'Viva Barça!', *Independent on Sunday,* February 13, 2005. http://findarticles.com/ p/articles/mi_qn4159/is_20050213/ai_n9532613 Accessed March 10, 2010.

Index

4461828R00103

Printed in Great Britain
by Amazon.co.uk, Ltd.,
Marston Gate.